£10

STark.

STark.

PAINTING ○ COLOUR ○ HISTORY

COLLECTION PLANNED AND DIRECTED BY
ALBERT SKIRA

ITALIAN PAINTING

FROM
CARAVAGGIO TO MODIGLIANI

CRITICAL STUDIES BY LIONELLO VENTURI

HISTORICAL SURVEYS BY ROSABIANCA SKIRA-VENTURI

TRANSLATED BY STUART GILBERT

ALBERT SKIRA

GENEVA - PARIS - NEW YORK

CONTENTS

LIST OF ILLUSTRATIONS

WHILE FULLY RECOGNIZING THE ETERNAL youth of Giotto, Masaccio and Piero della Francesca, those artists of all time whose work can never lose its aspect of modernity, and the ageless perfection of the art of the great Cinquecento painters, we may say, none the less, that it was in Rome at the beginning of the XVIIth century that the basic principles of our modern art were formulated. For the XVIIth century broke definitively with the past—not only with all previous methods of representation but also with the so-called classical, that is to say religious, subject—and reality forced its way, un-abashed, into painting. Caravaggio personified this new realism which, while linked up with the ideals of the Creators of the Renaissance, sponsored a wholly new way of seeing. And from both realism and classicism conjointly there arose, in the fullness of time, that glorious decorative art which found its full flowering in Tiepolo. In the XIXth century a group of Italian artists, known as the Macchiaioli, though they may not have had any decisive repercussions on the future, made nevertheless a very real contribution to world art. With the beginning of the present century came new ventures, new conceptions, in close association with the art movements developing in other countries: ventures that pointed the way to a drastic break with the traditions of the great Italian schools of art which had arisen under the aegis of Caravaggio in the XVIIth century. Thus a survey of the successive phases of Italian art from Caravaggio to Modigliani cannot but throw light on many of the sources of the art of today, and this has been, in fact, our aim in this last volume of our History of Italian Painting.

★

It is a pleasure to express our gratitude to the Superintendents, Directors and Curators of the various Museums and Galleries and to the many private collectors who have allowed us access to the masterpieces in their keeping, and whose generous co-operation has so greatly facilitated our task.

SEVENTEENTH

AND

EIGHTEENTH CENTURIES

CRITICAL STUDY BY LIONELLO VENTURI

BETWEEN the year 1573 when Caravaggio was born and the year 1920 when Modigliani died, the changes that came over representational art were nothing short of radical. Thus it is impossible to view these three and a half centuries as an 'historical' period, in the modern usage of that term. Nowadays in fact, Caravaggio is in high favor, and his work figures as a *point de repère* in our retrospect on art; but we have much the same feeling about Piero della Francesca, Masaccio and Giotto, far removed from our present-day culture though they obviously are. In short the art we now call " modern " took its rise at a point somewhere between the beginning and the end of the XIXth century, probably with the birth of Impressionism. All that preceded this is the art of " the masters of the past. "

As far as Italy is concerned it is obvious that great outstanding figures such as those of the XIVth, XVth and XVIth centuries (dealt with in the previous volumes of our History) become rarer and rarer from the end of the XVIth century up to the present day. None the less, long after the Renaissance, Italy, and Rome in particular, continued to be regarded as the fountainhead of art and infallible arbiters of taste. At the beginning of the Seicento young artists flocked to Rome, not merely to admire the statues of classical antiquity and Raphael's pictures but also, and above all, to study Caravaggio's works. Poussin drew inspiration from the Carracci and from Domenichino, and decorative painters throughout Europe conformed to the precedents of Rome and Venice. Even more than during the Renaissance the Courts of Europe felt it incumbent on them to have Italian artists paint the portraits of their notables and decorate their palaces. No longer centered in a few world-renowned personalities, Italian taste now found its expression in a profusion of works of art so vast in scope that the ceilings of churches and palaces seemed no longer large enough to contain so copious a flowering of the artists' decorative imagination.

The institution of the Italian Court Painter (alongside that of the Court Poet) came to an end with the French Revolution. In any case, from the middle of the XVIIIth century onward, Rome—now more than ever a lodestone for the artist and art-lover—owed her attraction much more to the works of antiquity to be seen there than to the genius of contemporary artists; indeed admiration of the latter diminished *pari passu* with the rising enthusiasm for antiquity. Unfortunately the Italian painters, far more than their French contemporaries, believed in the imitation of antiquity as the ideal training for the artist. They carried their imitative skill to a rare perfection—but at the cost of all creative originality. " Neoclassicism " crystallized into Academicism, to such effect that during the first half of the XIXth century it came to be thought that art and Academicism were identical.

The consequence was that the young enthusiasts who in the second half of the XIXth century were by way of producing original, vital works (I am thinking of the Florentine Macchiaioli) found themselves up against a prejudice in favor of the antique and the classical so deeply rooted that the very real value of their art passed unnoticed. In all ages Italy has given the world fine artists, but artistry alone, however brilliant, is of no avail if the tastes of an age are narrow, pedantic, blindly conservative.

From the beginning of the XIXth century Paris replaced Rome as the center of modern art and arbiter of taste. The Italians were slow to admit the artistic primacy of Paris, partly owing to their pride in belonging to a country that was " a nation once again," and also because they tended to divert their creative impulse towards political ideals and their realization. It was only at the beginning of the XXth century that they succeeded once again in winning a place in the vanguard of international art, by way of Futurism, Metaphysical Painting and, above all, the original genius of Amedeo Modigliani.

ROUND about 1600 tendencies which were to prevail in European art during well-nigh two centuries made their appearance, and they took a three-fold form: Realism as sponsored by Caravaggio, the Classicism of Annibale Carracci, and Baroque decoration, that pictorial aftermath of the architectural style of the same name, towards which tended the Carracci and their school no less than Rubens and Bernini.

Realism, in so far as this implies the representation of reality with a view to deepening man's apperception of the outside world, was an ideal of the Italian Renaissance in the Trecento and Quattrocento, and of Cinquecento Venetian painting. But Caravaggio's realism struck a new note (as against that of the Renaissance) owing to its being a vigorous attack on Mannerism, which had laid stress on formal lay-out, to the detriment of representation. Caravaggio, however, re-united form and representation by a forceful expression of plastic volume, relief, solidity.

The psychological background of his art is its humility *vis-à-vis* nature, thanks to which he could paint with equal zest a basket of fruit and a beautiful woman. Nevertheless he refused to stand for any conception of art inspired by classical models; this would have meant an intellectualization infringing both the artist's freedom and the respect due to nature. Thus Caravaggio's deference to nature made him hostile both to Mannerism and to Venetian chromatism, in which reality tended to be submerged in an orgy of colors.

He showed the same humility as regards the world of men. During a period in which the differences between the aristocracy and the lower classes were given a wholly Baroque emphasis, Caravaggio bore in mind the fact that the apostles were not princes of the blood and that pilgrims did not take a hot bath before paying homage to the Virgin. It was owing to his habit of using people of the working class as his models that his pictures were not considered ' elevated ' enough to serve as altarpieces. But it is for this very reason that some of his works, for instance *The Death of the Virgin*, rank amongst the finest examples of religious art in Seicento Italian painting.

Great colorist though Caravaggio was, few colorists have denied themselves so thoroughly the artist's natural joy in color. Indeed in Caravaggio's art the play of contrasts of light and shade superseded the colors to such an extent that he became the pioneer of ' Luminism,' that special type of art to which the Seicento owes so many of its masterpieces.

Such whole-hearted devotion to nature leads to a contemplative turn of mind and this is why (as Giorgione had done nearly a century earlier) Caravaggio began by painting busts with flowers or fruit and musical instruments—" genre pieces " as they were called; in other words, works having no distinctive names and without any historical context, whose value stems from the forms themselves and their vitality. Caravaggio's figures do not dream; they are alive, alert. In depicting a sacred scene, he does not use dramatic movement to stress its message; he achieves dramatic effect by centering on a moment of arrested motion that is the crux of the incident—on Christ's beckoning hand in *The Vocation of St Matthew* and the extended arms in *The Conversion of St Paul*.

It is in his powerful chiaroscuro that the essentially dramatic nature of Caravaggio's art makes itself felt. With it he imparts a new kind of unity to the representation which, no longer filling a limited, defined area, seems to move freely in infinite space. This reduction of form and color to contrasts of light and dark gave a new coherence to the artist's vision, and through it Caravaggio effected what was nothing short of a revolution in European taste. Indeed in the history of taste he marks a turning-point. All the same, the truest value of his art lies in his humility, involving as it did a special way of envisaging man and nature.

It is one of the most tragic ironies of destiny that a man naturally endowed with such high moral qualities should have been led by the hostility of those around him into becoming a sort of 'public enemy' and subject to a persecution mania leading to an act of murder.

NONE of Caravaggio's disciples had the genius or the spiritual endowments of the master. Yet they proved themselves good painters, not only by their masterly handling of color and light and their fidelity to nature, but also in their happy choice of subjects appropriate to their technical means.

To Orazio Gentileschi, perhaps the greatest of them, was due the propagation of Caravaggio's style abroad and notably in the Low Countries. Brought up in the Tuscan Mannerist tradition, he had learnt to paint in bright colors and chose subjects naturally pleasing to the eye, and he kept to this even after adapting Caravaggio's style. True, his colors are over-light and thus lack depth, but this is redeemed by his grace and elegance of form; indeed his *Woman Playing the Lute* is a work worthy of his great exemplar.

Carlo Saraceni, after thoroughly assimilating Caravaggio's style, employed it in a quite personal way; his works are agreeable trifles, sparkling with wit and imagination.

Young artists from all over Europe, from Germany and the Netherlands, no less than from France and Spain, came to Rome to learn the lesson of the master. Moreover, examples of his work were to be seen everywhere in Italy and these the local painters studied to advantage. Two cities especially—whose contributions to Italian art had been relatively slight during the Renaissance—now came brilliantly to the fore: Genoa and Naples.

Though in Bernardo Strozzi, who hailed from Genoa, we may detect a streak of vulgarity, there is no denying that his pictures make good as works of art, such is this painter's sincerity and forcefulness. On the other hand Bernardo Cavallino, a Neapolitan gifted with a very delicate poetic sense, used biblical scenes as pretexts for depicting the natural kindliness and simple, forthright ways of the Neapolitan populace. More than any other painter he identified himself with the revolutionary methods of Caravaggio. Realism, as the Renaissance practiced it, had meant depicting men's personal peculiarities rather than their conduct in a social context. Caravaggio, however, had understood the social message implicit in the Gospels, and it was Cavallino who expressed this in his art in, so to speak, colloquial terms and with a warm sympathy for the lives of the common people.

Domenico Feti, who migrated from Rome to Mantua and Venice, brought tidings to these cities of the new, realistic tendencies in art, which he illustrated in scenes full of wit and colorful exuberance.

Several decades had elapsed since Caravaggio's death when Michelangelo Cerquozzi, a Roman painter, brought into fashion the special kind of realistic picture, launched by the Dutch painter Van Laer, which came to be known as the *Bambocciata* (a term derived from Van Laer's nickname " Il Bamboccio "). This gave rise to a new and vigorous campaign led by the classicists against realism in art. A very gifted, sensitive painter, Cerquozzi handled Caravaggesque effects of light and shade with fine discretion in his depictions of everyday incidents or fantasies based more or less on visual experiences that had come his way; sometimes he even ventured into uncharted territory and painted scenes of real 'low life,' undeterred by their vulgarity. He soon became extremely rich, for the Roman aristocracy relished such pictures, which enhanced their sense of their own superiority over the 'lower orders.' If we compare these *bambocciate* with the homely, amiable scenes of daily life painted by the contemporary Dutch painters, we can gage the sad estate of the Roman populace in those days.

Thus the Bambocciants specialized in a particular kind of subject, and in fact this habit of specialization which artists now developed was a natural outcome of Caravaggio's realism. For instance it was noticed that he had begun by painting pictures of flowers and fruit, and his imitators now proceeded to turn them out in large numbers, often troubling themselves little about problems of ' style.'

From earliest youth Caravaggio had shown a special fondness for musical instruments, probably because their geometrical structure appealed to him as calling for the utmost objectivity on the artist's part. This was the genre which the Bergamask painter Evaristo Baschenis made peculiarly his own, and he succeeded in imparting to it at once elegance and not a little dignity.

CARAVAGGIO came to Rome in or about 1593, Annibale Carracci in 1595 and it was in Rome that he ' discovered ' Classicism. For in Bologna where he had had his early training, he had been saturated with the traditions of Northern Italian art, in which chiaroscuro played a leading role; indeed we may say that the background of the Carracci was much the same as that of Caravaggio. But hardly had Annibale arrived in the Eternal City than he fell under the spell of the past and began to introduce into his painting the plastic values of the Graeco-Roman statues, the monumental composition of Roman Renaissance art and those elaborate illusionist effects which as far back as Vasari's time ranked as the crucial test of an artist's skill. Today we are far less sure that these conceptions were really in accordance with the classical spirit, but Annibale Carracci's contemporaries were convinced that this was so—and hailed him as a new Raphael.

There was a very serious danger latent in the procedures of the Carracci: that of eclecticism. By the close of the XVIth century, following a bad example set them by the writers of the day, most artists had taken to eclecticism; that is to say, they borrowed freely from other painters and their work became a concoction of different, ill-assorted styles, taken over as a rule from Raphael and Correggio, Michelangelo and Titian. Obviously this patchwork effect becomes apparent only when the borrowed elements are not fully integrated into the artist's own style and thus their origins are plain to see. The Carracci stand head and shoulders above the other eclectics, for they achieved a truly personal style—even if occasionally they betrayed the sources whence they drew their inspiration. And since the art theory behind eclecticism was not merely approved of but extolled as the noblest of ideals during this period, the Carracci, as being the artists who put it into practice most successfully, were regarded as the greatest painters of the day. But they were also regarded as the reformers of Mannerism, for they always kept the mannerist elements in their painting well in hand.

Thus the classicism practiced by the Carracci was a fusion of realist conceptions, mannerist procedures and the classical ideal. In the decorations at the Farnese Palace we see their art at its apogee. The subjects, taken from classical mythology, are a pretext for an orgy of ' illusionism '—imitation marble, imitation bronzes, imitation tapestry; all the same the composition holds together wonderfully well, the artists' skill is undeniable and the overall effect is one of sheer magnificence, combining vigorous movement with dignity. Here in fact was proof that while drawing his inspiration from antiquity, from Raphael and Michelangelo, an artist could none the less achieve effects quite novel as compared with the art of the Renaissance.

But Annibale Carracci took his art more seriously and had a subtler insight than the decorations in the Farnese Palace—painted for Cardinal Farnese more with the intention of delighting than of impressing him—might lead us to believe. Probably we see him at his best in some of his pictures on sacred themes with landscape backgrounds. Examples are *The Samaritan Woman at the Well* (Vienna) and *The Flight into Egypt* (Doria Gallery, Rome). It was in the XVIIth century for the first time that the landscape was recognized as an independent branch of painting existing in its own right, and this was due to the tendencies towards Realism described above. For there is no question that the XVIIth-century Dutch landscapes have all the characteristics of the realistic genre picture. But Annibale Carracci had studied ancient art to good effect, with the result that he devoted much care to the tectonic structure of his compositions; thus his landscapes as a whole are architecturally ordered, even though individual details are treated realistically. The Carracci's disciples,

Domenichino especially, continued painting architecturally ordered landscapes and thus created the " classical landscape " as against the " realistic landscape " of the Dutch artists. (We need hardly mention the superb achievements, at a later date, of Poussin and of Claude Lorrain in the field of the classical landscape.) The classicism of the Carracci, discussed and defined by Monsignor Agucchi in his treatise on art and by Bellori in his *Lives*, was accepted as the criterion of ' high art ' in many European countries during the XVIIth century, for the good reason that it answered so well to the requirements of the Church, and some of the Carracci's disciples, Domenichino and Guido Reni for example, were ranked among the very greatest masters.

Uncompromising classicist though he was as regards the formal structure of his pictures, Domenichino was far from narrow-minded, nor did he shut his eyes to the realities of everyday life and their psychological implications. As for Guido Reni, most highly gifted of all the followers of the Carracci, beauty was his mistress—beauty of form, of gesture and of well-ordered composition—and his style recalls, if at a far remove, that of Raphael. It is an interesting point that today we cannot bring ourselves really to like the art of the Carracci, Domenichino or Guido Reni, the reason being the hypocrisy we sense behind it. True, there is ample evidence that these painters showed far more earnestness and sincerity in the practice of their religious duties than did several of the Renaissance artists whose religious works move us so deeply. All the same we cannot shake off the impression that the Carracci and their school painted their pictures as so many specific tasks assigned them by the Church. In fact such art was, in the last analysis, propagandist, and though they were convinced of the excellence of the cause that they were serving, the mere fact that they had consciously to act as propagandists somehow imparted a false note to their work; it became strained, over-emphatic. The creative genius of Caravaggio, allied with his strong sense of moral and social responsibility, had given his art, as against that of the Counter-Reformation, a compelling sincerity and independence. But the works of the Carracci were products of the Counter-Reformation and much as they did to sponsor a lofty standard of taste and to preserve what remained of the classical spirit of the Renaissance, they were unable, owing to the force of circumstances, to foster new developments; in other words they had a cultural rather than a creative value.

The case of Guercino is the exception that proves the rule. There is no question about his painterly genius and he imbibed the style of Lodovico Carracci before the rise of Classicism. Thus his style, in his early phase, was luminist and if in several respects it resembled that of Caravaggio (minus, needless to say, his driving force), it was none the less individual and independent. But when in 1621 Guercino went to Rome to work for Pope Gregory XV and came in contact with the classical art then flourishing at Rome, he let himself be diverted from his natural path and, to please his patrons, aimed at a more delicate, refined art. And though he continued to turn out some excellent pictures, that first fine rapture which had led to the creation of the Ludovisi *Night* had left him, never to return.

In the latter half of the XVIIth century Naples came to the fore with the Calabrian painter, Mattia Preti, whose work covered much the same ground as Guercino's. Some of Preti's chiaroscuro effects have a richness and an intricacy no other painter has ever surpassed, and we are justified in regarding him as the most brilliant exponent of Caravaggesque procedures during the last half of the century. However, the decorative tasks assigned him forced him to turn away from Caravaggio and to incorporate Baroque methods in his style.

V AST as was the success and widespread the influence of Caravaggio's realism and the classicism of the Carracci, the fact remains that Baroque decoration covered as wide a field and aroused still more enthusiasm. Since its very *raison d'être* associated it with architecture, Baroque painting was as it were a natural outcrop from the Baroque architectural style. But there were other reasons for its great prestige and popularity. Caravaggio's realism was too heavily charged with moral and social implications to allow him freely to indulge in flights of fancy. Classicism, on the other hand, was too uncompromising in its objective representation of reality, and likewise in its idealizations, not to provoke reactions on the artists' part—proof of which is the feeling of stress and strain given us by the work of Andrea Sacchi, a perfect representative of mid-XVIIth century classicism. Baroque decoration avoided these pitfalls, by choosing subjects that lent themselves to virtuoso handling and brushwork of the freest order. In the large-scale decorative works they undertook the XVIIth-century artists could throw caution to the winds and break quite new ground, and we can see why their best performances were their paintings on the ceilings of churches and palaces. The technical skill they thus acquired incited them to paint scenes boldly rendered in a " perspective from below "—the " frog's-eye view " as it is called—and to create illusionist vistas of boundless space. As a matter of fact this kind of painting had already been practiced by the Renaissance decorators; all that the Mannerist and Baroque artists did was to bring to it a greater talent and a livelier usage of illusionist effects. Once the illusion of infinite space was complete and ceilings were transformed into visions of heaven and paradise, the artists came to impart movement not only to individual figures but to whole groups. Thus they created the illusion of crowds of figures floating freely in the upper air, and what began as a display of virtuosity ended in that creative freedom which belongs to all great art.

The ceiling of the ' salon ' in the Barberini Palace, painted by Pietro da Cortona, is an example of Baroque decoration at its best, while that of the Church of Gesù, by Baciccio, illustrates a more sophisticated form of art and shows a finer sense of color, even though it lacks the boldness that characterizes the true pioneer.

The feats of illusionist perspective brought off by Andrea Pozzo were yet more brilliant, but they made no new contribution to the art of decoration. At Rome, Naples, Genoa and Florence alike decorative works followed hard upon one another, but it was only with the coming of Tiepolo that this form of art made a great forward stride.

The Seicento witnessed the climax of the great period of pictorial decoration. The century had begun with a new conception of reality, originating not as a reaction against the Counter-Reformation but frankly disregarding it; at the same time it encouraged the imitation of classic models, and this led to a certain rigorism both as to the forms employed and as to the subjects deemed ' natural '—i. e. corresponding to the idea of nature then obtaining. Yet in spite of this Italian artists did not let themselves be hampered by any excessive concern either with realism or with classic perfection of form, and gave free rein to their prodigious talent for decoration of a fancifulness verging on the extravagant. Though in time " Baroque decoration " came to be synonymous with " bad taste " we should be hard put to it to find in any other art such exuberant freedom, and Baroque was far more than a case of the imagination running wild. It was, rather, an expression of the XVIIth century mentality, its illusion of man's abounding, absolute power —an illusion which was deliberately shattered in the following century. The communion of the artist with a large section of the community— that is to say, the diffusion of his way of seeing and feeling through a broad stratum of society—is in itself a proof that Baroque decoration stood for a contemporary ideal and a means of communication between the artist and the world of his day.

IN Italy two painters stand out as representative of the transition from the XVIIth century to the XVIIIth. A great change had come over social conditions, though it had not as yet made itself felt in painting. These men are Giuseppe Maria Crespi, of Bologna, and Alessandro Magnasco, of Genoa. At first sight Crespi may strike us as being still a Seicento painter, a follower of Guercino, one of those many artists who were by way of transforming religious art into genre pictures. But we know how independent was his attitude towards his patrons and how strongly he asserted the autonomy of his art. Indeed he went so far as to include, quite naturally, charming young women even in his *Massacre of the Innocents*. One of his finest works shows us nothing more than a confessional-box, another a well-stocked bookcase. With him the prevailing taste for illustration gave way to one for the creation of form; form, in fact, is his leitmotiv, unifying subject and background within an all-pervading dusk. The interplay of light and shadow rendered with quick, deft brush-strokes makes objects stand forth and recede; and so smoothly, naturally, do they emerge that we can sense the artist's delight in his facility, and even share in it. Lightness of heart and lightness of touch blend happily in Crespi's style; we feel his joy in being rid of that gravity and sense of responsibility which had weighed so heavily on the style of the XVIIth-century artists.

Magnasco outdid Crespi in one respect; he made up his own subjects, and these, including as they do scenes of magic rites, wizardry and even Black Masses, were equally different from those of the previous century. Indeed they might well have got him into trouble with the Inquisition had he lived in that less ' enlightened ' age. Actually, however, people of his day were ceasing really to believe in sorcery; thus Magnasco's witches are obviously mere toys of the imagination, sportive *diableries*. His subjects, in a word, carried no meaning—and this very whimsicality was exactly what was needed for the liberation of form.

The characteristic of Magnasco's form is the breaking up of the line in terms of light, a procedure familiar to etching from Rembrandt onwards. Magnasco stressed the effect of his broken line by using very tall, thin figures involved in constant movement whose rhythms pervade even the landscape and indeed every object represented on the canvas. But this movement was not called for by any ' action ' essential to the subject; its sole purpose was the purely formal pleasure it afforded. For a long time color meant little to Magnasco, contrasts of light and shade were all he needed. A day came, however, when colors broke through, so delicately and so suavely illuminated that in his *Garden Party* they well might seem to celebrate the coming of age of the XVIIIth century, the end of shadows and obsessions, the triumph of serenity, affability, a life of leisured elegance. Indeed Magnasco's color became pure poetry, an art in itself, and of so high a quality that in this respect his only rival is Guardi.

THIS lightheartedness we find in the art of Crespi and Magnasco speaks for a new way of living. Whereas the XVIIth century, dominated by Spanish influence, had been intensely, almost aggressively serious, obsessed with melancholy broodings on the problems of life and death and the clash between Church dogma and the claims of normal life, the XVIIIth century, under French influence, was all for carefree frivolity, the *joie de vivre*, religious skepticism and freedom of thought.

The philosophy of the XVIIIth-century Enlightenment sums up this attitude, with its confident rationalism and its direct, unbiased observation of nature. This rationalistic view of the world did poor service to art and merely grafted on to it the would-be scientific notions it sought to popularize and render agreeable and entertaining to the public. In 1739 Francesco Algarotti wrote his *Newtonism for Ladies*. In the same way Settecento decoration was based on a use of illusionist perspective whose aim was, *inter alia*, to exalt " the female form divine " and to please women by its virtuoso brushwork—procedures which certainly did not commend themselves to Pietro da Cortona. This much can be said in favor of the Enlightenment, that it enabled art to approach nature boldly and unequivocally, feeling no need either to idealize the natural world or to defend it. We have only to compare the XVIIth-century *Bambocciate* with Ceruti's or Longhi's works to see the gulf that separates them; a difference pertaining not to the history of art but to that of culture.

During the first half of the XVIIIth century there was vast enthusiasm in Italy for all things French—French ideas, French fashions, French modes of living. Yet the changes that came over Italian art owed nothing to French painting. While French Rococo, anyhow in its inception, showed leanings towards classicism, Italian art tended towards an interpretation of reality freer and more fanciful than that of the Seicento. It was not until round about 1730 that the two varieties of Rococo, the French and the Italian, coalesced. The fundamental difference between the arts of the two countries during the XVIIIth century becomes evident when we recall the fact that Watteau's was the outcome of an abrupt swing-round in taste and that he was a leader of the admirers of Rubens and the sponsors of the theories of De Piles; whereas the transformation of Italian art took place gradually and was not based on any theories. If we now turn to the nations which claim that their art evolved 'historically' (such as Spain, Flanders and the Netherlands), we find that after having achieved greatness in an anti-classical realism, they surrendered to classicism at the end of the XVIIth century and lapsed into mediocrity. France, on the other hand, after practicing classicism in the XVIIth century achieved a real triumph in the field of art with the imaginative realism we find in Watteau and Chardin.

In Italy a shift took place as regards the centers of artistic productivity. At Rome there was as much activity as ever, but limited first to Classicism, then to Neoclassicism; realism and XVIIIth-century decoration played no part there. The importance of Naples, Genoa and Bologna as art-centers dwindled to a considerable extent. Lombardy, then entering on an era of prosperity in various fields, made a name for itself in painting too. But the outstanding art-center was unquestionably Venice, whose very name became a household word for art-lovers throughout Europe. For a century Venetian art had been under an eclipse; it could neither retrieve its own tradition nor fall in line with classicism. But from the beginning of the XVIIIth century onward, following the lead of Crespi and Magnasco, it advanced from strength to strength in the fields of decoration and realism. Indeed the magnificence of Italian Settecento art was enshrined in Venice.

It was in the art of Giambattista Tiepolo that this magnificence found its supreme expression. From his youth he enjoyed the favor of the highest in the land, but after enjoying more renown than any other painter, he lived to witness in Madrid (where his death took place) the gradual paling of his star before the dawn of Neoclassicism. He was soon forgotten and for almost a century his art was cruelly belittled. Then, with the coming of the inevitable swing-back towards realism, Tiepolo regained his old prestige and his work is now regarded as one of the pinnacles of art—though he still has his detractors, even in our time. No one however gainsays his creative genius and the spontaneous inspiration manifested, in particular, in his sketches, though he is often reproached with insincerity, not to say meretriciousness, in his big decorative works and altarpieces. That insincerity is not to be denied, but the fault lies less with the artist than with the conditions of his age. Indeed one of the most flagrant errors of our modern criticism is this failure to realize that Tiepolo expressed to perfection and quite spontaneously the spirit of the world around him, a world compact of artifice and insincerity; and that to condemn him on moral grounds or by 'classical' standards is to do him grave injustice.

Tiepolo painted many religious pictures, and it is obviously absurd to ask of an XVIIIth-century painter the intense religious fervor of the XVth-century Italians. None the less the charge of hypocrisy should not be leveled against Tiepolo's art. It may be justified in the case of a man like Guido Reni who was constrained by his patrons to play the hypocrite to some extent; to express emotions conjured up 'to order,' and not naturally his. It came equally easily to Tiepolo and was as much a matter of social etiquette to bow before the Virgin as to pay homage to Cleopatra's beauty; and both alike were excellent pretexts for painting young women full of grace and charm, with a lavish palette and a wealth of glittering adornment. Thus while the content—that is to say the artist's starting-off point— had nothing to do with our conception of the Virgin as the Mother of the Redeemer, it by no means follows that behind Tiepolo's portrayal of her there was not real feeling, sincerity of a special kind.

For some time I had been thinking of suggesting that a certain community of taste existed between Tiepolo and Metastasio. I have recently noticed that this similarity has struck others too (Mazzariol). Thus if we view Tiepolo's big scenes as frankly melodramas, we get a good idea of their true nature and their limitations—but we also see their flashes of poetic inspiration. Vernon Lee regards XVIIIth-century opera as a fusion of tragedy and the Carnival; a fusion that, tending to submerge the tragic elements, lent an ideal value to aspects of the Carnival. Seen from this angle, Tiepolo's art is a perfect expression of the spirit of that festival, the freest, most spontaneous, least didactic rendering of it that any painter has achieved. And here, I think, we have a criterion enabling us to select, in the vast output of this prolific artist, his most happily inspired productions.

What impresses us in the works of his youth is their remarkable vivacity, the fullness of the volumes, the sense they give of real masses existing in space. For, as an admirer of Bencovich and Piazzetta, Tiepolo had not yet broken with the XVIIth century. Next he observed to good effect Rembrandt's and Magnasco's broken line, Sebastiano Ricci's bright palette, and, at a greater distance, Veronese and the effectiveness of theatrical lay-out. By now his taste was already formed, but not as yet his artistry. He then concentrated, in a small expanse of canvas, harmonies of colors, and took to building up forms in terms of color, discovering in some muted tone the sudden thrill of beauty, in a ray of sunlight a means of transcending reality, or in a harmony of warm tonalities an apt expression of his abounding joy in life. ' Enthusiasm ' as it was called was an aesthetic motif particularly dear to the XVIIIth century, and no one since Rubens had shown such orgiastic zest for color. So it was only natural that his contemporaries were both amazed and enchanted by Tiepolo's innovations.

After having tried out these procedures in sketches Tiepolo used them to good effect in frescos and altarpieces. Obviously these richly concentrated color-patterns lost something of their intensity when diffused over a large area. But in the ceilings he now painted was an aerial brightness no artist before him had ever achieved, diversified here and there with the smiling grace of some celestial figure. And, curiously enough, the remoter are these figures in the blue depths of the sky, the more complete, more exquisite appears their beauty. His output was prodigious and he painted with an unconstraint and a lightness of touch perhaps unique in the world's art. For whenever he turned his mind from his daily task as an artisan of genius and lingered on a figure or a passage of color, the creative artist in him got the upper hand.

As regards his altarpieces we might say that the larger they are the more vivid the impression of prodigious skill they give us, and the smaller they are the greater is their natural artistry. (A revealing example is *The Communion of Saint Lucy* in the Holy Apostles Church at Venice.)

Some minor pictures, too large and ' finished ' to be regarded as sketches yet too small to have served as altarpieces, show his art at its splendid best; such are the *Last Supper* (Louvre) and the *Crucifixion* (National Gallery, London). A theatrical art if you will, but none the less deeply felt. For even on the stage emotion can run deep and its visual effect be heightened by the very conditions of the theater. From these small pictures there issues as it were a clear, sweet melody, and even XVIIIth-century opera has given the world none more entrancing.

THE form assumed by XVIIIth-century Realism was usually that of depictions of contemporary life. Thus, in Lombardy, Ceruti illustrated with remarkable *finesse* the life of the common people, washerwomen, beggars and the like. There is not a trace of class prejudice in his approach; he saw no reason for looking down on the so-called lower orders and this is why he depicted them so objectively, as they really were, with none of the condescension of the Bamb__occianti. This attitude was a result of the new conception of life and of the scheme of things sponsored by the *Illuminati*.

When mention is made of the change that came over the Italian artists' way of seeing the world during the XVIIIth century, the first name that occurs to us is that of the Venetian Pietro Longhi. When we compare him with Chardin, it is obvious that the latter not only handled color more delicately and adroitly but also had a deeper insight into reality; nevertheless there is an almost indefinable quality about Longhi's art that is lacking in Chardin's and indeed in that of all other XVIIIth-century painters. It is not in his hunting scenes or pictures of the Venetian populace that Longhi's genius is seen at its best; on the contrary we cannot help feeling that their elegant simplicity is somewhat superficial. But when his subject is the daily life of the families of the aristocracy, their frivolity, insincerity, not to say immorality, we sense an underlying spiritual significance in these scenes, despite their seeming forthrightness. Not that the artist emphasized the physical or moral traits of the people he depicts; any stress on the former would have given the scene a certain coarseness, on the latter, have made of it a sermon. Yet somehow these figures, seemingly so dull, inert and apathetic, convey a sense of irony, implicit, never insisted on by the painter, and permeating the scene as a whole: an irony which for its very reticence is all the more effective. Longhi has been likened to Parini, but it is obvious that Parini's moralizing had no place in Longhi's art. It was not that Longhi failed to see the profligacy of the life around him; rather, he was too much disheartened by it to stress it in his pictures. Indeed it is to this detachment that they owe their delicate appeal. Also, his color, low-pitched though it be, is handled with a subtle refinement adding that ' finishing touch ' to the forms to which they owe their charm.

It is an interesting point that depictions of inanimate nature always have a touch of contemporaneity. This may come as a surprise, for we are apt to imagine that the Roman or Venetian scene, no less than landscapes showing rivers and mountains, should be unaffected by the lapse of time; they stand for permanence in an ever-changing world. But this is not the case. Indeed even the way of seeing the ruins of Rome varies from one century to another and the artist's response is always that of his own age. In the XVIIIth century there was a special fondness for views of cities; for one thing, it was a century of travel and the artists tended to cater for the interest travelers naturally felt in the cities they visited. A picture of the ruins of Rome was an agreeable keepsake for the man who had visited the Eternal City or, if he had not, an invitation to come and see it. Moreover, the very aspect of the ruins, their broken surfaces and irregularities, appealed to that taste for the picturesque which steadily gained ground in the XVIIIth century. Already, in the previous century, Claude Lorrain had painted the Roman Forum, but it was left to Pannini to produce a host of depictions of the Roman ruins in a style essentially ' picturesque.' This cult of the picturesque was not confined to Italy. We need only mention the work of the French artist, Hubert Robert, whose way of seeing was similar, and yet more refined than Pannini's.

DURING the XVIIth century a German artist, Heinz the Younger, took to painting views of the Grand Canal at Venice, often including figures, and thus launched a fashion which was followed by Luca Carlevaris, and which, taking their lead from him, Canaletto and Guardi turned to good account. For neither Heinz nor Carlevaris had given their productions any true artistic value—they were ' views ' and little more. There is no question that the first painter to elevate this type of picture to the status of a work of art was Antonio Canal (known as Canaletto). So as the better to create the illusion of space he took to employing the ' camera obscura,' but we need not regard this as more than a technical expedient. Happily he also saw Venice with the eyes of a true artist, quick to respond to the strange enchantments of her skies, lagoons and waterways, and the harmonious outlines of her palaces. Moreover he could treat his subject lucidly, objectively, while none the less enraptured by its beauty. In his early works Canaletto obviously took special pleasure in strong contrasts of light and shade, which not only lent the picture a monumental grandeur but also a suggestion of mysterious depths beyond depths. Later on, however, he aimed at clarity, an explicit rendering of the beauty of forms. After his stay in London and his paintings of English scenes, his colors became lighter and more brilliant, without being balanced by passages of shadow; this gave the picture a gem-like luster, but also, it must be admitted, a certain shallowness.

Canaletto's nephew, Bernardo Bellotto, aimed constantly at a just balance between light and shade; while closely modeled on Canaletto's, his work displays a very personal use of color and a remarkable richness of surface.

Because Guardi's most famous pictures are views of Venice, his name and Canaletto's have persistently been coupled together. Yet au fond the two artists were very different. Guardi's training, personality and way of seeing were quite other than Canaletto's; in fact there is no point in looking for resemblances and, if we are to understand Guardi, we must approach him with an open mind. It should be noted, to begin with, that he came of a family more closely associated with Vienna than with Venice, and though his home was always in the latter city, during his formative years he came more under the influence of Viennese Baroque and Magnasco than under that of Canaletto. It may well have been Tiepolo, his brother-in-law, who inspired him with that predilection for intense color and dashing brush-work which characterizes his art. Finally, there is no denying that Guardi quite unblushingly " stole " from other artists motifs that had caught his fancy. And though in the XVIIIth century plagiarism did not incur the odium it has today, this habit suggests a certain creative indolence on Guardi's part. It is a remarkable fact that despite these handicaps, if such they were, and his failure to make any considerable name for himself in his lifetime, such was Guardi's genius that he may probably be regarded as the greatest artist of the whole Italian Settecento.

It is still a moot point whether the decorations of the organ-loft of St Raphael's of Venice are by his hand or the work of his brother Gian Antonio. The presence of figures proves nothing, for Francesco often used figures in his pictures. The decorations of this choir are certainly the masterwork of Venetian XVIIIth-century painting so far as the rendering of figures is concerned, and excellent painter as Gian Antonio was, we can hardly believe him capable of having reached such heights. During a period when melodrama was the order of the day and the artists were interpreting life in terms of the theater, these scenes are a delightful exception, such is their discretion, one might almost say humility. The silvery colors seem to whisper timidly of what is happening in the picture rather than voice it openly; brushstrokes are broken so that line and light are unified. Though no doubt similar procedures had already been used by Magnasco and Tiepolo, they are sublimated here to a pitch of delicate spirituality that has never been excelled.

In this context another illustration of Francesco Guardi's painterly discretion comes to mind; I am thinking of his *Gondola on the Lagoon* (Poldi-Pezzoli Museum, Milan). All he shows us is a strip of sea with a gondola in the foreground, in the distance a slender line of buildings, and a glimmering expanse of sky. Nothing could be simpler, yet this very simplicity gives the picture its universal significance. All nature is revealed to us in a few tones of blue, and everything is bathed in that exquisitely serene beauty which is peculiar to the light, the waters and the skies of Venice, miraculously rendered in one of those ecstatic moments when nature and the artist's vision are in happy unison.

The masterpieces—drawings no less than paintings—we owe to Francesco Guardi can be reckoned by hundreds; indeed it seems as if he had but to take up his pencil or his brush for him to produce some perfect work and for his whole style to spring to life at their mere contact with the paper or the canvas. Often one almost feels that he is unaware of his genius and squanders it with the noble lavishness of those to whom wealth means nothing.

The refinement of Rococo was bound up with the life of that aristocratic class which was swept away by the French Revolution. An interesting feature of Guardi's art is his gift of imparting an aristocratic elegance and grace to everything he paints: not only to the stones, lagoons and skies of Venice, but also to the most commonplace scenes that caught his fancy. Indeed the representation he gives us of the daily life of his time is fuller, richer in intimations, than that given by any other painter of his century.

CARAVAGGIO (1573-1610).
THE MAGDALEN, CA. 1590. (41½×38″)
DORIA GALLERY, ROME.

HISTORICAL SURVEYS
BY ROSABIANCA SKIRA-VENTURI

1

SEVENTEENTH CENTURY

★

CARAVAGGIO

A NEW INTERPRETATION OF VISUAL EXPERIENCE

AFTERMATH OF CARAVAGGIO

GENTILESCHI SARACENI BASCHENIS FETI STROZZI

CAVALLINO CERQUOZZI

CLASSICISM AND BAROQUE PAINTING

THE CARRACCI GUERCINO DOMENICHINO PRETI

BACICCIO PIETRO DA CORTONA

CARAVAGGIO
A NEW INTERPRETATION OF VISUAL EXPERIENCE

VASARI in the last (1568) edition of his *Lives of the Most Eminent Painters, Sculptors and Architects* admitted to a certain anxiety as regards the future of painting. " I feel convinced," he wrote, referring to the XVIth century, " that art has now done all that it is possible for an imitator of nature to do and reached so high a pitch that we have more reasons for fearing a decline than for hoping it will make progress." And there is no denying that the glorious achievements of the recent past weighed heavily on the century that was drawing to its close. Michelangelo and Raphael, Correggio and Titian exercised what was nothing short of an obsession on the XVIth century, an obsession that was destined to renew itself time and again in the course of art history. How, indeed, could those who shared Vasari's belief that Michelangelo had attained the acme of perfection hope that any advance was feasible and not share his fears for the future of art ?

It is common knowledge that the charge of decadence has often been brought against XVIIth-century art and that a whole art period used to be stigmatized under the then opprobrious label of " Baroque." Today, however, we can admire its very real merits, its adventurousness and the feverish intensity of its conceptions, foreshadowing the Romanticism of a later age. Though Italy no longer took the lead in the artistic flowering of the century, it was in Italy that the art problems of the future were envisaged and new paths opened up. Hardly nine years after Michelangelo's death a great painter was born, a man of a reckless, passionate disposition, whose genius was destined to have a decisive influence on the next generation. That man was Caravaggio.

His career was brief, but long enough to enable him to break with the past and play havoc with all accepted rules. In revolt against the politico-religious government of his day, and loathing hypocrisy of all descriptions, in art no less than in public morals, he fixed his eyes on the real world and it was on reality he called to breathe life into his compositions. Despite his natural arrogance he was humble enough where his painting was concerned, making direct, spontaneous expression his aim ; and though his work was often viciously attacked by contemporaries, such was its persuasive power that they were forced to recognize its value. We today are not biased in our judgment of Caravaggio's art by the life he led, that of an outlaw stung to violence by the least provocation ; but naturally enough it was otherwise in his lifetime. It might indeed be said that, seen in time's perspective, the artist's unruly way of life helps us to comprehend the psychological tension pervading all his work.

Michelangelo Merisi was born in the village of Caravaggio near Milan, whence he derived his name, in 1573. After the death of his father, architect to the Count of Caravaggio, he was apprenticed in early youth to the painter Peterzano, a pupil of Titian. On leaving

him (in or about 1593) he went to Rome where to begin with he had a hard struggle to keep afloat. We may assume that he had quarreled with his family, for no remittances came from them and he had to earn his living by menial tasks. Falling ill, he was admitted to the Hospital of the Consolation, where he did some painting for the Prior. Soon after this his fortunes took a turn for the better. A painter in high favor in ecclesiastical circles, Il Cavaliere d'Arpino, commissioned him to paint some still lifes, and before long two eminent art-patrons, Cardinal del Monte and the Marchese Giustiniani, took the young artist under their wing. In or about 1597 he was given a commission for a series of pictures for San Luigi dei Francesi. Thus Caravaggio's rise to fame was rapid ; starting from next to nothing, he had made a name for himself within four years. This does not seem so surprising when we remember the vast demand for pictures emanating from the dignitaries of the Roman Church. Men like d'Arpino and Baglione were snowed under with orders, but whilst these artists kept to the Mannerist procedures of the day, what Caravaggio stood for was nothing short of a revolution, a wholly new approach to painting. This, however, passed unnoticed until the San Luigi dei Francesi pictures were exhibited, and their appearance promptly brought a storm of abuse on the young painter's head.

A noteworthy feature of Caravaggio's art during his early period is the simplicity of the subjects he favored and the enthusiasm he showed for *motifs* often without figures, even mere baskets of fruit, was something completely new to art. It needed a very real devotion to nature and an ardent interest in painting for its own sake for a painter at the dawn of

CARAVAGGIO (1573-1610). BACCHUS AILING, CA. 1590. (26×20½″)
BORGHESE GALLERY, ROME.

CARAVAGGIO (1573-1610). BACCHUS AILING, CA. 1590. DETAIL.
BORGHESE GALLERY, ROME.

the XVIIth century to dispense so readily with the "noble subject" and the big historical theme. Indeed the chronicler Bellori was quick to hail Caravaggio as the inventor of a new genre, and the painter's declaration that "it cost him quite as much effort to make a good picture of flowers as one of figures" must have sounded like a manifesto at the time when it was made. The works of this period which have come down to us, with their smooth play of light on bright tonalities, show at once an amazing forthrightness and an obvious delight in rendering fruit and leafage suffused in, or reflecting, radiant light. When Caravaggio paints the *Maddalena* he lingers lovingly on the translucencies of the glass and the pearls, the sudden gleams on the young woman's auburn hair, and indeed transposes the religious theme on to the plane of everyday life. Faithful to his principles, he rules out that rhetorical emphasis on the Magdalen's personality which his contemporaries would have certainly indulged in. His treatment of the background as a wall isolating the subject and the low-pitched colors create an atmosphere at once poetic and serene, if faintly tinged with sadness. Whereas in *La Derelitta*, his picture of a woman excluded from her world by a wall and a fast-shut door, Botticelli had stressed the pathos of her lot, Caravaggio makes no secret of his joy in the mere act of creation and his love of life.

To this period belong several other religious pictures, including the *Rest during the Flight into Egypt* in which the composition is arranged symmetrically on both sides of the Angel. The peaceful group of the Woman and Child, the *finesse* of the landscape, the details so delicately rendered evoke an almost homely scene of family life. Also in such subjects as his *Bacchus*, the *Bacchus ailing* and the *Basket of Fruit* Caravaggio displayed a marvellous inventiveness and freedom of expression. Most famous of this group of works is perhaps the Basket, in the Ambrosiana (Milan), in which the clean-cut forms of the vineleaves and fruit telling out against a bright, uniform background, compose a finely rhythmic pattern. The light exalts each detail, infusing a wonderful sense of *joie de vivre* into the entire composition and harmonizing the brilliant colors. Considering the period when this picture was painted, the subject seems so unlikely that some have seen in it a detail of some larger picture, but there is nothing whatever to support this theory. Caravaggio uses similar motifs in his depiction of the young god of wine. He is expressing his juvenile delight in all the beauties of nature ; and he displays the same poetic exaltation whether he paints a bunch of grapes, an apple or a human figure.

The dating of the pictures painted by Caravaggio for the Contarelli Chapel in San Luigi dei Francesi was for long a moot question ; they are now assigned to the years 1597-1600. These are *The Vocation of Saint Matthew, The Martyrdom of Saint Matthew*, and *Saint Matthew and the Angel*. The first version of the last-named picture, owned by the Berlin Museum, was destroyed in 1945 ; the others are still in the church. According to contemporaries these were the painter's first " public " works ; in their day they encountered amazement and hostility, if tempered with a hint of admiration, and the artist's pride was galled by their reception. Nevertheless they now rank as major works in Caravaggio's *oeuvre*, the *Vocation* being probably his best known picture.

In his *Lives of the Modern Painters, Sculptors and Architects* (1672) Bellori has an anecdote *à propos* of Caravaggio's " realism." Looking at statues by Pheidias and Glycon, the painter's reaction was " to point with his hand towards a crowd of persons near by, thus indicating that Nature had sufficiently provided him with Masters." It is in a Customs office, serving for the occasion as a gaming-room, and amongst fashionably dressed young men—Caravaggio's boon companions—that, in *The Vocation of Saint Matthew*, Christ's outstretched hand beckons the apostle-to-be. But the portrayal of this relatively simple incident has become a miracle of light ; indeed light is its true protagonist, building up and revealing forms, and we are reminded of a phrase of music suspended for a moment in a brief lull of silence. Light ripples along the wall ; no ordinary light but one that wells up from an unseen source outside the picture. Its magic brings the figures to life, stressing individual responses yet uniting them in that vivid, almost physical sensation of a miracle which is produced by the picture as a whole.

Though many characteristics of Caravaggio's earlier art are present in this canvas light had never been used before in quite this manner, even by him. True, there are suggestions of a moralistic purpose, a covert attack on the social order, yet so sincere is the painter's devotion to his art that the overall effect is one of the purest poetic fervor. His genius was freeing him from the thrall of the knowledge he had amassed, and at the same time he was learning to control the unruly promptings of his pride. The truth expressed in this canvas is absolute, stripped clean of any literary sentiment or afterthought ; Caravaggio knew that any man might be the subject of a miracle.

The hostility and incomprehension of his *milieu*, and particularly the enmity of the Church, caused him much distress. He was particularly unfortunate with *Saint Matthew and*

CARAVAGGIO (1573-1610). THE FORTUNE-TELLER, CA. 1590. DETAIL.
ACCADEMIA CARRARA, BERGAMO.

CARAVAGGIO (1573-1610). THE VOCATION OF ST MATTHEW, 1597-1600. (129 × 137")
CHURCH OF SAN LUIGI DEI FRANCESI, ROME.

the Angel. " This work," Baglione writes, " was removed by the priests, who asserted that the leading figure had neither the attitude nor the aspect of a saint, sitting as he was cross-legged, with his feet shamelessly exposed to view." It can have been small consolation to the painter that the picture was acquired by the Marchese Giustiniani. Given his readiness to take offence, the affront done him by the Church must have exasperated him and intensified his temperamental instability.

From 1600 onwards the records have much to tell of the brawls in which Caravaggio's fierce temper involved him, the sword wounds of ever increasing severity he inflicted and received. In 1603 the painter and writer Giovanni Baglione (to whom we owe a detailed account of the artist's life) brought an action for libel against Caravaggio. Thanks to the good offices of the French Embassy he was released from prison, but he was forbidden to set foot outside his house without a permit. The records of the trial include an interesting declaration made by the painter on the subject of art. Speaking of painters, whom he styles *valenthuomini,* he explains that this term implies the artist's mastery of his craft ;" I call that painter *valenthuomo* who can excellently imitate natural objects." His contemporary Van Mander gives an interesting description (1603) of Caravaggio's swashbuckling habits, how he " always walked abroad with his sword dangling at his side, attended by a servant, and went from house to house, always ready to pick a quarrel, and was so choleric that it was difficult to have any dealings with him." All the eyewitness accounts tell of his arrogance and pugnacity, also of his habit of working by fits and starts, as the fancy took him.

None the less he was given many orders for pictures both religious (such as *The Conversion of Saint Paul* and *The Crucifixion of Saint Peter* for Santa Maria del Popolo, the *Madonna dei Pellegrini* for Sant' Agostino and the *Deposition* of the Pinacoteca Vaticana) and secular, such as the *Love Triumphant* (Berlin).

From now on a straining after expression stepped up to its maximum intensity makes itself felt more and more in Caravaggio's work ; the action is more dramatic and takes place simultaneously on two different planes, chiaroscuro is more and more accentuated, even the richness of the colors being subordinated to effects of light and shade. The painter tends to show the ' action ' in the picture as a struggle and exalts the atmosphere of storm and stress, convinced of its inherent beauty. His figures fight amongst themselves, hurl defiance at each other, and even when stricken to the earth are unsubdued. Though he himself was suffering deeply, tears and compassion were ruled out of his pictures during this phase. In the *Deposition*, for example (greatly admired by his contemporaries), the triumphant beauty of Christ's body and the grandiose orchestration of the shafts of light playing on all the figures show at their splendid best the artist's plastic vigor and indomitable vital energy. There is no denying that he aims at theatrical effect, there are definitely Baroque tendencies apparent in his art, and though Caravaggio's painterly sincerity prevents him from indulging in the extravagances of his successors, this theatricality constitutes a flaw. Sometimes, indeed, a detail has for us a purer, more compelling significance than the composition as a whole ; a musical instrument, a child's figure or objects on a table convey more happily that sense of simple, almost humble craftsmanship which gives *The Vocation of Saint Matthew* its delightful naturalness.

In 1605-1606 Caravaggio painted a series of works in which his ' Luminism ' became more discreet and his quest of movement less pronounced. Thus in *David and Goliath* (Borghese, Rome) the shadows mantling the faintly luminous body of David impart poetic overtones rarely found in his earlier works. According to Bellori we have in the grim, scowling face of Goliath a self-portrait. But surely it would be more plausible to see in the face of David, already faintly tinged with sadness, a nostalgic evocation of his lost youth. Similarly, in *The Death of the Virgin* (Louvre) the poignancy of the scene is enhanced by the play of shadows converging on the dimly lit body of the Virgin. Painted for the Church of Santa Maria della Scala, this picture was not deemed worthy of a place above the altar because " the Virgin's body was too bulky." It was bought by Rubens for the Duke of Mantua and finally found its way to France. This was not the only work rejected, but these rejections did not deter Cardinal Scipione Borghese, nephew of Pope Paul V, from voicing his admiration of Caravaggio's work and buying several of his pictures. Yet though the artist did not lack admirers he was embittered by the setbacks he encountered and grew more and more reckless in his conduct. He was imprisoned twice in 1605 ; then, having wounded a local lawyer, took refuge in Genoa where, however, his stay was brief. Though commissions flowed in steadily he was always in financial straits, the reason probably being that he so often neglected to fulfil his undertakings. Subject to what we now call persecution mania, and mentally unbalanced, he could never control his propensities to violence. Thus, on May 29, 1606, as the result of a quarrel over a game of rackets, he became involved in an affray which cost two men their lives and in which he, too, was wounded, with the result that he had to flee from Rome. This was the beginning of a hunted, nomadic life ; but though constantly in trouble for breaches of the peace and harried from town to town, Caravaggio continued to paint indefatigably, and there was now a new note of compassion in his work.

CARAVAGGIO (1573-1610). THE CONVERSION OF ST PAUL, 1600-1601. (90×69″)
CHURCH OF SANTA MARIA DEL POPOLO, ROME.

CARAVAGGIO (1573-1610). THE CRUCIFIXION OF ST PETER, 1600-1601. (90×69")
CHURCH OF SANTA MARIA DEL POPOLO, ROME.

33

For some time he remained in hiding near Rome, hoping that his friends would succeed in having the sentence on him quashed on the grounds that he was guilty only of " justifiable homicide," and that he would be allowed to return to the capital. After roaming from one town to another (little is known of his movements at this time) he went to Naples in the spring of 1607. We have records of several paintings of this period : the *Madonna of the Rosary* (perhaps another work rejected by the Church authorities) and, notably, the *Seven Works of Mercy* (Naples, Pio Monte della Misericordia)—a landmark in Caravaggio's output both as regards his own development and that of Neapolitan painting. " Amongst other things," Bellori writes, " we see the feet and limbs of a dead man being carried to the sepulchre; rays from a torch carried by the man who is holding up the body light up the white robe of the priest, while the glow kindled in the colors gives the whole composition its compelling strength. " The illumination of the canvas issues from different points and the result is an arabesque of lights and shadows from which the figures emerge with almost startling suddenness. The intricate, if slightly confused, construction shows that the painter had an elaborate compositional scheme in mind. Set in the midst of a tangle of draperies, of glistening wings and subtle glints of light playing upon the bare flesh of the angels, the figures of the Madonna and Child have a gentle, natural grace that strikes a note of exquisite repose. Elsewhere a woman's face, bathed in vivid light and charged with a mute appeal almost lacerating in its stark vulgarity, looms out above a crowd of wretched creatures milling in an inky darkness laced with silvery gleams. We feel that Caravaggio was determined to prove to himself that, however turbulent his private life, he had his painterly resources well in hand.

In 1608 he painted the portrait of the *Grand Master of the Order of the Knights of Malta* (Louvre) and was awarded the Cross of the Order of Knighthood, an honor which he greatly coveted since it enabled him to feel on an equal social footing with his rivals, notably the Cavaliere d'Arpino. While in Malta he painted several pictures (cited by Bellori). But as usual his unruly temper landed him in trouble, this time with a high official of the judicature, who had him thrown into prison. On October 6 he escaped, took ship and landed at Syracuse. On the verge of a nervous breakdown he wandered about Sicily, visiting Messina and Palermo, before venturing to return to Naples. The existence he was leading, of a man ' wanted ' by the police, had not prevented his painting some outstanding works in Sicily : *The Burial of Saint Lucia*, *The Resurrection of Lazarus* and *The Adoration of the Shepherds*. The prevailing tonality of these works is somber, all movement seems arrested in a few, brief flashes of dazzling light, and the figures have the look of phantoms isolated from the world by a wall of clotted darkness. Surely no more poignant rendering of utter grief exists than the form of the Madonna clasping the Child in her arms (in *The Adoration of the Shepherds*, Museo Nazionale, Messina), and in the rapt gaze of the shepherds we seem to read a mute interrogation : Why should such suffering be ? In his brief, tragic career Caravaggio paid a heavy price for the ability to express so intensely in his art the lot of the outcast, forsaken by all. While at Naples he was so severely wounded by one of his enemies that he was left for dead ; indeed on October 24, 1609, the report was circulated in Rome that : " News has come from Naples that the well-known painter Caravaggio has been killed ; some, however, say he is only wounded." At death's door he embarked on a felucca bound for Rome. Wishing to make sure that he could count on a pardon from the Pope, he halted at Porto Ercole, a Spanish possession, where by a mistake he was imprisoned for two days. This judicial error had disastrous consequences for the artist, for when released he was completely destitute, the boat having meanwhile sailed with all his belongings on board. On July 18, 1610, a fatal attack of malaria cut short, at the early age of 37, a life which was surely the stormiest in the whole history of painting.

Caravaggio had opened up a new field of painting and foreigners as well as Italians drew inspiration from him. Considering the dramatic power of his art and its direct appeal to the spectator, the great influence he exercised on subsequent painting is easily understandable. True, what is known as Luminism was nothing new in Italy and there had been

CARAVAGGIO (1573-1610). DAVID AND GOLIATH, 1605-1606. (40 × 39 ½″)
BORGHESE GALLERY, ROME.

many great visionaries of light, from Cimabue to Tintoretto ; it was, however, left to Caravaggio to give light the leading rôle, that of creating and revealing life. Indeed the peculiar dynamism of his compositions derives from oppositions of light and shade, which not only stress the psychological climax but conjure up suggestions of events, adumbrated rather than expressed. Unlike Titian, Caravaggio set much store on rendering volumes, his early works show that he gave close study to the problem of conveying a sense of real mass existing in space ; in his later work he indicates them by the play of light alone.

In the *oeuvre* of Caravaggio his contemporaries and successors found a rich mine of discovery. Thus his so-called realism was taken over wholesale, schematized or sometimes toned down, according to the temperament of the artist concerned ; likewise his use of strong contrasts of light and shade was carried by some artists to excessive lengths. But, above all, we must not forget how much such masters as Velazquez, Rembrandt and Vermeer learnt from Caravaggio. Indeed it was not in Italy that the revolutionary qualities of his art were exploited to best effect ; for, owing perhaps to the special historical and religious conditions of the times, the Italian painters employed Caravaggio's realistic Luminism with much caution and a characteristic suavity that glossed over its rebellious vehemence.

CARAVAGGIO (1573-1610). ADORATION OF THE SHEPHERDS, 1609. (123 ¼ × 82 ¾")
MUSEO NAZIONALE, MESSINA.

AFTERMATH OF CARAVAGGIO

GENTILESCHI SARACENI BASCHENIS FETI STROZZI CAVALLINO CERQUOZZI

WE can get some idea of what Rome meant to XVIIth-century painters by comparing her artistic role with that which Paris played during the first half of this century. It was to Rome, as in our time to Paris, that artists of all nations flocked for instruction and inspiration, it was there that ideas proliferated and interest in art was keenest. From the end of the XVIth and throughout the following century the Popes, well aware that art could be one of the most effective forms of propaganda, promoted and commissioned a host of ventures in the various fields of art, especially architecture. Baglione tells us that Gregory XIII " used to say that building edifices was an act of public charity. " Thus, besides the vast restorations and embellishments carried out at St Peter's, a surprising number of churches were built at this time, and the ' new style ' then developed spread all over Europe. " Vignola's Church of Gesù, " wrote Marcel Reymond at the beginning of the present century, " corresponded so well with all that one could wish a church to be that it has served as a model up to our own times. " Sculpture, too, made great strides ; we need only recall the career of that famous sculptor Bernini, architect and painter too. Thus papal patronage enhanced the prestige of Rome as an art center and all the most eminent artists flocked to the city. To name but two, Poussin and Claude Lorrain found here exactly the climate needed for the flowering of their art. The great and small of the art-world lived in such close contact with one another and shared the same sources of inspiration to such an extent that today it is sometimes practically impossible to sort out the work of certain lesser artists with precision. Some of them, indeed, would be of definitely minor interest, did not their works testify so clearly to the impact of Caravaggio's artistic personality and to Rome's position as a fountainhead of new ideas. It was they, moreover, who carried abroad the doctrines of the new ' luminist ' art.

Orazio Gentileschi belonged to the same generation as Caravaggio. Born at Pisa about 1563, he went to Rome when still a boy. His contacts with the art of Caravaggio undoubtedly had more effect on his development than the works in the Mannerist tradition he saw in Florence and those of the School of Bologna (though he was much impressed by Guido Reni). Gentileschi's *Woman playing the Lute* (Prince of Liechtenstein's Collection) has a finely balanced harmony of bright tones, to which the gracefulness and ease of its construction lend a particular charm. This is due not only to the artist's technical ability ; his sensitive handling of the highlights in the colors is in perfect keeping with the musical subject. Though some have attributed this canvas to Caravaggio, it obviously lacks the compelling power which distinguishes that artist's work, and this attribution is highly questionable, to say the least of it. Generally speaking, Gentileschi favors a lighting that sharply defines volumes, while bringing out colors and intensifying their sheen.

Besides painting a large number of works for the churches of Rome, he was employed in several cities of the Marches. From 1621 on he was at Genoa, whence he left for France upon the invitation of Marie de' Medici. In 1626 he settled in England, where he worked at the Court of Charles I ; there he remained until his death, which is believed to have taken place in 1647.

Gentileschi carried the tidings of Caravaggio's innovations to the north of Europe and thus left his mark on Dutch painting. His painter daughter, Artemisia, following in his footsteps, assimilated some of the features of Caravaggio's art and propagated them in the south of Italy, at Naples in particular.

Whereas, in Gentileschi's painting, the influence of Caravaggio is grafted on to the Florentine mannerist tradition, the early work of Saraceni shows this painter's fondness for Venetian color. (We may note *en passant* that likewise Caravaggio's art took its rise in a mannerist climate before he developed a vision somewhat like that of Giorgione.)

Carlo Saraceni was born at Venice in or about 1580; he came to Rome in the early years of the XVIIth century and died in 1620. He may be assimilated to those 'little masters' who, anticipating Rembrandt, were experimenting with effects of luminous shadows. He belonged to the same cultural group as the German Elsheimer and the Frenchman Jean Le Clerc, an intimate friend with whom he worked in close collaboration at Venice. After Saraceni's death, Le Clerc undertook the completion of the decorative compositions begun by his friend at the Ducal Palace.

The characteristics of Caravaggio's way of seeing play a large part in Saraceni's art. However, Saraceni never showed a desire for dramatic expression ; he concentrated on the anecdotal aspects of his subjects and what delights us in his compositions is the elegant movement of the figures and the exquisiteness of the tones. And if, like Caravaggio, he sometimes devotes much care to depicting objects such as musical instruments, what really interests him is their pleasing appearance and the rhythmic possibilities of their structure. Thus his handling of light also takes a particular form ; he shows much adroitness in using it to give its utmost value to a bright passage or to set off juxtaposed colors to the best effect. In his *Judith and Holophernes* Saraceni brilliantly plays off opposing tones and values against each other. From a haze of shadows floating around the woman's figure softly rises the quiet beauty of her face ; the head of Holophernes evokes no sense of tragedy or horror, but like some queer, grimacing mask faintly emerges from the gloom, while the spectator's gaze is held by the sparse touches of color on the white drapery and the shadowed face. Whereas Caravaggio's *David* is charged with poetic feeling, Saraceni charms us with the grace and elegance of his figures' attitudes ; his work as a whole seems devoid of real emotion and the religious theme is a mere pretext for pictorial effects.

The movement towards portrayals of home life and a choice of subjects which, though commonplace, were felt to have a truth lacking to more pretentious themes enabled the Dutch artists to achieve a sober grandeur in keeping with the earnestness of their Protestantism. In Italy, however, the Counter-Reformation had won the day and the Catholic Church, with an eye to edification, assigned to painting loftier aims than the illustration of daily life and common objects. All the same some Italian painters of the period — those who have been called " painters of the everyday " — began to show a certain interest in such subjects, and this new development owed not a little to Caravaggio.

In one of Caravaggio's pictures the sole theme is a basket of fruit, and in other canvases he laid much stress on accessories such as flowers and fruit. Inspired no doubt by these precedents, Baschenis devoted himself whole-heartedly to the still life, and especially to musical instruments, and he never wearied of grouping and regrouping them in telling combinations. Indeed, such is the loving care which he devotes to bringing forth the ' living presence ' of the objects of a still life that his work bears a real stamp of originality.

Evaristo Baschenis came of a very old Bergamask family which, generation after generation, from the second half of the XVth up to the XVIIth century, produced painters specializing, for the most part, in church decorations. Born at Bergamo in 1617, Evaristo

ORAZIO GENTILESCHI (1563?-1647?). YOUNG WOMAN PLAYING THE LUTE, CA. 1626. (56¾×51″)
COLLECTION OF THE PRINCE OF LIECHTENSTEIN, VADUZ.

elected for a career in the Church, but spent most of his time painting. His life was uneventful ; simple-minded, studious and contemplative by nature, he seems never to have left his
native city, where he died in 1677.

  We sometimes find figures in his pictures, but always either set off with flower motifs
or shown playing the virginal or the viol ; and though now and again he painted a still life
of fish or shellfish, it was as a ' portraitist of musical instruments ' that Baschenis excelled.
There are recalls of Caravaggio in his way of using contrasts of light to make volumes tell

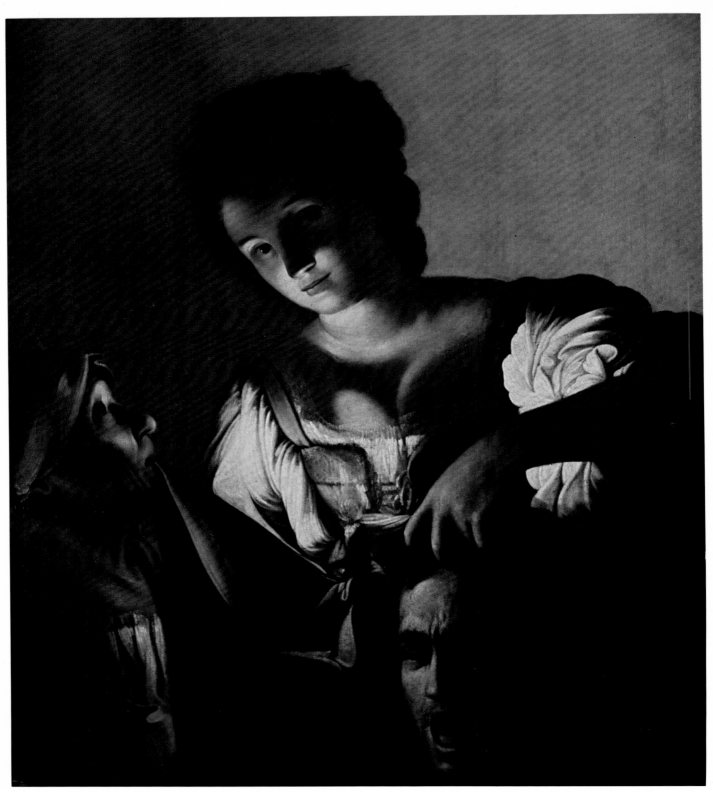

CARLO SARACENI (1580-1620). JUDITH AND HOLOPHERNES, 1610-1620. (35½×31″)
MUSEUM, VIENNA.

out against a dark background, and he imparts to colors a bright, particular sheen sharply
defining the contours of objects. He is careful to render the exact texture of each element
in his composition : the different kinds of wood with which the instruments are made, the rich,
lustrous surface of draperies ; likewise he indicates not only the individual stitches in a tapestry, but even the layer of dust on woodwork and the notes of a musical score. For all his
literalism, however, Baschenis so well understood the secrets of harmonious lay-out and the
balanced distribution of volumes that he builds up as it were a world apart. His colors kindle
sudden gleams amidst the shadows, bringing out the gloss of varnished wood ; almost we
fancy that echoes of the music these instruments have been discoursing linger on the air.
It is not known whether the painter was also a musician. But it is significant that

among his contemporaries, hailing from the same part of Italy, were the most famous lute-makers of the day, men like Nicola Amati, and the great Stradivari, whose marvellous violins have never been surpassed. Baschenis took a passionate delight in the beauty of these instruments ; he painted them again and again, weaving their rich curves into his compositions with unfailing zest, diversifying the pattern now and then with motifs of fruit or colored ribbons. He used light in such a way as to illuminate them from within, and his warm colors so as to exalt their shapely forms and structure. True, Baschenis' art was limited in scope and the spirit behind it is perhaps that of the provincial artisan, yet so intense is his feeling for the world of the still life that he sublimates it to the purest poetry.

André Malraux has recently observed that when painting for his own satisfaction " Rubens is less tragic, but more intensely a painter. With him, clouds, ascending saints, extravagant foreshortenings—all end up as heavily charged brushstrokes, and this irruption of purely plastic values destroys theatricality, because it destroys illusion." In Italy, more than elsewhere, the artist found it difficult to conceive of an art dispensing with illusionism and existing in terms of plastic values alone. It was asking too much of him that he should turn his back on the great allegorical and heroic themes favored not only by a long Italian tradition, but also by the authorities employing him. Even so, whenever he humbly set himself to solving the basic problems of the *métier*, he turned his attention to what later became known as the 'genre piece' and was brought to perfection by the Dutch. This kind of picture did not call for heroic gestures or metaphysical allusions. Its point of departure was sometimes the anecdote ; its essence was always the revelation of the painter's personality in his way of treating a group, an interior, or some common household utensils.

EVARISTO BASCHENIS (1617-1677). MUSICAL INSTRUMENTS, CA. 1650. (29½ × 42½")
ACCADEMIA CARRARA, BERGAMO.

We may now glance for a moment at three Italian painters — Domenico Feti, a Roman, Bernardo Strozzi, a Genoese, and Bernardo Cavallino, a Neapolitan — who though widely differing in temperament and background, illustrate, each in his way, this new development in painting and who, though they failed to give full expression to it, produced works that are significant of the changing climate of the epoch.

DOMENICO FETI (1589-1624). MELANCHOLY, CA. 1614-1621. DETAIL.
LOUVRE, PARIS.

BERNARDO STROZZI (1581-1644). THE PIPER, CA. 1623-1625. (34 ¼ × 26 ¾″)
PALAZZO ROSSO, GENOA.

Feti, who figures in Baglione's *Lives*, was born in 1589. When still a boy he frequented the Roman artistic *milieu* and from 1611 on was employed by Ferdinando Gonzaga, soon to become Duke of Mantua. In 1613, following his patron, he settled at Mantua, with the post of adviser on artistic matters and curator of the Duke's art collection, at that time one of the largest in Italy (it was subsequently sold in its entirety to Charles I of England). In 1621 Feti made a trip to Venice to purchase works of art for the Duke; next year he made his home there, and it was in Venice that he died, in 1624. During his lifetime the artist's reputation was of the highest. Nowadays he is known chiefly for a series of small pictures he painted to illustrate the parables of Christ; most of these are now in Dresden.

Feti's lighting effects stem directly from Caravaggio, while his brushwork seems to owe something to Rubens. His practice of building up the picture in contrasting touches and planes was obviously a method involving the risk of lapsing into over-emphasis. From this, as a matter of fact, Feti was saved by his refined sensibility, thanks to which his pictures are vibrant with a life of their own in which no idealization of the subject on heroic or classical lines plays any part. His *Melancholy* (Louvre) is like a sentimental theme on which the painter has embroidered ingenious variations, intent on making each color accent or contrast of luminous planes in deep recession tell out on the canvas.

Bernardo Strozzi was born at Genoa in 1581 and died at Venice in 1644. His was a different temperament altogether, headstrong and sensual, and his execution was of a coarser order than Feti's; yet this very vulgarity led him to a greater vitality of expression. At the early age of fifteen he devoted himself exclusively to painting, and though at seventeen he entered the Order of the Capuchins, he soon applied for a dispensation permitting him to give his whole time to art. His request was granted and, renouncing the monastic life, he quit his native city and moved to Venice. This did not, however, prevent his remaining in good odor with the Church authorities and in 1635 he was given the title of Monsignor.

Strozzi was trained in the Mannerist traditions which, at the time of his youth, were still flourishing at Genoa. But it is clear that he was no less influenced by Rubens' works, a considerable number of which could then be seen in that city. The first-hand contact he later had with the work of the great Venetian painters gave him a chance to freshen and vivify his style. We see Strozzi's real personality not so much in his religious pictures as in such genre scenes as *The Cook* and *The Piper* in the Palazzo Rosso at Genoa. In the last-named picture the figure of the musician displays the almost brutal force and seething vitality typical of Strozzi's manner; particularly striking is the skillful play of contrasts and the calculated emphasis of the musician's attitude. Strozzi's art has its shortcomings, for it never quite reached the goal he had set himself: of conjuring up with his brush homely and direct expressions of the life around him. All the same we owe to him one of the most interesting ventures in genre painting in XVIIth-century Italy.

While Feti makes us think of an occasionally brilliant composer of small prose poems and Strozzi of a realistic story-teller, Cavallino might be described as a poet in a minor key, sentimental and delicately perceptive.

Bernardo Cavallino was born in 1616 at Naples and continued living there until his death in 1658. He obviously owed much to Caracciolo, one of the leading Neapolitan imitators of the style of Caravaggio. There were many artistic cross-currents in Naples during the period of Cavallino's active career, noteworthy being a vast enthusiasm for decoration. Cavallino's practice seems to have been to take over some elements from each of the various tendencies then in vogue and assimilate them into his own personality. But, sensitive as he was and something of an introvert, he preferred intimate expression to the portrayal of spectacular events. By a dextrous handling of light he imparted to his colors a gemlike luster, while his crisp, simplified form foreshadows in some respects the art of the following century. Thus Cavallino gives an impression of standing out against the tendencies then prevalent in Naples and, thanks to the poetical quality of his work, cuts an attractive figure amongst the small group of painters who aimed at creating a non-official art exempt from any doctrinaire intentions.

BERNARDO CAVALLINO (1616-1658).
ST CECILIA AND THE ANGEL, CA. 1645. (24½×19½″)
PINACOTECA, NAPLES.

MICHELANGELO CERQUOZZI (CA. 1602-1660). THE ROMAN BATH, AFTER 1647. (48½×67¾″)
COLLECTION OF ELEONORA INCISA DELLA ROCCHETTA, NÉE CHIGI, ROME.

A general survey, however summary, of the various movements which associated or antagonized the painters working in Rome during the first half of the XVIIth century, must take into account a group of artists centering on the Dutch painter Van Laer, who owing to a physical deformity was nicknamed Bamboccio by the Italians, with the result that his followers came to be known as the " Bamboccianti." They specialized in painting street scenes and picturesque glimpses of the life of the common people. While borrowing much from Caravaggio, the work of the Bamboccianti was sadly lacking in the vigor and majestic power of Caravaggio's art ; its chief interest consists in an entertaining, pleasantly descriptive realism, combined with much executive skill and shrewd observation. Michelangelo Cerquozzi (1602-1660) is the Italian painter who displays most originality in his handling of the Bamboccio style. He specialized in battle-pieces, to such effect as to be grandilo-quently styled the " Michelangelo of Battles "—but less flattering contemporaries later called him "our Michelangelo of Bambocciate." This wholly new development, coming at a time when the other Roman artists were haunted by visions of the grandiose and the sublime, was a salutary diversion from the beaten path. The Bamboccianti were much esteemed in their day; indeed the aristocratic families crowded the walls of their residences with their pictures, in which the petty trades and the daily avocations of the average citizen were depicted with a faintly supercilious whimsicality. In Cerquozzi's *Roman Bath* the collaboration of Codazzi in laying out the perspective is authenticated by the oldest records. It has been suggested that in respect of some of its elements (especially the naked woman reclining in the foreground) this picture pointed the way to certain aspects of Dutch painting and also of Velazquez' art. There is a pleasant touch of humor in the artist's treatment of his unpretentious subject. While the glints of color in the chiaroscuro add much vivacity to the *ensemble*, discreetly stated highlights bring out the translucency of certain details, such as the vase of flowers at the window. The tirades of the champions of Classicism against these Bambocciianti have a quite modern ring. Thus, in reply to a letter from Sacchi lamenting the decadence of painting, Albani, another classical painter, after a half-hearted acknowledgment of the painters' technical skill, goes on to say : " Your invective has kindled in my heart as well so fierce a flame of scorn and indignation that I would wish my voice were that of Jove the Thunderer and my language lightning. Can such things be ? Are we to see our noble Queen, divine art, dragged down into the stews and pigstys ? " One almost seems to hear a spokesman of the XIXth-century French middle class declaiming against the " Bohemian " obliquities of the young French artists. But the Bambocciianti lacked the driving force to carry their art beyond the stage of the merely quaint and picturesque, and to conquer a new field of art.

MICHELANGELO CERQUOZZI (CA. 1602-1660). THE ROMAN BATH, AFTER 1647. DETAIL. COLLECTION OF ELEONORA INCISA DELLA ROCCHETTA, NÉE CHIGI, ROME.

GENERAL VIEW OF THE DECORATIONS IN THE FARNESE PALACE, ROME.

48

CLASSICISM AND BAROQUE PAINTING

THE CARRACCI GUERCINO DOMENICHINO PRETI BACICCIO PIETRO DA CORTONA

WHEN, leaving Caravaggio out of account, we study the currents and cross-currents of art at the beginning of the XVIIth century, we seem to discern a certain deeply seated psychic disequilibrium in the artists' apprehension of their *métier*. Between their endeavors and intentions, on the one hand, and their actual achievements on the other, there is a hiatus, which cannot be attributed either to a lack of serious purpose or to inadequate talent. But the creative impulse seems to be stifled, unable freely to exert itself ; the moral ' climate ' of the age precluded this and the painters sometimes fell back on a classical ideal—that which had given rise to masterpieces in the remote past—or sometimes over-stressed emotions they no longer felt. In both cases, they broke contact with life, with the world in which their lot was cast and with which they had to reckon. Michelangelo, too, had been acutely conscious of the moral drama of his age, but he had nourished his art with his tragic sense of life. Raphael had worshipped classical art but, though full of enthusiasm for the resuscitation of ancient Rome, he had created in his painting forms that were his alone and in complete accord with his personality. But in the XVIIth century classical antiquity came to mean an ' ideal ' or a thesaurus of pictorial recipes, and when the artist sought to body forth the drama of his age, he lapsed into mere theatrical effect.

Hence the cross-currents we so often find in the art of the individual artist and the incoherence often manifest in his choice of his means of expression; often, a strain of Baroque extravagance mingles with aspirations towards classicism, and the vague awareness of these inner conflicts imparts to some XVIIth-century works a feeling of nostalgic regret, of a poetic surrender to illusion. It is perhaps this quasi-romantic quality that most appeals to us today. But it was not so in the XVIIth century ; the writers and art-lovers of that period took a very different view. Thus the classicism of the Carracci was regarded in Italy, France and England—and for fully two centuries after their death—as an authentic revival of the great Italian tradition. Bellori speaks of Annibale as " that very great genius, thanks to whom Art, long moribund, flowers anew." Indeed the school of the Carracci was held to have been " the salvation of Italian painting."

These three men whose works and teachings exercised so vast an influence and enjoyed such fame were the two brothers, Agostino and Annibale Carracci, and their cousin Lodovico. In 1582 the three Carracci (who came of Lombard stock) founded an art school at Bologna : L'Accademia degli Incamminati. After a humble start this school, between 1590 and 1595, rose to immense celebrity ; indeed Bologna came to be styled " the new Athens." Of the trio, Lodovico (born 1555) seems to have been the organizer, Agostino (born 1557) was more drawn to engraving, had literary tastes and acted as the theoretician of the school, while Annibale (born 1560) was the most naturally gifted as a painter. At Bologna the school,

ANNIBALE CARRACCI (1560-1609). THE FLIGHT INTO EGYPT, CA. 1603. (47×88¼″)
DORIA GALLERY, ROME.

collaborating with immense ardor, decorated several *palazzi* (Fava, Magnani, Sampieri) and carried their sense of fellowship to the point of answering, when asked what part of a work was done by each, " We did it all of us together." However, in 1595 the Carracci parted company, Annibale going to Rome (whither Agostino soon followed him), while Lodovico stayed at Bologna, where he retained his post of director of the Accademia until his death in 1619.

Meanwhile the Carracci made several journeys (the dates are not known) with a view to widening their knowledge : to Parma to study Correggio, to Venice to study the great masters of color : Titian, Tintoretto, Veronese. Thus they followed conscientiously the paths which, to their thinking, led inevitably to art's perfection. For if the criteria of all great art were observance of the rules, harmonious proportions, observation of nature (interpreted by the reasoning mind) and the exaltation of Man, lord of creation, as the ideal figure—if these assumptions were correct, it necessarily followed that " to constitute a supremely perfect art " (for they aimed at nothing short of this) all that was needed was to combine the drawing of one great master, the color of another, and the light effects of a third. It also followed that the style of these eclectic classicists did not keep to a quite coherent line of development.

The magnum opus to which Annibale Carracci owed his vast renown was his work at the Farnese Palace. Cardinal Farnese had summoned him to Rome in 1595 and commissioned him to paint the decorations of the ' Camerino ' and the ' long room ' of his Palace whose building had been supervised by Michelangelo. The decoration was to be a glorification (allegorical, needless to say) of the great deeds done by the Cardinal's famous father, Alessandro Farnese.

Agostino made haste to come to Rome and help his brother, but dissensions soon arose between them. It seems probable that Annibale had too strong a personality not to chafe at the constant presence and advice of a colleague more gifted as a theorist than as a painter. Perhaps, too, he realized that if they both had a hand in it, the work as a whole would lack that overall coherence on which he set much store. In any case Agostino moved to Parma in 1600, and Annibale carried on the work without him, seconded only by his pupils, one of whom was Domenichino.

Praised to the skies in its day, this great *ensemble* still impresses us by its gorgeousness, the sense of opulence it conveys, and it did much to shape the taste of subsequent generations of art-lovers. While there is no denying the artist's decorative talent and the wealth of his imagination, we cannot help feeling that he sacrificed the latter to a rather tedious display of culture and, following a practice of the day, multiplied details to excess. Hence the impression of over-crowding we get from the composition as a whole ; also of needless complication in the distribution of the picture-space. By way of recalling the sculpture and bas-reliefs of antiquity, the fresco is studded with *motifs* imitating stucco ornaments and bronze medallions. The various scenes are presented as though glimpsed through windows opening on the sky. In the 'long room' the stuccos are in white and gold, while caryatids painted to look like statues in grey marble seem to uphold the gayly colored vault decorated with mythological themes. This ceiling is a mass of figures seen in strong foreshortening against the blue of the sky and the painter has lavished all the resources of his craft on stressing the splendor of the scene. Yet this work gives us a feeling that the artist was troubled by conflicting purposes ; he wanted to convey rapid movement and the interplay of vivid colors and at the same time to realize the classical ideal of a static equilibrium. Hesitating between these two alternatives, Annibale failed to get the best out of himself and perhaps, like so many eclectics, to understand that for the production of good painting good intentions are not enough. Where, however, he gave rein to his natural sensibility, especially in his renderings of nature, he displays a fine sense of rhythmic composition. Thus in *The Flight into Egypt* (Doria Gallery, Rome) the landscape (much the best part of the picture) seems tranced in an all-pervasive, dreamlike calm. Here indeed we have the " ideal equilibrium " dear to the classical artist, combined with something new in art ; that intimate feeling for nature which Poussin, too, achieved in his most famous canvases. This picture formed part

GUERCINO (1591-1666). LANDSCAPE, 1621. FRAGMENT OF A DECORATION.
VILLA LUDOVISI, ROME.

of a set of illustrations of biblical scenes made for a chapel in the Villa Aldobrandini. Dated approximately 1603-1604, it was one of Annibale's last works, being painted after he had fallen ill and when he was depending largely on the aid of his assistants. Nevertheless in *The Flight into Egypt,* by far the best work in the set of decorations, the master's touch is unmistakable. With its colors so subtly pervaded by the dominant tonality and so well harmonizing with the greenish-blue evening light, this composition is obviously no casual inspiration but the fruit of long meditation on the Bible story. In this connection an observation made by Valenciennes, a French landscape-painter of the early XIXth century, with reference to Poussin (in his *Théorie du paysage*) may be quoted: " The color of the artist's feeling should take precedence of his feeling for color." This dictum, which throws light on the aspirations of the classicist painters, holds good not only for Poussin but for this work of Annibale Carracci, in which his feeling for the sacred subject of the picture is expressed by the idealistic rendering of the landscape and the poetic emotion imparted to every detail. We can well understand the widespread influence of this work on the subsequent development of this genre of painting, which aimed at bringing out the " noble " side of nature. In other landscapes attributed to Annibale, though we see the same aspiration towards balance and serenity, it is difficult to determine precisely the shares of the master and his pupils.

Annibale Carracci's last years were darkened by an ever-increasing hypochondria and misanthropy. For one thing, he had been very badly paid for his work at the Farnese Palace

DOMENICHINO (1581-1641). GIRL WITH A UNICORN, CA. 1602.
PALAZZO FARNESE, ROME.

and this preyed on his mind. In 1605 he had a stroke but he continued painting, in self-imposed solitude, nursing his grievances, until his death four years later.

The large place assigned to the school of the Carracci in art history is also due to the great number of painters it turned out ; indeed their production, especially in the field of decoration, was nothing short of prodigious. Domenico Zampieri, better known by the slightly pejorative diminutive of Domenichino, was born in 1581. After studying under the Carracci at Bologna he moved to Rome, where he took part in painting the frescos at the Farnese Palace, one scene of which, the *Girl with a Unicorn*, is generally regarded as being entirely by his hand. The simplicity of the theme and the daintily executed landscape, all in soft, pale tones, lend the scene not only a naïve descriptive charm, but create the atmosphere of an old-world fairy-tale.

Gifted with a fine sensitivity, this artist achieves a delicate harmony of gay colors, while preserving a classic balance of design—a combination far to seek in most of the painting of the XVIIth century. This is doubtless why Domenichino has been described as "a Quattrocento painter who somehow strayed into the Seicento." Unfortunately he lacked the strength of personality that would have enabled him to hold his own against the various art tendencies of the age into which he had been born.

In the course of his career he seems to have met with more than his share of setbacks and disappointments, and this soured his temper. Yet there were many who thought highly of him and he did not lack for commissions. His *Flagellation of St Andrew* first brought him into the public eye and he was later chosen to decorate the Farnese Chapel in the Abbey of Grottaferrata, near Rome. The *Communion of St Jerome*, the frescos in the Church of San Luigi dei Francesi at Rome and the *Bath of Diana* are among his best known works and they still have their admirers.

Around 1630 he was called on to decorate the Chapel of the Treasure in the Naples Cathedral. His experiences in Naples were disheartening ; he made *faux pas*, was plagued with endless intrigues and petty vexations. The truth is probably that the Neapolitan public had been by now so completely won over to the art of Caravaggio and the Spanish painters that Domenichino's work struck them as tedious and insipid. The painter himself, moreover, was temperamental and by no means easy to get along with. By 1634 things had come to such a pass that he had to flee from Naples. When, later, he returned to that city, his troubles began all over again ; nevertheless he remained there until his death (in 1641), poisoned, rumor had it, by his enemies. Even Bellori, warm admirer of Domenichino though he was, had to admit that the work he did at Naples was certainly the least successful part of his *œuvre*.

If the greatness of a painter is to be evaluated by the adulation and enthusiasm of contemporaries, or by an esteem that remained untarnished for nearly two centuries after his death, surely the palm would go to Guido Reni. The *literati*, it is true, did not endorse the admiration lavished on him by the public, by the official circles of the Church and the great foreign Courts of the day. The fact remains that Guido Reni succeeded in producing exactly the kind of painting that his contemporaries—and many generations to come—most greatly relished. Indeed this artist became the object of a veritable cult. The sublime grace of his figures, the skill with which he visually interpreted the passions of the soul, the pathos he evoked without ever clouding the cup of beauty—surely such endowments were beyond the scope of any ordinary mortal, and could only be the result of divine inspiration ! The riddle of man's life on earth and his anguished yearnings after God were read into Guido Reni's works, and so lovely were his figures, so graceful their attitudes, that it seemed to those who saw his pictures that they were being given glimpses of Paradise itself. This, in fact, is how Guido's contemporaries, with that habit of overstatement characteristic of the age, did not hesitate to put it. For us today Guido Reni is perhaps chiefly memorable for initiating that luscious type of painting later known in France as *la peinture de Saint-Sulpice*. Though no artist should be blamed for the misdeeds of his followers and imitators, we are bound to recognize that the germs of future excesses were

GUERCINO (1591-1666). NIGHT, 1621. DETAIL. FRAGMENT OF A DECORATION.
VILLA LUDOVISI, ROME.

already present in his work. Thus the vigorous reaction against him which accompanied the rise of Romanticism is easily understandable. In justice, however, to the artist it should be pointed out that the abject flattery of his admirers, coupled with the weakness of his character, may have done much to handicap his very real talent. Be this as it may, it is hard for us really to like Guido Reni. Used to freer flights of the creative imagination, we are allergic to forms that strike the modern eye as stiff and lifeless, however superlative the painter's technical ability. Yet we cannot afford to condemn this kind of art off-hand or to ignore the very great influence Guido Reni had on the artists of his day—and on many later generations. Indeed we might go so far as to say that the very anomalies of his art throw much light on this period of art history when so many high hopes came to nothing, so many very real gifts were squandered.

Guido Reni was born in 1575 at Calvenzano, near Bologna, where he went in early youth to study painting, his first teacher being Denis Calvaert. In 1595 he quit this master and enrolled in the Academy of the Carracci. He very soon made his mark, and in 1600 migrated to Rome. Three years later, as a result of a dispute with a prelate, he left the city abruptly and returned to Bologna. The incident, famous in its way, throws light on Reni's character; we are told that when the prelate commented adversely on his painting, the artist retorted that, while there were plenty of priests in the world, there was but one Guido Reni. From 1605 to 1622 he was again living in Rome, though during this period he made trips to Ravenna, Naples and back to Bologna, in which city he finally settled for good, and it was in Bologna that he died, in 1642.

Thus, throughout his career, the painter never faltered in his devotion to the city where he got his start, indeed he went so far as to decline an invitation from the King of France to come to that country. True, he much appreciated flattery, official honors and substantial payments for his work; nevertheless his chief desires seem to have been to be allowed to paint in peace and to indulge in his propensity for the gaming-table. This may surprise us in an artist so gifted by nature, whose chief concern was to represent with ideal grace and in terms of classical forms and rhythms, the loftiest sentiments of man. Whilst in Caravaggio's case his addiction to gambling and violence was quite in keeping with the truculence of his art, which flouted all the tastes of his time, Guido Reni, we might almost say, was flouting his own temperament when he forced himself to paint in a manner congenial to the public, nobility and clergy alike, and it was himself that he was trying to escape when he indulged in the excitements of the gaming-tables.

He was not the only artist of the day to court success by pandering to the tastes of the age. But because he was, by and large, more gifted than the others, his *œuvre*, with its achievements and its flaws, throws much light on the art of this century of contrasts. His prolific output reflects the variety of tendencies he espoused; now he makes play with clashes of light and shade, now with bright tonalities harmonized to the rhythms of the forms. His famous fresco *Dawn* at the Villa Rospigliosi has a finely rhythmic sweep of movement, while in *Atalanta and Hippomenes* the graceful counterpoint of moving bodies and vivid colors telling out against a dark background show a lively sense of plastic values. Yet there is something curiously artificial about it all. Reni's art was the fruit of a social order that was all too apt to conceal its true nature under a veneer of elegant attitudes and studied refinement.

Guido owed his vast renown principally to his amazing versatility in rendering facial expressions. It is recorded that the artist himself boasted of the variety of ways in which he could depict a saint gazing heavenwards, and, in the last analysis, his *œuvre* is little more than a long sequence of mawkish, melodramatic depictions of this order. For it was impossible to adhere to a set program, as Reni did, and at the same time paint a human face that should really live. Only now and then, when he broke with the conventions of the day did he make proof of the very real sensibility that certainly was his. The picture usually known as the *Portrait of the Artist's Mother*, for example, shows the natural dignity with which he could imbue a face when he kept faith with his true painterly instinct.

Another pupil of the Carracci, though at second hand, was Guercino, whose real name was Giovanni Francesco Barbieri (he owed his nickname to the fact that he was blind in one eye). He was born at Cento in 1591 and did not go to Bologna until 1617, after studying under several little known masters and painting a *Madonna and Saints* (1616) which caught the public eye. Immediately upon his arrival in Bologna he won the admiration of the Carracci. Lodovico voiced his enthusiasm for the young artist in a letter which described him as " leaving the best painters of the day dumbfounded." It was about this time that he won the favor of Archbishop Ludovisi (later Pope Gregory XV), who throughout his life remained Guercino's patron and protector. After a trip to Venice, where he studied the work of Titian's last pupils, he was summoned to Rome (1621) by the Pope and commissioned to make the decorations of the ' Casino Ludovisi '—one of his finest achievements.

The artist showed from the outset a remarkable skill in handling contrasts of light and shade. He imparted a particular intensity to his compositions by the use of glancing lights and constantly varying tonalities. Under his brush even dark patches lose their density and, while his figures do not seem actually to move, he imparts a curious vibration to the composition as a whole. There is a briskness in the air, a lively play of color, in keeping with the fantasy and narrative ease of the scenes he favors. There is no doubt that this artist's natural high spirits and vivacity of execution disqualified him for any profound interpretation of religious themes or the human personality, and Stendhal's vast admiration for Guercino—he likened him to Shakespeare !—seems preposterous. All the same we cannot but be captivated by the spontaneity and poetic charm of Guercino's art.

It is in the decorations at the Casino Ludovisi that the painter gave perhaps the best of his talent, sustaining an unfailingly poetic vision throughout a free and fluent rendering of the various themes. Thus his *Dawn* is a symphonic arrangement of black and white horses against a background of sky and clouds. In the lunette representing *Night* Guercino imparts a faintly nostalgic charm to his rendering of a theme lending itself so well to that flickering interplay of patches of light and color in which he delighted. His creative imagination is perhaps seen to best advantage in his landscape backgrounds. He never felt called on to readjust nature to that ideal, well-balanced order prescribed by the classicists. On the contrary he sacrificed formal patterns to the chance effects of trees and airy buildings depicted in illusionist perspective against a backcloth of open sky. Passeri, a contemporary writer, tells us that " having seen how successful the Carracci were in compositions which included landscapes, Guercino decided to try his hand at them. But while following in their footsteps, he developed a quite different style. The countryside and rustic sites of his birthplace provided an excellent starting-off point, and he schooled himself to depicting a type of landscape in keeping with the figures in his pictures." Hence the fact that, as compared with Annibale Carracci's, Guercino's landscapes have much more to tell us ; indeed they already show signs of that fondness for ' the picturesque ' which was to be one of the traits of the following century.

In 1623, after the Pope's death, Guercino returned to Cento. His style now underwent a gradual change under the influence of Domenichino, tending towards a more classical ideal. He made no secret of his desire to please the public, and accordingly brightened his palette and toned down his contrasts. But going thus against his natural manner, his work lost something of its happy ease. He made a journey to Piacenza to finish work on the apse of the Cathedral, then to Bologna, where he settled permanently in 1642. After the death of Guido Reni, he made a bid to step into that artist's shoes and inherit his renown. Thus he took to working harder than ever, trying to keep up with the steady flow of commissions that came to him from Rome. He died at Bologna, in 1666.

In Guercino's career we have yet another illustration of rich gifts that never quite fulfilled their early promise. True, the painters of this century had at their command all the technical acquirements an artist could wish for ; yet, lured from their path by ' idols of the market-place,' they seem to have lacked that one thing needful, an instinctive faith in the absolute value of their art. They continued to turn out altarpieces, but while they drew their inspiration

MATTIA PRETI (1613-1699). THE PRODIGAL SON, 1656-1660. DETAIL.
PINACOTECA, NAPLES.

from the Jesuit doctrines of the age or from classical models, " they always worshipped the same gods, the gods of the theater," as André Malraux has pointed out. Their religious faith may well have been sincere and their intentions lofty; the trouble was that their expression no longer had its roots in real life, while their smoldering unrest had not yet given place to that bland detachment, tinged with melancholy, which was to characterize the art of the next century.

Mattia Preti's is usually considered one of the most interesting personalities of the late XVIIth-century art world. Little authentic information is available regarding his career; we have only legends to go on. Even the dates of his works are for the most part merely conjectural. His art, like that of Luca Giordano, belongs to the period when elements of the Baroque style which had flourished in the painting of the preceding generation were being noticeably modified, especially at Naples.

Preti was born in 1613 at Taverna, in Calabria. Round about 1630 he went to Rome, where he lived with a brother of his, also an artist. All that is known of his activities as a painter relates to a much later period; the oldest writers agree in stating that he moved from place to place, studying art at Bologna, Parma, Modena and Venice. In 1640 we find him back in Rome.

Next year, having been made a Knight of the Order of Malta, he began to frequent aristocratic circles. As a result of this distinction Preti is often referred to in old chronicles as the " Calabrian Knight." In Rome he executed a number of commissions; at Modena, where he lived from 1644 to 1650, he painted the vaulting of the choir and the apse of the Church of San Biagio, where his depiction of Paradise follows the illusionist procedures in favor with the painters of the day. In the course of his travels he had many opportunities of studying the most significant art forms of his own and the preceding centuries. The artist to whom he owed most seems to have been Guercino; Preti's use of strong contrasts and clashes of light for heightening the emotive tension is paralleled by the effects of all-pervasive vibrancy and movement Guercino obtained with his chiaroscuro. His paintings in the Church of Sant' Andrea della Valle (finished probably in 1651) delighted the Roman public. In the three big pictures representing the martyrdom and burial of St Andrew we see Baroque taste at its most tempestuous. In this phase the artist was still too much preoccupied with expressing emotion through gestures and attitudes, and failed successfully to integrate his subject-matter within a dramatic chiaroscuro, as he was to do in some later works. In 1656 he was at work at Naples, painting the gates of the city with votive frescos to commemorate the ending of the plague. Although the work itself has been destroyed, two sketches are extant, and they show how effective and convincing Preti's art could on occasion be. In one, in particular, the whole scene is built up in terms of chiaroscuro; the bodies of the plague-stricken are dramatically suggested by alternating passages of light and shade following in quick succession. By nature hot-headed and somewhat uncouth, Preti imported much of his temperamental violence into his work. His dark tonalities hint at depths beyond depths, the thickly laid-in color has a dusky glow. In this luminist vision of the world, the restricted space in which the figures have their being conveys a sense of heaviness, a feeling of oppression. Drama is there, but held in leash, almost as if the artist's emotion were too tragic, too poignant to be given full expression. Grace and refinement meant nothing to Preti, who was the typical South Italian peasant of the day, little cultured and unexpansive; thus he treated religious themes on forthright, matter-of-fact lines, though with a deep feeling, rare at the period, for the underlying moral significance of the Bible stories. In his *Prodigal Son*, for example, the chiaroscuro has an exquisite sheen, and he varies the intensity of the lighting, tempering zones of brightness with a counterpoint of shadows. In his compositions we feel that each figure is closely and consciously involved in what is happening, and is a truly living presence. Given the rank of a Knight of Grace in the Order of Malta in 1661, Preti made a trip to the island and decorated the Church of St John at Valetta. Except for a brief stay in his native Calabria, he continued living in Valetta until his death in 1699.

Baroque tendencies are perceptible in the art of such painters as Caravaggio and even in the classicism of the Carracci, no less than in the work of most XVIIth-century artists. The word *Baroque* is thought by some to derive from the term *baroco,* a mnemonic for one of the more ' eccentric ' figures of the syllogism ; by others, to come from the Portuguese *barroco,* meaning a rough pearl. Academic-minded critics at the beginning of the XIXth century used it to designate and condemn all such art forms of the XVIIth century (with special reference to architecture) as seemed to them bombastic, over-florid or theatrical. Today, however, we can take a less biased view and realize that these Baroque tendencies towards ' excess ' were signs of a healthy reaction against the frigidity of Mannerism, and attempts—extravagant no doubt at times—to widen the scope of art and extend its freedom. There is no denying that this vast movement was carried to extreme lengths in Italy over a long period ; it found a purer and deeper expression in the painting of Protestant Holland.

In this connection we must not forget that the XVIIth century was the Golden Age of papal domination in Italy, and that it was to the ecclesiastical authorities and the new religious orders then springing up—of which the Jesuits were the most powerful—that the artists looked for their livelihood. Hostile to anything that might imperil religious faith, the Church deemed it necessary to set rigid bounds to the imagination and even indeed to induce a sort of mental coma excluding, so far as possible, any intervention of the reasoning faculty. Thus the painter was enlisted as a propagandist, and never before had art sponsored subjects of so violent and gruesome an order : martyrdoms and flagellations, corpses and skeletons. Gazing wildly heavenwards, male and female saints gesticulate and writhe in the throes of mystic ecstasies. Architecture was given swelling curves and dramatic perspective effects, while statuary became a swirl of outstretched, gesturing arms and convulsed limbs. There was a liberal use of polychrome marble, painted stucco, metal inlays, gilding. Indeed, the church was by way of becoming an abode of sheer sensationalism, and one wonders how it could have been possible to meditate and pray in such surroundings. Under these circumstances it is not surprising that technical skill and *maestria* were the qualities most prized in the painter's art and that the artists felt more at ease in large-scale decorations than in painting easel-pictures. At the turn of the century, however, there came a change of heart ; religion began to weigh less heavily, men's eyes were reopened to the joys of life—and Baroque decoration found in Tiepolo one of its most brilliant exponents.

What XVIIth-century painters aimed at for the most part was the acquirement of a technique enabling them to create the illusion of a boundless ideal space within a fixed architectural setting. Above all they wished to convey an impression of the limitless recession of the sky, and, beyond the scenes of action called for by the ostensible subject of the picture, they depicted great fields of swirling light, broad zones of color. Obviously the realization of these grandiose visions involved a disregard of the formal considerations which had counted for so much in earlier art. Moreover, baroque decoration in Italy was frankly theatrical. During this century the theater came to play a prominent part in contemporary life, and we find even Cardinals and other Church dignitaries composing the scripts of the melodramas then in vogue, while the most eminent artists were called in to paint the scenery and to parade their skill in creating illusionist perspectives. (Bernini, for example, worked for the Barberini theater.) Public squares, churches and *palazzi* were laid out on the lines of stage sets. In fact painting, sculpture, architecture and scenic decoration tended to coalesce ; the barrier between reality and illusion grew so tenuous that artists could move from the former to a world of sheer imagination and *trompe-l'œil* with an unparalleled facility.

It is not surprising that, in an age when there was certainly no lack of talent, displays of mere virtuosity tended to supplant the truly creative spirit. The desire to exhibit their skill in solving technical problems was a common failing among artists of the day ; this, however, did not prevent them in their best works from displaying genuinely spontaneous enthusiasm in their renderings of dazzling light, imparting a vibrant life to their visions of transcendence, and thus fully integrating their very real gifts for decorative expression.

PIETRO DA CORTONA (1596-1669). SKETCH FOR THE CEILING OF THE PALAZZO BARBERINI, ROME, CA. 1629-1637.
(65 ½ × 44 ½") NATIONAL GALLERY OF ANCIENT ART, ROME.

BACICCIO (1639-1709). SKETCH FOR THE CEILING OF THE CHURCH OF GESU, ROME, 1674-1679.
(71×44″) SPADA GALLERY, ROME.

Thus in the big central reception-room at the Barberini Palace, the ceiling painted by Pietro da Cortona impresses us as a superb achievement in the Baroque style ; drawing on his architectural experience, the artist has created a striking lay-out in terms of illusionist perspective. The personality of Pietro Berrettini (1596-1669), named Pietro da Cortona after the town where he was born, is typical of the epoch. After the Barberini Palace he decorated the Pitti Palace at Florence, the vault and dome of the Chiesa Nuova in Rome and the ' long room ' of the Pamphili Palace for Pope Innocent X. His fame soon spread through Western Europe ; Mazarin invited him to the French Court and Velazquez to the Spanish. Though he had to decline these invitations, he sent abroad several works (amongst them plans for the construction of the Louvre) which contributed to propagating Baroque procedures beyond the frontiers of Italy.

While Vignola's Church of Gesù stands as the prototype of XVIIth-century architecture, Baciccio's decoration of the ceiling of that church, *The Triumph of the Name of Jesus*, may also be regarded as one of the most typical creations of the period. The light flooding from the sky seems to draw up, in a tremendous vortex whose apex vanishes into infinite distance, a soaring mass of bodies, billowing draperies, foreshortened figures. And, by a supreme illusion-miracle, the bodies disappearing into the sky beyond the vault seem to overhang the cornice, on to the actual structure of the dome. In short the boundaries between architecture and painting are effaced and space, whether architectural or pictorial, is done away with. The preliminary sketch reveals to us more clearly than the finished work the painter's plans for making the dark passages tell strongly out against the luminous background and arranging the groups in an almost geometrical pattern.

Baciccio (Giovanni Battista Gaulli) was born in Genoa in 1639 and died in Rome in 1709. Essentially a cultured artist he had begun by a careful study of the work of Rubens and Van Dyck in his native city and when he came to Rome devoted much attention to Raphael's decorations in the Stanze, whence so many artists of the day drew inspiration. He lived permanently in Rome, which he left only for occasional study trips, notably to Parma to see Correggio's works. He was a friend and *protégé* of Bernini and the influence of sculpture is manifest in his art. Baciccio owed much of his renown to his portraits, whose life-likeness delighted his contemporaries.

2

EIGHTEENTH CENTURY

✶

TOWARDS THE EIGHTEENTH-CENTURY SPIRIT

CRESPI MAGNASCO

TIEPOLO AND THE LAST PHASE OF

BAROQUE DECORATION

LONGHI, PAINTER OF THE VENETIAN BOURGEOISIE

THE VENETIAN SCENE

CANALETTO BELLOTTO GUARDI

GIUSEPPE MARIA CRESPI (1664-1747). GENRE SCENE (THE FLEA), 1707-1709. (18 × 13 ¼")
UFFIZI, FLORENCE.

TOWARDS THE EIGHTEENTH-CENTURY SPIRIT

CRESPI   MAGNASCO

FROM the XVIth century onward what is known as 'Luminism' tended to play a leading part in Italian painting. Titian worked miracles with his handling of light, his powerful chiaroscuro, his sudden gleams that flash out abruptly, then sink back into pools of shadow shot with glittering specks of color. Indeed his visionary genius gave, it has been justly said, a new impetus to painting. At the beginning of the XVIIth century Caravaggio used strong effects of light and shade for making volumes tell out and emphasizing form. Towards the close of the century new methods of handling the vibrancy of light in an all-pervading atmosphere of gloom were introduced by two painters of differing ability, Crespi and Magnasco. Their active careers bridged the last years of the XVIIth and the first half of the XVIIIth century, and they mark the transition from the tastes and tendencies of the one century to those of the other.

Born at Bologna in 1664, Giuseppe Maria Crespi died in the same town in 1747. He was commonly known as 'Lo Spagnolo' owing to his habit of wearing a Spanish cloak and also to certain eccentricities of behavior which his fellow-townsmen vaguely felt to be 'foreign.' Thus in his *History of the Clementine Academy* (Bologna, 1739) Zanotti observes that "Crespi's manners were certainly extravagant," and gives us to understand that he behaved exactly as the fancy took him without regard to the opinion of others. In short, his temperament and attitude to life were out of tune with the spirit of the XVIIth century and this may explain why, though he duly studied the work of the Carracci at Bologna, Crespi deliberately turned his back on the art tendencies of the age into which he was born and his tastes affiliated him, rather, to the XVIIIth century. Even when the subject of a picture lent itself to violent action — an example is *The Massacre of the Innocents* which in about 1702 he presented to Prince Ferdinand of Tuscany, at Florence—Crespi handled it with a singular serenity. One of the best-known works by this artist is the picture sequence named *The Seven Sacraments*, all in rich tonalities, sparkling with sudden silvery glints. In general his composition consists entirely of gradations of the chiaroscuro. But it is not built up by the play of the highlights ; these never linger on a detail but slide off it, forming a film of light around the subject. In the picture generally known as *The Flea* (Uffizi) the playful handling of light effects adds a slightly burlesque quality to this delightful fantasy. Crespi's realism differs from that of many XVIIth-century painters by reason of its sprightly good humor and the obvious lack of any sociological intent. For he never sets up to be a moralist (his 'Luminism,' too, is in a class by itself) and he charms us by his spirited, unforced renderings of daily happenings in an unpretentious *milieu*. His art is as far removed from the erudition of the classicists as from the passionate soul-searchings of Baroque, and with his lively wit and whimsicality, he cuts a unique figure in his age.

ALESSANDRO MAGNASCO (1667-1749). ST ANTHONY THE HERMIT, CA. 1720. DETAIL.
PRIVATE COLLECTION, FLORENCE.

During the second half of the XVIIth century some painters, notably Salvator Rosa, launched a new style of landscape painting, on anti-classical lines. Salvator Rosa's fame owes more to his powers of imagination and the fact that he inaugurated the romantic landscape than to any real painterly ability ; he was, above all, an initiator of that cult of the ' picturesque ' which makes itself felt in so much XVIIIth-century art. His landscapes, with their carefully contrived array of ruins and beetling crags that cast a cavernous dusk, interspersed with strong contrasts of light and shade, upon the scene, point the way to the tempestuous imaginings and fantasies of that far more original artist, Magnasco.

Alessandro Magnasco, also known as Il Lissandrino, was born in 1667 at Genoa. After the death of his father, also a painter, he went in early youth to Milan to study art. Except for a few journeys and a longish stay in Florence he lived permanently at Milan until 1735 when he returned to Genoa, where he died, in 1749. Relatively little is known about his life. Though he enjoyed no small success in his day, he was one of those artists who are doomed to undergo a long eclipse after they are dead. Indeed it was not until the beginning of the present century—at the same time that El Greco was ' discovered '—that the remarkable originality of Magnasco's work was recognized. The fact that the resuscitations of the two artists synchronized is probably more than a chance coincidence ; it was only after the Impressionists and men like Van Gogh had familiarized the public with a new and bolder way of seeing that such art as theirs could be appreciated. Though the true

ALESSANDRO MAGNASCO (1667-1749). GIPSIES AT THEIR MEAL, CA. 1715. (21 ½ × 27 ½″)
UFFIZI, FLORENCE.

value of Magnasco's discoveries and inventions was lost on his contemporaries, some Italian artists of the XVIIIth century were undoubtedly impressed by his use of light in sudden bursts and in the guise of ' accents,' and also by his dislocations of contour-lines. For these procedures are particularly suitable for depictions of a world of the imagination ; thus it is not surprising that Tiepolo and Guardi owe not a little to Magnasco.

In the course of the second half of the Seicento, imagination came to play a larger part in painting, and a range of sentiments heralding Romanticism found brilliant expression in the half macabre, half mocking visions of Magnasco, as, later, in the *Prisons* of the engraver Piranesi and his famous ' apocalyptic ' renderings of architecture. An XVIIIth-century writer, Ratti, who is one of the few to give us definite information about Magnasco, says that after painting portraits (none of which has survived) he " took to a special kind of painting with tiny figures." It was, indeed, in this " special kind of painting " that Magnasco made proof of his high originality ; in those compositions in which the figures are rarely more than a few inches high and move in a restricted space, crowded to repletion with picturesque details, held together and organized by the overall play of light. The subjects, considering the period, often strike us as peculiar to say the least of it. Magnasco frequently depicts, with " his peculiar mingling of austerity and verve " on which Louis Gillet comments, the characters of the Italian comedy, especially the gangling Punchinellos playing their pranks and jerking about as if they had just touched a live wire. There had already been odd characters and grotesque scenes in Jacques Callot's engravings ; Magnasco's originality lies in his skill in mingling the burlesque with the tragic and imparting to scenes of farcical comedy something of the anguish pervading XVIIth-century Baroque.

What immediately strikes us in Magnasco's art is the state of mental agitation it reveals, to which he gives expression by a highly special treatment of light. Indeed light, in its impacts on the dark tonalities in which most of his pictures are composed, is their most vital element ; thus forms are distorted, even shattered, so as to give their full effect to the few, vivid flashes of light striking through the prevailing gloom. His figures, capering manikins, are denizens of a world in which all nature—ocean, rocks and trees—is in perpetual movement, as though great gusts of wind were sweeping across the picture. In a setting of ruined buildings all these people, men and women alike, indulge in the most extraordinary antics, as though engaged in some nefarious voodoo rite. Soldiers in camp, gipsies engaged in heaven knows what mysterious activities, Inquisition scenes—such are Magnasco's favorite subjects, though sometimes, too, he paints landscapes peopled with a few inoffensive fishermen. And in all alike the motifs, even those taken directly from nature, seem to belong to some grotesque world of his own devising.

Another of Magnasco's themes is monastic life. The Baroque vision had led painters to depict a world of limitless space, in which the human elements, too, seemed strangely buoyant, airborne, always on the brink of darting outside the limits of the composition into the blue beyond, and this induced in the spectator a curious malaise, a sensation almost of dizziness. Magnasco had the original idea of associating this Baroque atmosphere with scenes of ordinary life—hence his curious combination of frenetically dramatic action and ironical effects. Whatever the setting—monastery library, refectory or chapel—the monks move, or rather slink, about, tall gaunt automata, in a throbbing dusk, and even the architectural features seem endowed with an eerie life of their own. Men and architecture alike suggest an elemental, unstable world, the creation of a mind at once sarcastic, capricious and obsessed. The picture surface is traversed by streaks of light, splashed with rapid brushstrokes in which gemlike colors sing out through the gloom. The denizens of this strange dreamworld seem haunted by atavistic fears. The pale, wraithlike forms of monks burying a member of their community sway to the rhythms of a *danse macabre*. Brothers doing penance or beset by temptation are perpetually haunted by visions of hell. Yet though Magnasco's personages seem convinced that men cannot hope for pardon, there is a touch of mockery in his depictions of them. Thus while its spiritual unrest links his art up with that of the XVIIth century, its fantasy and eccentricities foreshadow the XVIIIth.

ALESSANDRO MAGNASCO (1667-1749). PUNCHINELLO AND HIS SON, CA. 1720. (13¼ × 12″)
GATTI-CASAZZA COLLECTION, VENICE.

With an exquisite palette of soft, light hues Watteau immortalized the faintly nostalgic glamour of the fashionable life of his day, and one of Magnasco's last works, too, suggests a sort of appeasement, the surrender to a gentler mood. In the *Garden Party* we share his pleasure in a vista of hills stretching out to a far horizon, the gay costumes of ladies engaged in mild flirtation. This charming scene is quite in the mood of French XVIIIth-century art, with its embarkations to Cytheras of untrammelled love and beauty and its view of life as one long golden afternoon, unclouded by forebodings.

ALESSANDRO MAGNASCO (1667-1749). MONKS IN A LIBRARY, 1720-1730. DETAIL.
ITALICO BRASS COLLECTION, VENICE.

ALESSANDRO MAGNASCO (1667-1749). A GARDEN PARTY AT ALBARO, AFTER 1735. DETAIL.
PALAZZO BIANCO, GENOA.

GIAMBATTISTA TIEPOLO (1696-1770). THE CARRYING OF THE HOLY HOUSE FROM NAZARETH TO LORETTO, 1743.
(49¾ × 33½") ACCADEMIA, VENICE.

TIEPOLO AND THE LAST PHASE OF BAROQUE DECORATION

AFTER a hundred years' eclipse Venetian art regained the prestige lost during the XVIIth century. Unlike Florence whose creative energy had spent itself for good at the close of the Cinquecento, XVIIIth-century Venice once again gave the world a new art, full of strange enchantments. After an interval of over a hundred years Tiepolo rediscovered the secrets of those gemlike colors and festivals of light which had made the art of Veronese so joyously alive. Born at the close of the XVIIth century, Tiepolo was eminently a man of his own time and he imparted to the Baroque spirit a breath of fresh, abounding life that perfectly reflected the trend of XVIIIth-century taste. During this century the Venetian Republic entered on a rapid decline ; the year 1797 witnessed the abdication of the last of the Doges, and Venice came under Austrian rule. But meanwhile the Venetians, taking no thought for the disastrous morrow, made the most of a life that was one long round of festivities, carnivals, theatrical performances. Tiepolo's art is a mirror held up to this life, carefree, gay, heedless of all but the pleasure of the moment.

Giambattista Tiepolo was born at Venice in 1696. His parents were well-to-do trades-people and he was youngest of six children. From earliest youth he was conscious of his vocation and after studying only a few years under a mediocre painter, Lazzarini, set up for himself. Da Canal, a contemporary, writes (in 1732) : " Tiepolo, who now is highly thought of, studied with Lazzarini. But very soon, breaking with academic methods, he took to a dashing, highly personal style of painting, in keeping with his fiery, strongly imaginative temperament." Indeed even in his quite early works we find that *brio*, that rapidity of execution and, above all, that wealth of decorative imagination which never failed him throughout his career.

By the beginning of the XVIIIth century the Venetian painters had had their fill of Mannerism and, no longer obsessed by the great masters of the past, were endeavoring to break new ground in art. Piazzetta, for example, went to Bologna, became a pupil of Crespi and studied the effects of light in an atmosphere of obscurity, with a view to exploiting the emotive possibilities of contrasts of light and shade. Open to new ideas and eager for new fields to conquer, Tiepolo was much interested in these ventures, and in his early work we find carefully planned contrasts in the lay-out and a predilection for ' shock tactics.' But this manner was irreconcilable with the fluent brushwork and, still more, with the natural inventiveness which were his greatest gifts, and he soon departed from it, finding a more congenial field of activity in the decorations which the religious congregations and the great patrician families commissioned him to paint. Evidently success came to him quickly ; we find Da Canal writing of him as the painter most in favor with the Doge Cornaro (who died in 1722). " He was put in charge," Da Canal adds, " of all the decorative work in progress in the Doge's sumptuous residence." And he mentions the jealousy this success aroused among Tiepolo's fellow-artists. Round about 1725, at Venice, Tiepolo painted the walls and ceiling of the Great Hall in the Sandi Palace, did ten large pictures dealing with episodes of Roman history for the Dolfin Palace, undertook the decoration of a chapel in the Udine Cathedral and some frescos in the Archbishop's Palace in the same city. The last-named work (finished probably in 1728), though it does not display the artist at his mature best, has passages of much vivacity showing his excited brushwork at its most characteristic.

We may note that, almost from the start, Tiepolo showed no interest in the action of the picture, whether physical or psychological. What interested him was the arrangement of the scene, the lay-out of successive zones of color and the interplay of shafts of light—qualities which often give his work the appearance of a stage performance or, rather, a ballet. Whether the subject is taken from Roman history, from the Old or the New Testament, Tiepolo transposes it into an imaginary world where human emotions count for nothing and the artist's sole concern is to delight, indeed to enchant, the eye. Moreover, his art tends constantly towards an ever greater purity and in his last years he attained a remarkable simplification, by no means devoid of a certain dramatic tension.

In 1731 Tiepolo painted two very large works in Milan : one (destroyed in the recent war) at the Archinto Palace with mythological subjects, and another at the Dugnani Palace, where the murals relate episodes of Roman history and the ceiling decoration is an *Allegory of Magnanimity*. Each scene is presented as if taking place on an enclosed stage and being one of the ' tableaux ' of some spectacular play, while the characters, wearing helmets and flowing robes and carrying lances, look like actors dressed up for their roles. In short, what Tiepolo gives us here is a representation of one of those elaborate entertainments so popular with the Venetian *élite* of his day, who liked nothing better than getting into fancy dress and parading would-be heroic sentiments by playing the parts of Scipio Africanus or Sophonisba drinking the bowl of poison. And we feel that here the artist, too, has applied his fine and sensitive craftsmanship to rendering emotions which he is often far from feeling, personally. Though when he depicts the vastness of the sky, depth upon depth of pearly light, he can convey a sense of religious exaltation, it is otherwise when he forces himself to paint, for example, *The Beheading of St John the Baptist* (Colleoni Chapel, Bergamo, 1733), and the effect is merely melodramatic.

After spending three months at Vicenza in 1734 engaged on " a big job " at which he " toiled practically day and night without a break " (as he described it in a letter), the artist devoted himself to coping with an ever-increasing flood of orders. In 1736 the Swedish Minister to Venice wrote to his King describing Tiepolo as just the man to decorate the Palace at Stockholm. " He is full of wit and zest, easy to deal with, bubbling over with ideas, has a gift for brilliant color and works at a quite prodigious speed. " However, Tiepolo declined this proposal.

He did paintings for the churches of Santa Maria del Rosario at Venice and Sant'Ambrogio at Milan, and in 1739 the Carmelite Congregation at Venice commissioned him to decorate their Scuola. This large work (which was not completed until 1743) aroused vast enthusiasm. The central panel of the ceiling, painted on canvas, shows the Virgin appearing to St Simon Stock. Under Tiepolo's brush the Baroque rendering of infinite space acquires a wonderful translucency in the vast expanse of sky that fills the whole scene with its radiance. The figures are shown with their backs to the light and the angel in the foreground, a dark, denticulated form standing out against the all-pervading brightness, is the starting-point of an illusionist recession that vanishes into the billowing remoteness of the clouds. Here Tiepolo has given the Baroque style an airy lightness hitherto unknown to it and brightened it with a wealth of delicately shimmering hues, while his overall arrangement of color patches produces an effect of serenity far to seek in XVIIth-century Baroque.

After finishing this work Tiepolo returned to Milan (1740) where he painted the ceiling of the Clerici Palace, the subjects being an allegory *The Four Parts of the World* and *Apollo with the Pagan Gods*—admirable pretexts for the fantasies his inventive mind improvised so easily and happily. Here, as so often in the years to come, he arranged the composition

GIAMBATTISTA TIEPOLO (1696-1770). TELEMACHUS AND MENTOR, CA. 1740. DETAIL.
RIJKSMUSEUM, AMSTERDAM.

in such a way as to leave clear the greatest possible extent of open sky, moving his figures back towards the cornice whence, by an illusionist device, he makes them seem to be stepping forth. The steady flow of light through the clouds and his distribution of the groups in well-balanced patches sets up a constant vibration in the picture space. As with Veronese, even the shadows are colored ; but Tiepolo's knack of juxtaposing tones of different pitch so as to increase the brightness of his blues and yellows was peculiar to himself.

One of the artist's most prolific, happily inspired periods centers on the year 1740, when he painted, for example, the *Telemachus and Mentor*, once owned by Théodore Duret, the eminent French critic. Duret was one of the earliest and warmest admirers of Impressionist art and it is not surprising that he appreciated the luminosity of the atmosphere and the fluent, unconstrained drawing which give its special charm to this scene of Greek mythology. (The catalog of the Tiepolo Exhibition at Venice in 1951 mentions the interesting fact that in one of Vuillard's portraits of Duret the little picture is seen hanging on the wall.)

The Family of Darius before Alexander is a sketch for the decoration the painter executed at the Villa Cordellina near Vicenza. Its date (1743) is fixed by a letter from Tiepolo to the Italian man of letters Francesco Algarotti ; a letter revealing something of the artist's character, his simple tastes and his whole-hearted devotion to his work. " I can assure you it would please me far, far more to spend a day with you quietly talking painting than to be involved in the round of gaieties into which I am plunged just now. " He also complains of not being able to get along with his work in peace because of a bustling crowd of foreign visitors. The composition of this sketch has much in common with the lay-outs practiced by Veronese and, as in other works by Tiepolo, we see the Negro servants, dogs and horses which figure so often in the *œuvre* of the great Cinquecento Venetian. But Tiepolo's treatment of them is quite different ; he lets his brush glide freely, lightly, over the canvas, thus giving a wonderful mobility to all the details bathed in color-light, while the line is at once vivacious and delicate to the point of evanescence.

The ceiling painted during the years 1743-44 in the Scalzi Church at Venice shows the painter in full possession of his powers. It is noteworthy that though Tiepolo often treated similar themes he never repeated himself ; never are there any signs of flagging of his creative energy, indeed in each successive work we find an ever-increasing freedom of execution and a wider imaginative range. The Scalzi fresco was destroyed during the first world-war but besides some fragments that have been salvaged, the Academy of Venice has a sketch which makes us realize the fine poetic inspiration of this fresco and the skill with which antitheses of dark and bright tones, dazzling and glimmering planes of light, were built up round the " Holy House of Loretto " arising like the fabric of a dream in an imaginary Space. The creation of this enchanted world of light necessitated a special kind of drawing, a breaking-up of outlines, so as to enable the colors to glitter like many-faceted jewels. Indeed Tiepolo shows even greater freedom and vivacity in the manipulation of his rich, variegated palette in his sketches than in the full-size decorations. Many pictures are extant which seem to be first impressions of the themes he subsequently used for his big compositions, in which the exigencies of form and considerations of the spatial lay-out lessened the immediacy of his ' attack.' Some episodes, for example, of the story of Antony and Cleopatra are the subjects of small pictures in which the sudden, impetuous brushstrokes make the colors sparkle like gems in sunlight. The same themes reappear in the decorations of the Palazzo Labia, where they are treated with the lavish magnificence to which these compositions owe their fame, and in which the painter makes skillful play with illusionist effects, giving an impression of actually incorporating the scenes into the architectural framework.

In December 1750, with his two sons Domenico and Lorenzo, Tiepolo set out for the German Duchy of Franconia. (In 1719 he had married a sister of Francesco Guardi, and by her he had nine children, amongst them Domenico, who often collaborated with him, and Lorenzo who also aided him, but showed less talent than his brother.) His destination was Würzburg, whither he was invited by the Prince-Bishop von Greiffenklau, who had asked him to decorate the Emperor's new palace.

GIAMBATTISTA TIEPOLO (1696-1770). THE FAMILY OF DARIUS BEFORE ALEXANDER, CA. 1743. SKETCH. (22 × 16")
COLLECTION OF DR JACOB M. HEIMANN, BEVERLY HILLS, CALIFORNIA.

GIAMBATTISTA TIEPOLO (1696-1770). THE RAPE OF HELEN, CA. 1757-1762. (13¾×15¾″)
COLLECTION OF COUNT ALDO BORLETTI, MILAN.

He began by painting the ceiling and walls of the Great Hall, and with such success that he was given another contract, in 1752, for decorating the ceiling of the Grand Staircase. In the Great Hall are depicted incidents in the career of Barbarossa, while the ceiling, surrounded by a delicate tracery in stucco, displays *Apollo leading to Barbarossa his Spouse, Beatrice of Burgundy*. Here once again the painter's imagination has conjured up an imaginary world of softly glimmering colors and all-pervading radiance. Light as gossamer, the figures seem to tread on air, while Apollo's chariot, emerging from a great burst of light, is drawn by four mettlesome steeds so dazzlingly white that they, too, seem creatures of the air. The Baroque artists of the previous century had often depicted horses appearing in the sky but, insisting as they did on volumes and dramatic chiaroscuro, they never quite achieved this effect of airy lightness. As the years went by Tiepolo tended more and more to draw his inspiration from a world of glamorous make-believe, where all was gaiety, no tremor of anxiety ruffled its smiling ease. Here space is depicted as an immensity of tranquil light, while the vast diversity of figures—courtiers, natives of Asia, Africa and the Americas— surrounded by flowers and animals of every description and massed along the cornice, testifies yet again to the painter's copious imagination.

During his stay in Würzburg Tiepolo painted a number of easel-pictures, intended for the most part to serve as altarpieces. Notable amongst these is *The Adoration of the Magi* now in the Munich Museum; here deft, quick brushstrokes make the colors scintillate,

while the lights converging on the Madonna and Child produce a curious effect : at once of grandeur and of almost homely intimacy.

On his return to Italy in 1753 Tiepolo was given a number of commissions ; amongst others, for frescos at a Villa near Treviso and at the Villa Contarini, and for the ceiling of the Pietà Church at Venice. The frescos at the Villa Valmarana (Vicenza) were painted in 1757, this being the date inscribed by Domenico, who worked on (and signed) some of the decorations in the Hunting Lodge, while his father painted the so-called ' Olympian Hall, ' and worked chiefly in the rooms of the Villa itself. The subjects chosen were taken from the Aeneid, *Gerusalemme Liberata* and *Orlando Furioso* ; in these a great variety of colors, ranging from soft greys and purplish-blues to yellows and almost strident tones, implements a restless play of light on fleecy clouds, naked forms of goddesses, helmets and armor. Occasionally, indeed, these mythological fantasias approach that decorative art which arose when Baroque moved on to Rococo.

Tiepolo's frescos in the Palazzo Rezzonico are a justly renowned *ensemble*. Though the themes were such as he had often employed before, they give an effect of newness, such is the inventiveness with which he distributes touches of color and renders the play of light. We feel that in the period following his return from Franconia he was keener than ever on imparting an airy lightness to the rhythms of the composition—indeed it often gives one the impression of being improvised rather than thought-out. That small canvas, for instance, named *The Rape of Helen* which he painted between 1757 and 1762 (at which date he left Italy again) illustrates to perfection the rapidity and vivacity with which Tiepolo could ' register ' the fleeting moment. The drawing is spirited, but color plays the leading part ; it has a smooth, enamel-like brilliance and the contrasting tones, yellows, reds and blues, sing out across the light.

Until 1762 Tiepolo was kept busy with the decorations of various *palazzi*, notably that of Canossa (at Verona) and that of the Pisani family (at Stra). Early in 1762, accompanied as usual by his two sons, he went to Madrid where King Charles III had commissioned him to decorate three rooms in the Royal Palace. Though he now was 66 he put all his

GIAMBATTISTA TIEPOLO (1696-1770). THE BUILDING OF THE TROJAN HORSE, 1757-1762. (15¼ × 26¼")
NATIONAL GALLERY, LONDON.
REPRODUCED BY COURTESY OF THE TRUSTEES

GIAMBATTISTA TIEPOLO (1696-1770). THE DEPOSITION, CA. 1758-1760. ($25 \times 16\frac{3}{4}''$)
NATIONAL GALLERY, LONDON.
REPRODUCED BY COURTESY OF THE TRUSTEES

wonted zest into this work and completed it in an amazingly short time. Thus in 1764 he signed and dated the fresco on the ceiling of the Throne Room, measuring no less than twenty-six by eleven yards. This is an allegory of the Spanish monarchy and nowhere else, perhaps, has Tiepolo imparted such effulgence to his rendering of a vast expanse of sky, which under his brush becomes a vision of infinite space, ineffably serene, becalmed in its high remoteness. Here, whether illuminating clouds or figures floating in the sky, the light is everything, and it is not the common light of day but that of a dreamworld of abounding joy. After his work on the Throne Room (for it would seem that he began with it) Tiepolo painted the ceilings of two smaller rooms, the Ante-Chamber and the Hall of the Halberdiers. When he had finished these (in or about 1766) the King asked him to paint seven altarpieces for the Aranjuez Church. These were completed in 1769 but next year, after the artist's death, they were replaced by works in the neo-classical style then in vogue. For Raphael Mengs was now in high favor in court circles and it is easy to imagine how distasteful Tiepolo's idiosyncrasies—his excited brushstrokes and unexpected, almost impromptu accents—must have seemed to the new school of uncompromising classicists.

Whether it was that the incomprehension of his art at once exasperated Tiepolo and spurred him on to further efforts, or whether, now that his life was ending, he felt freer to express himself, the fact is that in his last years his art achieved a sensibility surely unique in the history of art. In this last phase his amazing light effects, with their accents constantly syncopated and constantly renewed, add a dramatic element to the lyricism of his vision and, if the range of colors is somewhat reduced, the passages of pure white develop a luminosity that is little short of magical.

PIETRO LONGHI (1702-1785). THE DANCING LESSON. DETAIL.
CA' REZZONICO, VENICE.

LONGHI, PAINTER OF THE VENETIAN BOURGEOISIE

THE Venetians of the Settecento saw their churches and palaces transfigured into " something rich and strange " by the luxuriant imagination of Tiepolo. With his bright, gay colors, his dashing execution and the reckless prodigality of an artist completely master of his craft, he revealed to his charmed contemporaries a world of gorgeous scenic effects and delightful fantasy. But if essentially a man of his age, Tiepolo was also of the lineage of the great Venetian painters ; and indeed we can sense a spiritual continuity between his work and that of Veronese. Already the Venetian *élite* was losing that adventurous spirit to which the Island Republic owed her rise to power and prosperity, and giving itself up to the pleasures of the moment, and in Tiepolo's art we have as it were the sunset glow of the great aristocratic age of Venice. His theatrical effects and the illusionist vastness of his skies were exactly to the taste of the Venetian nobility, which preferred to shut its eyes to the drab realities of life. But now that the aristocracy was losing its power and indeed its *raison d'être*, the middle class, thanks to its pertinacity and acceptance of hard facts, was in the ascendant. Thus, abandoning the sublime visions of a Titian or a Tiepolo, art tended to fall back more and more on representations of everyday life and allowed little scope to the decorative imagination. More even than during the previous century the painter seemed best served by a humble setting when he gave play to his sensibility in happily inspired color relations and telling incidences of light. This was the case, in France, with Chardin ; in Venice it was Guardi above all who, in depicting the sky and the lagoon, succeeded in imparting to the picture surface its utmost vibrancy and magical effects of shimmering light. Some other painters as well, amongst them Longhi, limited as was their range, show in their best moments a very real gift for composing delightful color harmonies.

Pietro Longhi (1702-1785) was born and died in Venice. His life was uneventful ; like that of many other artists of the day his attitude to the *métier* was that of the artisan. After studying under Balestra he went to Bologna, where he came in contact with Crespi. He returned to Venice in 1732 and thenceforward never left his native city. From now on he devoted himself exclusively to genre painting, and in his work we have a pleasant visual chronicle of a bygone age. From his *bottega* on the Rio de la Frescada (just behind San Rocco) came a steady flow of small pictures showing Venetians in their homes, paying visits, at the dentist's, sharing in the Carnival or gazing at the side-shows of the public fairs, and these pictures turned out by Longhi and his assistants were in great demand.

We find many descriptions of the life in Venice at this time in contemporary literature : in the works of playwrights, satirists and writers of memoirs. Goldoni tells us that everybody was fond of singing and farces and masquerades were all the rage, while Carlo Gozzi writes that " in Venice you could see all the costumes and hear all the tongues of Europe and the East ; idlers from every land rubbed shoulders with the pedlars and mountebanks." " While the common people were taking their pleasure in the streets," Pompeo Molmenti observes ironically, " the members of the aristocracy and the rich middle class were busy ruining themselves at the gaming-tables."

" Pietro Longhi was born at the beginning of this century of cheerful impropriety, gay masqueraders, promiscuous love-affairs, and the most elegant and sumptuous performances of the Commedia dell'Arte. " This remark of Octave Uzanne's might lead us to expect that an artist who set out to depict the manners of this age would illustrate the ceaseless appetite for pleasure and the butterfly existences of those around him. Actually, however, when we compare Longhi's pictures with these literary descriptions of the Venetian scene, we are surprised to find that the persons figuring in them are quite well-behaved folk going their ways in a no less staid environment—and here we see at once the strength and the limitations of his art. For Longhi did not aim at interpreting his visual experience in terms of poetry or *galanteries*, but at depicting the social life of the day as it really was (" his brush was at the service of the truth," Goldoni said of him), and, paradoxically enough, he ended up by creating a world of marionettes. His masked, richly attired figures, preening themselves in their drawing-rooms, seem to be playing parts, as though they were not yet quite used to this life of luxury and *dolce far niente*. There is always a touch of caricature and irony in Longhi's work, amiable though we feel him to be. " This," he seems to be telling us," is the world I know only too well, since I belong to it." Thus he depicts quite naturally and simply what he observes: how awkwardly their gaudy costumes, frills and furbelows sit on those portly bourgeois and worthy housewives playing at being great ladies. There is much *finesse* in his handling of the relations of his pastel tones ; eschewing clashes of light and shade, he skillfully juxtaposes tonalities so as to ensure their maximum effect. Pinks, blues and soft greens harmonize pleasantly with greys, while touches of brighter tones impart color values even to the white passages. Space itself is kept within strict bounds ; rooms are small and sparsely decorated, while the subdued neutral tints create a curious impression of airlessness. The strange thing is that his contemporaries should have enjoyed seeing themselves thus portrayed—for they were loud in praises of his art. Though perhaps a minor painter and at times overmeticulous, he nevertheless had something of that vitality which we find, far more abundantly, in Guardi's art.

THE VENETIAN SCENE

CANALETTO BELLOTTO GUARDI

THE Venetian landscape-painters justly have pride of place in XVIIIth-century Venetian art. In their time Canaletto's canvases were much sought after by the dilettanti and visitors to Italy, and they have never lost their picturesque appeal. Indeed the picture that the name of Venice conjures up in our minds today owes much to the views of their native city bequeathed to us by Canaletto and by Guardi. Moreover they rank high in that group of painters who in the Settecento heralded the advent of a new way of seeing nature.

The XVIIth-century classicists, followed by Salvator Rosa and at a later date Magnasco, imported something of their personal feelings into their renderings of nature, though they viewed her from very different angles. While the classical painters aspired to an ideal harmony, Salvator Rosa stressed the more unusual and fantastic elements of the natural scene and Magnasco re-created *motifs* in terms of his desire for dynamic expression. The Settecento painters seem to synthesize these various trends, when they see in nature the making of a stage décor and convert the landscape into a ' view.' Now that the human element was no longer paramount, it was used for purely anecdotal or incidental purposes. What matters to the artist is the scene itself; he builds it up and selects the items to be included in it. Yet, while assigning the role of a mere ' accent ' to the human figure, he gives prominence to the works of man; indeed nature as the Settecento landscapists see it is always ' inhabited ' and intended to evoke emotive overtones. Hence their predilection for ruins, their recourse to architectural oddities—in a word the stock-in-trade of the picturesque. Sometimes, however, this stock-in-trade is transmuted by the alchemy of the painter's brushwork into the purest poetry and what was initially a ' view ' becomes the stuff of an inspiring picture : a miracle brought off frequently by Canaletto, occasionally by his nephew Bellotto, and supremely by Francesco Guardi, though on different lines.

Antonio Canal was born in Venice in 1697. In early youth he worked with his father as a scene-painter and it was to distinguish him from his father that he was called Canaletto. When he was twenty-two he ceased working for the stage and devoted himself exclusively to a new genre of landscapes, known as *vedute,* then in high favor. He entered the school of the painter, mathematician and art-theoretician Carlevaris, an expert in the lay-out of mathematically correct perspective. It is said that Carlevaris initiated him into the mysteries of the camera obscura, an optical apparatus that facilitated drawing in true perspective. Perhaps at Carlevaris' suggestion Canaletto went to Rome, where he is almost certain to have met Pannini, who specialized in painting ruins and official ceremonies, had cardinals and noblemen amongst his patrons, and was regarded as one of the foremost painters of the day. Pannini's instinctive feeling for the picturesque, seconded by the vivacity of his brushwork, served him well ;

ANTONIO CANALETTO (1697-1768). VIEW OF VENICE : THE STONE-MASON'S YARD. (47 ½ × 63 ½″)
NATIONAL GALLERY, LONDON.
REPRODUCED BY COURTESY OF THE TRUSTEES

his fame spread beyond the frontiers of Italy and one of his admirers was that fine French
artist, Hubert Robert. Ruins supplied a theme particularly suited to the spirit of the age;
for one thing, they evoked sentiments of gentle melancholy, regret for " the days that are
no more," and, moreover, what form of nature provided the artist with so many sudden breaks
of the line and absorbed or reflected light upon so many facets ? Canaletto, too, was impressed
by these vestiges of antiquity rising in forlorn eminence amidst fields and trees, and they
quickened his imagination.

It was natural enough that the Eternal City, with its ruins, its venerable stones whose
very color was an invitation to the painter's brush, with their golden patina, the result
of long exposure to sun and rain, should have inspired the artists of the XVIIIth century
to so many representations, at once poetic and elaborate, of the Roman scene. But Venice,
with her vast open sunlit spaces, her low, remote horizons and luminous skies—forming an
ideal background to her canals and palaces—and especially the unique lay-out of her architecture, was more to the taste of Canaletto.

The *Stone-Mason's Yard*, now in the National Gallery, London, cannot be dated with
certainty. Referring to this picture André Lhote writes, in his excellent discourse on the art
of the landscape : " It gives us a welcome rest from the somewhat theatrical depictions of
Venice and her grandiose festivals. The rigidity of its structure is softened-out by the chiaroscuro." Canaletto has a special way of handling patches of brilliant light ; he renders them
with less emotional tension, less restlessness, than Guardi, and this imparts serenity to his
vision of space. Lingering on details, and bringing them into prominence, he gives a more
objective view of the lagoons, which he throngs not only with gondolas but with large sailing

boats, bringing out the delicate tracery of the rigging, and even indicating the languid, all-pervasive rhythm of the waves. The feeling of careful balance we get from his renderings of architecture owes much to the precision of the drawing and the forthrightness of the colors, and in his perspectives casual brushstrokes play no part.

On his return to Venice between 1719 and 1721 he devoted himself to painting views of the city, the palaces and canals. His innate sensitivity led him gradually to dispense with would-be scientific conceptions, *à la Carlevaris*, of " the City of Venice seen in true Perspective " and to apply himself to rendering directly its contrasts of warm colors bathed in vibrant air. In fact light and atmosphere came to play the leading part in his pictures; he never wearied of depicting the gleaming surfaces of marble, the brightness falling from the air like golden dust into the lagoon, while for an enchanted moment all movement was held suspended in a luminous calm.

Canaletto's chief works are usually assigned to the period between about 1730 and 1746 when he went to England at the invitation of the group of English art-lovers who, through the British Consul in Venice, had purchased so many of his works. Except for a few months' stay in Italy he remained abroad for eight or nine years. Absence from Venice and new artistic contacts modified his way of seeing. In one respect his new manner seemed to assign a larger place to imaginative description and the play of fancy; yet, on the other hand, he also made his pictures more precise, indeed they sometimes display a meticulous exactitude worthy of a topographical survey. This was, perhaps, the penalty he paid for his immense popularity; he was deluged with commissions and so as to cope with them employed assistants, and moreover he tended to defer too readily to the predilections of his public. After his return to Italy Canaletto remained in Venice until his death, which took place in 1768.

Bernardo Bellotto (1720-1780), Canaletto's nephew and one of his most gifted pupils, left Italy for good when he was only twenty-five. He resided for the most part at Dresden

BERNARDO BELLOTTO (1720-1780). VIEW OF LA GAZZADA NEAR VARESE, 1744. (25½ × 39¼")
BRERA, MILAN.

FRANCESCO GUARDI (1712-1793). THE PROCESSION OF THE DOGE, CA. 1763. DETAIL.
LOUVRE, PARIS.

and Warsaw, enjoying the patronage of the local courts, and visited several European cities, amongst them Vienna and St-Petersburg. Only a few pictures by his hand can be seen in Italy : views of cities and country towns and, in some cases, scenes of imaginary ruins inspired by Roman monuments. Bellotto employed a very special kind of light, at once cold and brilliant, which makes the air crystal-clear and sharply defines contours. The pigment is smooth and translucent, while the chiaroscuro subtly gradates brown and green tones through varying shades of intensity. In the pictures painted after he left Italy the architectural elements are drawn with scrupulous exactness, at once implementing harmonies of linear patterns and bringing out ' picturesque ' features of the subject, while their overall tonality, so skillfully and delicately gradated in the chiaroscuro, creates an atmosphere of almost romantic emotion.

His contemporaries were far from being as enthusiastic over Guardi's work as they had been for Canaletto's, and obviously if what they wanted in paintings of this nature was the reproduction of scenes that gave them pleasure, they found much more accuracy and a far closer approximation to reality in Canaletto's pictures than in Guardi's more subjective treatment of similar subjects. In the XIXth century, however, the positions were reversed ; Guardi's superior skill in rendering the magic of the light that plays on Venice, his delicacy of touch and his gift of creating the atmosphere of some enchanted land of dreams were recognized and his pictures became much sought-after by collectors and art-lovers.

Born in 1712 in Venice, Francesco Guardi came of a family of artists. His father Domenico (who hailed from the Trentino), after studying painting in Vienna, had established a *bottega* in Venice, probably in the first decade of the century. Nothing is known of his career and as he died while Francesco was still a boy it is impossible to say if the son's art owed anything to the fact that his father was a northerner. On Domenico's death the management of the *bottega* passed into the hands of the eldest son, Giovanni Antonio, under whose tutelage Francesco studied art.

It is hard to distinguish the personal share of each of the two brothers in their output. Thus in the case of *The Stories of Tobias* painted for the organ-case of the Church of San Raffaele, it is a moot question whether (as used to be supposed) these are by the hand of Francesco, or by the two brothers jointly, or, following a theory recently put forward, should be attributed exclusively to Giovanni. In any case they have that serene yet lively poetic feeling combined with a gossamer lightness of touch which, as we have seen, characterizes so much XVIIIth-century Venetian art. In a general way it would seem that the elder brother's influence took little effect on the development of Francesco's highly original personality. It surprises us today to learn that during Francesco's lifetime it was Giovanni who was thought the better artist. But we must frankly recognize that information regarding the lives and artistic careers of the Guardi brothers is scanty to a degree.

If the *Stories of Tobias* be ruled out, it is his *Caprices* and *Vedute*—or 'views '—that tell us most about the art of Francesco Guardi. Apparently he took to landscape painting somewhere between the years 1735 and 1740. The view, current in his day and often reiterated, that he studied under Canaletto has now been definitely abandoned. The fact that Guardi obviously borrowed the themes of a famous set of etchings by Canaletto for his picture sequence of Venetian fêtes merely illustrates the truism that in the work of art the actual theme is only of minor importance. In fact Guardi took his themes indifferently from nature or from other painter's works, or, sometimes, made them up himself in his imagination. For he does not aim at representation but at the discovery or invention of a *motif* suited to his personal vision. Though he catered to the contemporary demand for "views of Venice," so popular all the world over in his day, he refused to abide by any standardized procedures in his drawing and ended up by arranging his planes solely in terms of his personal reactions to light and color—with the result that many were shocked by his " faulty perspective."

Guardi, in fact, adjusted all visual impressions to a poetic vision of space, in which the elements, water, land and sky, seem to share in the incessant vibration of the air. Often his

FRANCESCO GUARDI (1712-1793). THE GALA CONCERT, 1782. (26¾×35¾″)
PINAKOTHEK, MUNICH.

composition is not 'centered' and follows no preconceived plan, but is determined entirely
by the ebb and flow of lights and vivid colors. Whereas Canaletto unifies his pictures by an
overall illumination, Guardi lights up and stresses every detail. He uses a pictorial language
sparkling with shafts of wit and strewn with delicate touches of color : its commas, periods
and accents, so to speak. Though Guardi's way of seeing has something in common with
Magnasco's, it has none of that savage irony which Magnasco expresses with his sudden
brushstrokes. For Guardi surrenders gladly to the enchantments of his native city, the tiny
ripples fretting the surface of the lagoon with a silvery haze of broken lights, the gay profusion of colors seen on the canals on fête-days.

After the group of canvases depicting *Venetian Fêtes* Guardi found a host of subjects
ready to his hand in the small or great occasions of Venetian daily life, and in the changeful
aspects of the lagoon, sometimes storm-bound but oftener dreaming in a languorous calm
in which the water seems to merge into the sky. He also recorded on canvas the visits of
the " Counts of the North " to Venice, that of Pope Pius VI, and the ascent of a balloon.
Though the impression given us by his pictures of the waterways crowded with gondolas
and colorful figures is one of gaiety, there are nostalgic, sometimes almost anguished undertones in his slate-blues and silvery greys. The very architecture of the island city lent itself
to sudden breaks of the line, blurrings of contours, renderings of glittering planes of light;
moreover any architectural regularity would have been uncongenial to Guardi. He softens
the transitions between earth and sky and frets the horizon with the silhouettes of distant
houses, his aim being to prevent the observer's gaze from lingering on any given object
and to hold it by the vision of a perpetual flux.

FRANCESCO GUARDI (1712-1793). THE PIAZZA DI SAN MARCO, VENICE. DETAIL.
ACCADEMIA CARRARA, BERGAMO.

His work has been likened to that of the Impressionists. Actually, however, the Impressionist ideology was very different from his. True, like Sisley, Guardi sought to render the effects of all-enveloping air, but his attitude to the visible world was always that of a spectator. He never seems to yield himself unreservedly to the natural scene, but builds up and balances the elements of his composition in terms of an ideal presentation. For Guardi was a man of his age and for him the landscape was but the starting-off point for an escape from humdrum reality into a world of happy make-believe. In short, that later conception of Nature as a living entity with an independent, mysterious life of her own, was not his.

But, here again, it well may be that the XIXth-century painters have stimulated our response to earlier forms of beauty, long unrecognized as such. " It was only yesterday," writes Louis Gillet, " that we realized Guardi's charm, which passed unnoticed until Corot and Boudin had opened our eyes."

Thus during the XVIIIth century landscape painting made quite amazing progress, a new field of artistic expression was opened up—a development that might be difficult to account for, did we not bear in mind that tendency towards the specialization of genres which had set in with the opening years of the XVIIth century. Never until then had anyone supposed that an artist could direct so exclusive an attention to one single aspect of the natural world, of which Man was the lord and master. We need only recall how Michelangelo felt about the landscape (as recorded by Francesco di Olanda in his *Dialoghi*) : " In Flanders they paint simply to trick our eyesight. Their painting is made up of futilities : houses in ruins, greenery and fields, shadows of trees and bridges, and rivers (' landscapes ' are what they call these), with a few human figures dotted about. Though this may seem beautiful to some eyes, these pictures have neither art nor sense, neither symmetry nor proportion, neither discrimination nor taste." Yet two centuries later one of the greatest Venetian painters

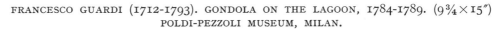

FRANCESCO GUARDI (1712-1793). GONDOLA ON THE LAGOON, 1784-1789. (9¾×15")
POLDI-PEZZOLI MUSEUM, MILAN.

FRANCESCO GUARDI (1712-1793). THE RIO DEI MENDICANTI. (17¼ × 17¼″)
COLLECTION OF COUNT ALDO BORLETTI, MILAN.

chose as his means of expression those very things that Michelangelo despised. Indeed we may say that these "futilities" were precisely what enabled Guardi to breathe new life into the great Venetian tradition of painting. In the "picturesque," so popular in his time, he found ready to his hand a means to the breaking up of form in despite of all set rules and logical balance. After Tiepolo he is the leading figure of this generation which saw the transformation of Baroque into Rococo.

It would seem that Guardi's creative power was perhaps narrower in scope than that of his brother-in-law and this is why he kept to a more limited field of art. Yet this very awareness of his limitations led him to scrutinize more closely his own resources and discover possibilities of re-creating themes that were familiar to art or using such as chanced to come his way. Instead of stressing picturesque aspects of the world around him he simplified them and, guided by his wonderfully delicate sensitivity, kept only what was best and purest.

In the famous *Gondola on the Lagoon* (Poldi-Pezzoli Museum, Milan), no trivial accessory mars the poetic beauty of the sky mirrored in the water, rimmed on the horizon-line by a slender line of sunlit houses, like the mirage of some city of a dream. Thus, too, when Guardi paints the front of the big building in the *Rio dei Mendicanti*, the play of shadows on the stone is so lightly indicated that the whole façade seems unsubstantial, on the brink of dissolving into the circumambient air. We can often detect an undertone of melancholy in Guardi's art ; perhaps he had a premonition that the splendor of Venice was soon to be no more. And when we look at the *Gala Concert* (Pinakothek, Munich), which also belongs to the last years of his career, we are struck by the curious manner in which he renders this scene of high festivity : with little specks of light, glittering whites and strangely luminous blacks telling out against a blue-grey background. Guardi's way of seeing found little favor with the art pundits of his day, indeed it was only quite late in life (in 1784) that he was elected to the Academy of Painting, of which his brother had for some time been a member. He died in Venice in 1793. Four years later the Republic lost its independence. Guardi's art is a last token of what Venice in her pride had been ; thereafter all was silence, the creative spirit of her artists, which had brought so much beauty into the world, had passed away.

NINETEENTH

AND

TWENTIETH CENTURIES

CRITICAL STUDY BY LIONELLO VENTURI

GUARDI died in 1793; Venice lost her centuries-old independence in 1797. For subsequent developments in art we must turn elsewhere, to Rome, the spiritual home *par excellence* of classicism and, by extension, of neoclassicism. For the classicism of the XVIIth century had continued into the XVIIIth, one of its most notable exponents being Pompeo Batoni. But Batoni's classicism was of a special order and French influences played a part in it; particularly the French ideal of charm, associated with the make-believe simplicity of a lost Arcadia, flawless good taste, and a cult of elegance and amiability ruling out any deeply felt emotions. Batoni's role was to carry on a cultural tradition which despite its limitations had not a little to commend it.

Neoclassicism was different; it was promoted by two Germans, Mengs and Winckelmann, who aimed at giving art an archaeological (or, as it was then called, " philosophical ") bias. The imitation of antiquity, basis of all classicism, was nothing new, though actually the classicists modeled their style on Annibale Carracci quite as much as on ancient statuary. The devotees of neoclassicism declared that there was no such thing as art outside classical antiquity, that in fact modern productions were not " art " at all, and that painters should hark back to the perfection of antiquity by way of an eclectic fusion of the styles of Raphael, Correggio and Titian. Thus it was not so much the program which the neoclassicists wished to change as the way of carrying it out; the artist's work was not to be spontaneous but premeditated—with the result that every striving of the creative spirit was stifled at birth.

Hence the fact that the only great artists who emerged at the end of the XVIIIth century were natives of those countries which were least imbued with neoclassicism and indeed hostile to it: Goya in Spain and Constable in England. France became steeped in neoclassicism, but it was soon expelled by the bayonets of the Revolution, and replaced by a realism which, however prosaic, was anyhow alive.

In Italy the phase of enthusiasm for all things French, which lasted throughout the first half of the XVIIIth century, was followed by a reaction against them. Foreigners flocked to Rome and duly admired Roman art, but they also insisted on proclaiming what was, to their mind, the proper way of admiring it. The Italians were quick to see that they had a tradition of their own to set up against foreign ones, and vigorously championed the supremacy of Italian art and literature. The polemics that ensued had at least one good result, the appearance of Luigi Lanzi's *History of Painting in Italy*, in which for the first time the essentially national values of Italian art were given prominence, as well as the views that were later propagated in France by Stendhal. This was the time when Italy was preparing to fight for her independence, and naturally enough for the Italian of the day the national emergency took precedence of all other interests. Thus the poets and painters attached to foreign Courts, hitherto reckoned amongst the glories of Italian art, fell into disrepute, despite their undoubted services to the cause of Italian prestige abroad. To this was due the eclipse of Metastasio's fame and Tiepolo's.

There was, however, one way in which neoclassicism might have blazed a trail towards the future, and this would have been by making antiquity contemporaneous so to speak; by responding to the grandeur of its ruins as they actually were and, in a rush of emotion, transforming it into art. In other words to get in tune with antiquity the artist needed to have a romantic turn of mind, as was the case with one artist of genius, Piranesi; but his example was not followed, perhaps because his medium was not painting but engraving.

Thus once again, as in the early XVIIth century, Rome became the art-lover's Mecca. But the cosmopolitan crowd who flocked there visited the Pio Clementino Museum, not the painters' studios. Likewise the Italian painters themselves grew more and more obsessed with their " glorious past," and waxed indignant if any foreigner dared to paint in his own manner. Under the aegis of antiquity Canova conquered Europe. Thus inevitably neoclassicism led to Academicism, and stood for consecrated, not creative values; for the static as against the dynamic. Even the best artists of the day, men like Appiani, Traballesi, Benvenuti, Sabatelli and Camuccini, produced nothing of lasting value, any more than did the Italian Purists who tried to launch in Italy a movement akin to that of the German ' Nazarenes.'

The romantic movement was equally unable to affect the course of Italian painting to any great extent. We all know what efforts it cost Delacroix to make good his coloristic painting as against the linearism of the school of Ingres. The Italian romantics did not dare to break with the academic line and thus to clear the way for expressive color. This is as true of Hayez as of Bezzuoli or Puccinelli (all of whom painted some good portraits). As for compositions including figures, mythology was now replaced by subjects from Italian history of the Middle Ages and the Renaissance—but to change the subject and add color to it was not enough. What was needed was to renovate drawing, color and theme alike, in terms of the new way of seeing. But Italian Romanticism steered clear of foreign " excesses " and not in painting only; it was timid, too ready to temporize, too parochial. Far more enterprise was needed if academic linearism was to be done away with. These are amongst the reasons why, with some rare exceptions (to which we shall refer later), there was no serious challenge to Academicism in Italy during the first half of the XIXth century. But meanwhile the artists were ' on velvet '; it was a time of perfect harmony between them and the public, and each Academy professor saw himself wearing the august halo of a modern Raphael. A happy age indeed. The pity was that no works of art came of it !

We have spoken of " exceptions." One was Giovanni Carnovali, known as " Il Piccio," who invented a style of his own, all in tenuous strands of light, admirably suited to rendering intimate glimpses of the real world and to creating scenes of charming make-believe. His typically Lombard genius was appreciated more by the artists than by the public, and it certainly had some influence on the technical development of such men as Ranzoni and Cremona. At Naples Giacinto Gigante was a landscape-painter of much distinction; he was intelligent enough to stop working on a picture at a point where other painters would regard it as a mere sketch; thus he was able to impart an overall coherence to his immediate responses to scenes of nature.

Antonio Fontanesi differed from these painters in his cosmopolitan experience, covering both romanticism and realism. He showed remarkable skill in handling large tracts of color, not with a view to emphasizing the colors themselves but so as to suffuse the composition in atmospheric light, and he makes us conscious of his pantheistic veneration of nature in even his humblest landscape scenes.

IT was not, however, until the century had run half its course and the War of Independence had supervened that a real change of taste took place in Italy. This change was towards realism, and its symbol was the *macchia*, or " patch." The centers of this new development were Naples and, above all, Florence.

At Naples, thanks to Vittorio Imbriani, art criticism acquired a new importance, on a par with Francesco de Sanctis' literary criticism. Imbriani upheld the view that the *macchia*, that is to say the patch of color making its impact felt throughout the composition, was the very stuff of painting; thus certain deeply-rooted prejudices which had hampered neoclassical painting and (in Italy) romantic painting as well must now be discarded once for all. By this was meant that the conception of the picture must no longer derive from extraneous or anecdotal elements, but solely from the first impression recorded sketchwise, as a general effect of light and shade. Obviously so radical a change of attitude towards the whole idea of painting set the artist no easy task, and it is not surprising that Domenico Morelli, who was the first to try to follow this program at Naples (in the second half of the XIXth century), was unsuccessful—owing to his approaching it from too ' literary ' an angle.

The painter who, at Naples, employed the color-patch with best results was Michele Cammarano; breaking with the romantic tradition, he achieved a rendering of visual experience all in contrasts of light and shade, without over-much precision but with a vitality whose zest and driving force made themselves felt throughout the composition. Though he obviously had an eye to the new art trends in France, his style was wholly original. In fact he typified the way in which an artist can assimilate outside influences to a purely personal idiom, and in particular how a Neapolitan could profit by French examples without detriment to the Neapolitan characteristics of his style.

Gioacchino Toma was an artist of a very different stamp. He handled Neapolitan realism with extreme caution, not to say timidity. Also he was always much interested in the ' subject ' and betrayed a weakness for sentimental themes. His career was not a happy one; he never achieved any real success, in fact even today he cuts a rather shadowy figure. None the less he possessed genius, indeed more genius than any other Neapolitan XIXth-century painter. Undeterred by the indifference and even hostility of those around him, he pursued his lonely path, giving expression to his wonderfully delicate sensitivity in harmonies of grey, whose quiet colors convey in undertones the artist's most intimate, most fleeting moods. We feel that he has pondered deeply on the human predicament and, though too gentle to rebel against it, expresses all its sadness with tender feeling. And his greys, keynote of his composition, seem an expression of his resignation.

A richly endowed artist, trained in the Neapolitan School, was the Roman Antonio Mancini. The luminist effects in his early works are exceedingly elaborate and while keeping in direct, vital contact with reality, he gave free play to a virtuosity which won him a great name not only in Italy but abroad as well.

Florence had been uncontestably the leading art center of Italy in the XIVth and XVth centuries and for part of the XVIth also, but all the vitality of painting seemed to ebb away during the XVIIth and XVIIIth centuries. The XIXth century, however, brought a great cultural revival and in the years following the 1821 revolution Florence regained her place in the vanguard of Italian culture. Indeed even academic art was less banal in Florence than elsewhere. Soon after the 1848-1849 war some young painters, later to be known as the " Macchiaioli," got together and to this group Italian painting owed its chief title to fame during the XIXth century.

The conception of the *macchia* in Florence differed from that of the Neapolitan painters we have mentioned and even from that of the theoretician Imbriani. True, its purpose was the same — that of focusing the painter's attention on effects of color-light, whose value replaced that of the picture's subject, and of thus diverting him from its literary or anecdotal content. But thereafter the ways parted between the Neapolitan and Florentine artists. For the latter inset the color-patch within well-defined contours (as was not the case in Naples), and moreover the Florentine Macchiaioli imparted to their color a quality and an intensity which not only made it a means of vivid lyrical expression but largely set it free from representational service. This led some critics to detect vestiges of the Baroque tradition in the Neapolitan color-patch, and in that of the Florentines a return to Fra Angelico. Both views were mistaken; they were far-fetched interpretations of two obvious facts:

realistic emphasis in the work of the Neapolitans and elegant design in that of the Florentines. With the triumph of realism the use of the ' patch ' had become generalized in European art, but it functioned differently in different countries and in the hands of individual artists. When we look back on those two decades (from 1865 to 1885 approximately), so rich in promise, of Florentine art, we get an impression that a truly great artistic movement, running parallel to that of the French Impressionists, was under way in Italy; unhappily it ended all too soon. Not that any outside pressure was brought to bear; the Macchiaioli deserted of their own free will the ' patch,' and sometimes too their special way of seeing, so as to come more into line with illustration. None the less within a remarkably short period they produced a number of masterpieces; this much the harshest critic may concede, without demanding of them what they could not give. What they could not give was a new trend to European art, the reason being the provincialism of Italian culture at this time.

Obviously it is possible to create an art perfect in its kind in a provincial, even parochial environment; but its repercussions are bound to be limited and its message is confined within narrow frontiers. This, too, is why no artist arose in the following generations capable of carrying the style of the Florentine Macchiaioli a stage further.

Giovanni Fattori was unquestionably the greatest of the Florentine Macchiaioli; the most vigorous draftsman, the most vivid colorist and, above all, the most poetic member of the group. He was intensely conscious of all such forms of life as are simple, austere, near the soil: horses, cattle, peasants. Aware of his lack of culture, Fattori shunned the over-intellectualized *milieux* of the city and preferred the solitude of the Maremma fens, which he liked for the same reason as the poet Carducci, his contemporary: because no one cared to live in that malarial climate. To this taste for simplicity and the primitive is due that epic quality in his art. The Macchiaioli were patriots to a man and Fattori took part in the political activities of the day, both in underground movements and in the firing line; and they brought the same fighting spirit to their revolt against Academicism.

Though Giovanni Costa, a Roman, was never a Macchiaiolo, he was in close touch with the group and especially with Fattori, to whom he suggested the use of certain tonal values. Silvestro Lega, a native of the Romagna, started off on rigorist, purist lines; the rather prim precision we find in his early works does not lack charm, and in it the ' patch ' plays no part. But he had a wayward, adventurous temperament, and once he was convinced that the ' patch ' symbolized a revolt against traditions of the past, none employed it with more fervor, freedom, boldness, than Silvestro Lega. As it so happened, this phase of his art synchronized with a tragic period of his personal life—which may explain the intensely dramatic handling of the ' patch ' which distinguishes his painting. Raffaello Sernesi and Giuseppe Abbati were ill-fated members of the group; both died young, the former on the battlefield, the latter in an accident. The few works by Sernesi that exist make us regret all the more keenly that he did not live to bring his art to fruition. For such is the beauty, such the purity, of his color that in itself it conjures up a world of glamorous enchantments, all nature is transfigured into a vision of some lost Arcadia. As for Vito d'Ancona, though he participated only indirectly in the Macchiaioli movement, he employed color-patch effects with remarkable vivacity, especially as regards the rendering of plastic volume.

Finally we may mention Telemaco Signorini; writer as well as painter, he was the theoretician and historian of the group, which he both championed and kept together. He was in touch with French painting, and even detected affinities between the *macchia* and impressionist procedures. He stood in the same relation to the other members of the group as Claude Monet to the other Impressionists, his position being that of their guide and leader (not that he was the best painter of the group, though he was probably the cleverest). He specialized in ' daring ' subjects with a view to giving his painting a sociological import; thus he painted asylums and brothels, with, however, considerable tact and sometimes with real distinction. Some of his works are certainly masterpieces of their kind, but it is clear that his interests were not purely painterly; he lacks that single-mindedness, that heroic self-dedication to art which we find in Fattori, Lega and Sernesi.

The lesson inculcated by the Macchiaioli was that of a forthright, engaging and some-times witty realism, and it served the turn of a number of lesser painters, among them Giuseppe De Nittis, Giovanni Boldini, Vincenzo Cabianca and Guglielmo Ciardi. A somewhat meager harvest, it cannot be denied, after the high hopes raised in the springtime of the movement.

BY the beginning of the present century all that was vital in the art of the Florentine Macchiaioli and in the realism of Naples and Lombardy had passed away. Like sculpture, painting had become a matter of clever drawing combined with rhetorical over-emphasis. Meanwhile—during the century's first decade, to be precise—the industrial, social and political evolution of Italy was rapid. The improvement in material conditions which, on the intellectual side, took the form of a philosophy of progress, led to an urge for regeneration of all the aspects of Italian life, seconded by a wave of nationalism.

The nationalists' program was simple; Italy was to make good her prestige in Europe. But in the field of painting Italy, as compared with France, was by 1910 obviously somewhat backward and any claim to leadership untenable. Futurism took both these factors into account. The Futurists stressed the ' Italianism ' of their art, not because they claimed to stem from any Italian tradition (on the contrary they completely broke with the past), but because they wished to make a name for themselves and for Italian art abroad. Obviously to bring this off in France—and elsewhere, for that matter—they had to take account of and reckon with the latest developments in Paris, Cubism in particular. But the only truly original feature which the Futurists could claim was their fierce revolt against the current conditions of Italian art, an aggressive dynamism which manifested itself not in any special treatment of form but in the glorification of life and movement. They were naturally interested by the Cubist procedure of exhibiting the various planes of an object as seen from different angles of vision, that is to say the taking to pieces of the object with a view to bringing up to the picture surface planes originally perceived in depth. But while the Cubists stood by compo-sitional demands of a rigid kind, the Italians were all for the imagination at its most volatile —and it was from the clash of these two attitudes that the best futurist works derived.

Three young painters, Boccioni, Carrà and Russolo felt like the others the need for a complete renovation of Italian art, but, having more courage than their colleagues, pressed the new conceptions to their logical conclusion. Joining forces with the poet Marinetti, who was a past master of publicity, they launched what was to be the art of tomorrow, ' Futu-rism.' An artist friend of theirs, Gino Severini, who lived in Paris, had like Boccioni leanings towards Divisionism (though on the lines of Seurat, not those of Previati). Severini was in touch with all the new developments in Paris and on learning that Marinetti wished to launch Futurism by a group exhibition in Paris, suggested that before taking any further steps they had better come there and look around for themselves. When his friends turned up in Paris, Severini was somewhat disappointed, not by the quality of Carrà's and Boccioni's paintings but by the fact that they were obviously so ignorant of the modern movement in art. For one thing (and this was borne out by their manifestos) they counted on the *subject* to furnish the major element of novelty in their campaign.

It is now common knowledge how Boccioni and Carrà, not to mention Severini, solved the problem. They discovered a new form of art which, however questionable on aesthetic grounds, matched their concept of untrammelled dynamism. And it soon was recognized, even in Paris, that the Italian Futurists had made a new contribution to art: the organization of dissociated planes in terms of movement. Certainly the French *avant-garde* were only half-hearted in their approval and kept most of their admiration for Delaunay and Marcel Duchamp, who had been influenced by the Futurists. All the same the Italians had won their spurs in Paris and there is no question that Futurism took effect on the subsequent developments of Cubism—not to mention its success in Germany where it proved a godsend to the adepts of the new theory of abstract Expressionism. It is a curious fact that while the influence of the Futurists in Italy was considerable, it was more because of what they brought back from Paris than for their own discoveries. The Italians were too keen-witted to be impressed by the crudities of Expressionism; they were better qualified to appreciate the new formal art that had arisen in Paris. Indeed the works of Boccioni (the most 'dynamic' of the Futurists) that were best liked were the most abstract. As for Severini, the most subtle and refined member of the group, his works won favor owing to his rhythmic handling of forms and his color harmonies.

The attitude of the Italians in general towards the Futurists is excellently illustrated by that of Soffici, who began by attacking them and later joined their ranks—that is to say he gave them his active support; actually his own paintings lack movement and violence and can best be described as neo-cubist. Despite its notoriety and a spate of manifestos Futurism was a short-lived movement. It is an interesting point that Boccioni, Carrà and Severini were all three theoreticians. Boccioni compensated for his cultural shortcomings by a clear understanding of the problems he was up against and their origins (which in a Futurist was all the more remarkable). Severini was a devotee of mathematics, which he regarded as the highest manifestation of the mind, and his passionate interest in them gave his art the driving force it needed. Carrà fancied himself as a philosopher, though really he was nothing of the sort; yet it is impossible not to be impressed by the zeal and earnestness he displays. Thus the esteem which Futurism enjoyed, and still enjoys, in Italy is largely due to the theories of art expounded by these three pioneers.

AT the time when the Futurists were creating a furore under the energetic showmanship of Marinetti, another Italian painter was discreetly forging ahead in Paris and attracting the attention of the most enlightened spirits of the day. This was Giorgio de Chirico. He did not cast about for any new way of juggling with forms or rendering life and movement; what he wanted was to bring to light something that had not even crossed the minds of the Parisian painters. The Cubists took natural objects to pieces so as to get down to their very essence, but what they represented was always physically existent. The Futurists also played fast and loose with the facts of vision, but with the object of imparting to them dynamic life. Giorgio de Chirico started out from entirely different premises. Though seemingly the first inspiration of his art came to him from literature, he had the faculty peculiar to the born artist of transmuting literary inspiration into poetic vision; it was due to this poetic approach to painting that he imposed on all the objects he represented a significance meaningful of something other than their normal selves. For he realized that under certain aspects an ordinary house or a public square can convey a sense of mystery. When studying at Munich, he had been much impressed by Böcklin and his earliest works are imbued with Böcklin's romantic presentation of the enigmatic. But the type of art that de Chirico subsequently evolved for himself owes nothing to the German painter; it is lucid, schematic, straightforward— and constantly amazing. Apollinaire and Picasso showed interest in de Chirico; they felt that his art belonged to their spiritual climate and opened vistas on the unknown more effectively, more magically, than Cubism in its early days.

De Chirico never had any doubts about his program. As early as 1913 he declared that painting must be liberated from the knowable, from subjects, symbols, all that is logical and rational, and present everything under a new aspect, as if bathed in the light of some far-distant planet.

Far from disintegrating objects so as to express his vision of a world invisible, de Chirico stressed their substantiality, solidity, stability. The things he represents seem petrified for all eternity; hence indeed their strange hallucinative power. If any style of painting may be described as metaphysical in the strict meaning of the term, it is certainly Chirico's; for his art takes its rise *beyond* the physical. No other artist of the generation preceding the first World War insisted to such effect on the vital need for poetry in painting. Today he has repudiated his early work, but his was one of the crucial influences in the development of surrealism. And though surrealism has ceased to yield appreciable results, there is no denying that in the period following the first World War, it was a movement of considerable scope and no little importance.

To begin with, Carlo Carrà had taken up with Futurism and even been one of its outstanding figures, but we now can see that, though he brought off some successes in this field, Futurism was never really congenial to him. Boccioni's was a happy-go-lucky genius, and he was a man of sudden, brilliant inspirations, whereas Carrà had a thoughtful, indeed sedate turn of mind. Once he understood that Futurism was not for him he reverted to the great Italian tradition, harking back to Giotto and Uccello. His extreme simplifications, his deliberate choice of commonplace objects and the way he arranges them in the picture reveal his purpose: that of suggesting what is not represented. Carrà had met de Chirico at Ferrara in 1915 and adopted his viewpoint. But those intimations of an unknowable reality behind reality which we find in de Chirico's *Nostalgia of the Infinite* (1911) have an intensity and immediacy not to be found in Carrà's art. Yet if Carrà's personal contribution to metaphysical painting was more limited in scope, it was in a sense more refined, since it linked up with a great art tradition. In any case he soon abandoned Metaphysical Painting and reverted to discreet, accurate, yet highly personal renderings of nature, which, however, lacked the international appeal of his futurist and metaphysical productions.

The artist who profited most by his venture into Metaphysical Painting was the lastcomer to the group, Giorgio Morandi, who joined them in 1918. He had never been to Paris, but, gifted with a rare sensitivity, he had sensed intuitively as it were the ideas behind Cubism and Futurism. What he brought to Metaphysical Painting was a wholly personal delicacy of color and a unique purity of form. In Morandi's art the " revelation of the unknowable," if limited in scope, is inherent in the forms themselves; whereas Carrà and de Chirico hinted at the mystery behind reality by startling combinations of incongruous objects, Morandi finds it in the objects themselves, because of his love for all existing things, even the simplest, such as bottles set in rows and household utensils. And such is his natural modesty and unassertiveness that he makes arrangements of these his leading themes. But the bottles and other objects are transmuted into symphonies of exquisite color, bathed in a light so tenuous that it seems to glance over rather than strike their surfaces, and vibrant with that subtle rhythm which gives Morandi's art its amazing power of suggestion. The contour-lines—that is to say the form—, the color and the composition have that supreme *rightness*, inevitability, to which Morandi owes his secure, if hardly won, place in the forefront of Italian art. His renown is world-wide, yet the strange thing is that in private life he is the most provincial of Italian artists; nothing will induce him to quit his native city, Bologna.

Finally we have Filippo de Pisis, who like Morandi began by an enthusiasm for Metaphysical Painting. But he spent many years in France and was affected both by Post-Impressionism and by Manet. It was to his lively interest in fortuitous, almost trivial aspects of reality and to his imaginative freedom, his refusal to be bound by any cut-and-dried theory, that he owed his subsequent success. For intellectual though he was, de Pisis was wise enough not to allow any schematic preconception to inhibit the flow of natural emotion.

AFTER bringing to French art the combativeness born of their strenuous fight for recognition in their own country, the Futurists turned their success abroad to good account in Italy. When de Chirico arrived in Paris his style was already mature, and he contributed more to French taste than he took from it.

Amedeo Modigliani, on the other hand, when he came to Paris (in 1906), had not yet found himself. He was twenty-two years old, had studied at Leghorn and Venice and his art training (which belonged to a period subsequent to that of the Macchiaioli) had not as yet been assimilated into a personal style. Thus, at Paris, he had nothing to contribute and everything to gain. He had in his favor, however, not only intense fervor and an all-consuming, heroic idealism of Nietzschean origin, but also a well-balanced mind, good sense and insight enough to give Futurist extravagances a wide berth and to profit by what he saw in Paris. Thus Modigliani's first impact on modern art was neither sudden nor spectacular. He advanced slowly, gradually accumulating a store of knowledge and trying out various paths, and in this quest of perfection his all-too-brief existence flamed itself away. His sculptures and caryatids are sometimes masterly, but they do not reflect his mature style; it was only after ten years of unremitting efforts that he achieved his definitive, unique form of expression.

What were the models that inspired him during those formative years ? He took over Cézanne's method of work (i.e. of proceeding from visual sensation to organized arrangement), his handling of planes and his richness of color—to such an extent that some of his works are literal copies of Cézanne. On the other hand he so completely transformed his other sources of inspiration that it is hard to say what they were. He was undoubtedly influenced by Picasso and his drawing of the ' blue ' and ' pink ' periods, though later he gave his line a totally different significance. He learnt something, too, from Negro sculpture, from Fauve and Cubist procedures and, it would seem, from the Italian Primitives as well; yet always observed these forms of art with the bland detachment of one who knows that their way is not his. By 1916 he had achieved a rich and varied style, which, however, cannot be said to stem directly from any one or even any combination of the elements entering into his cultural background. The truth is that his creative power welled up from sensual depths and all he had assimilated merely canalized it. Thus it is impossible to assign him to any group or movement of his day. He belonged neither to the Cubists, Futurists, Fauves, Expressionists or Surrealists. He was (as Baudelaire defined the artist) his own God, his own prophet and his own priest.

Modigliani's line is the criterion of his mature style, a line that controls and synthesizes all the elements of the composition. Whereas Picasso, in his ' blue ' period, had used his superb line to bind the volumes within his chiaroscuro, Modigliani's line served to partition the zones of color and emphasize their function. For this purpose a line that merely defined contours literally and objectively would be useless; this is why Modigliani's use of line is imaginative, not objective; it is a ' creative ' line involving and overriding all the elements of the picture. Hence Modigliani's famous ' distortions.'

As Severini remarked, " To *distort* is to *correct* nature in terms of the artist's sensibility." It follows that every true artist distorts, or, if we prefer, transforms the visible world. However Modigliani's distortions are, as it happens, more glaring and less easy to explain than those of most painters. Those of his friend Soutine, for instance, strike us as being spontaneous, direct emanations of his sensory responses. Modigliani's distortions, while no less spontaneous, seem less direct and more theoretical—in a word, more ideal. Their sole purpose is to minister to beauty, not Raphael's, yet a beauty parallel to it. We are reminded of Baudelaire's remark à propos of the beauty of Delacroix' women, in other words romantic beauty: " Here is a beauty all its own." Neither classical nor romantic, Modigliani's beauty is peculiar to his art. Born of despair and tragedy, in the years of moral and intellectual confusion before and during the first World War, it arose like a lonely flower in a wasteland, frail symbol of the painter's hope and his ideal. Hence that curious sense of a delicate, ever-threatened loveliness and the poetic quality we find in Modigliani's art.

This book opens with Caravaggio and ends with Modigliani: two great artists and two tragic figures. It may be rash to draw any arbitrary conclusion from this coincidence, yet does it not suggest that today no less than in the past the artist's path is darkened by adversity and suffering ?

HISTORICAL SURVEYS

BY ROSABIANCA SKIRA-VENTURI

1

NINETEENTH CENTURY

★

LIGHT AND STRUCTURE RENDERED BY THE COLOR PATCH

TOMA AND CAMMARANO

THE MACCHIAIOLI OF FLORENCE

FATTORI LEGA SIGNORINI SERNESI

ABBATI D'ANCONA

VITO D'ANCONA (1825-1884). WOMAN WITH A PARASOL, 1860-1870. (11 × 6¾")
NATIONAL GALLERY OF MODERN ART, ROME.

THE NINETEENTH CENTURY
AND THE MACCHIAIOLI OF FLORENCE

WHEN Tiepolo died in Madrid in 1770 Goya was twenty-four, and thus the art of the XIXth century was already knocking at the door. The Spanish painter who may justly be regarded as the first of the moderns was instituting that new tradition which, starting from the concept of human freedom, was to discover a new value, that of Man. We can hardly conceive of such artists as Delacroix, Daumier and Manet (to name a few of many) without thinking of Goya, and when André Malraux observes that " Manet and Van Gogh, Sisley and Gauguin joined forces in a glorious conquest of freedom," we glimpse instinctively the shade of the great recluse of the " Deaf Man's House " pointing their way.

But on Tiepolo's death no Italian painter came on the scene whose work symbolized that break with the past which made itself felt throughout Europe at the end of the XVIIIth century and brought so many new values to the Western world ; nor was there in Italy any artist whom Goya's art inspired (as happened in several other European countries) to a new, bolder creativity. Indeed it must be admitted that in the XIXth century the Italian contribution to the art world in the making was highly limited. True, there were some unquestionably gifted artists, several of whose works gave expression to the new sensibility, but they cannot rank as authentic pioneers. The truth is that the ' climate ' of Italy, which century after century had encouraged the flowering of so many great works of art, became in the XIXth century particularly oppressive, indeed hostile, to the artist. Thus even though in the second half of the century a group of painters initiated, in no spirit of bravado, but with deep sincerity, " a new way of seeing the world with a view to the discovery of the whole earth's past," (André Malraux) they do not seem to have fulfilled their very real promise as fully as we might have hoped.

Though, seen from a certain angle, the art of the Quattrocento may look like an art supplied ' to order,' that is to say bespoken by the powers that be, it constitutes one of the most vital elements of European culture ; and this holds equally good for the Cinquecento, though already in the XVIth century there were symptoms of a cleavage between art and the authorities. Still even Michelangelo, profoundly affected as he was by the new movement towards a purer form of Catholicism, never lost favor with the Pope and executed, even if it went against the grain, the commissions coming to him from that source. In the XVIIth century the fissure widened; the authorities were determined to keep art under their control; hence the banning of Caravaggio's pictures from the churches. Yet even Caravaggio, rebellious and independent as he was where his art was concerned, made no secret of his desire to have his work approved of by the authorities. True, the XVIIIth-century aristocracy found Tiepolo's art to their liking, and everyone admired Canaletto's carefully executed landscapes; nevertheless Guardi's delightful " impressions " left his contemporaries cold.

The political upheavals that accompanied the close of the XVIIIth century widened yet more the breach between art and the social order. Courting the favor of 'authorities' who had lost all real authority, artists succumbed to the bondage of the Academies and their dead conventions. Moreover the uncertainties of the social and political situation led to a certain timidity and lack of confidence, and those who might have given expression to the underlying trends of the age were too unsure of themselves to exercise that bold clairvoyance which is the hall mark of truly creative art.

While, exceptionally, such a painter as Pompeo Battoni succeeded in reconciling the spontaneity, vivacity and ease of his brushwork with the classical ideal of the previous century, the wave of neo-classicism which swept Europe at the end of the XVIIIth and the beginning of the XIXth century, evoked no vigorous response in Italy. Rome meanwhile was crowded with foreigners who had been infected with Winckelmann's antiquarian passion for Graeco-Roman art, and with the neo-classical theories which Raphael Mengs put into practice in his paintings. In fact Rome had become one vast museum and the Italian artist felt crushed by the burden of his heritage—so much so, indeed, that he ended up by seeing the artists of classical antiquity and even Raphael through the eyes of Mengs and when he wanted to paint a 'classical' portrait looked to David for guidance.

The glamour exercised by the works of the Italian past, or those which were to be seen in Italy, took another form in the art of the 'Nazarenes,' a group of German painters who came to Rome in 1809. Their aim was a revival of Christendom in its 'golden age' and they thought that by dint of copying the Quattrocento painters they could bring about a sort of XIXth-century reincarnation of the earlier art. Actually all they produced was an art that, in practice, fell between two stools; they deliberately pitted themselves against the neo-classicists, but their own doctrines were no less artificial. This movement—described by Goethe as a "masquerade"—had little direct effect in Italy, though it may have encouraged a stricter moral discipline, a more chastened esthetic. Its chief merit, perhaps, was that of drawing attention to forms of art other than Graeco-Roman or those of the High Renaissance. From the international viewpoint this 'Purist' movement foreshadowed, after its fashion, some aspects of the vast romantic movement; but Romanticism, too, failed to find a favorable soil in Italy. The "fine frenzies" of the North were cultivated by the Italian painters in a highly attenuated form (if at all) and one that was a sort of compromise between the illustrated anecdote and the canons of the Academies, the sole exception being that remarkable artist Fontanesi, who came somewhat later on the scene.

In this connection mention must be made of Carnovali, known as "Il Piccio" (1804-1873), a painter of very real originality. Of a restless temperament and deliberately keeping aloof from the fashionable art trends of the day, Carnovali traveled not only all over Italy but in Switzerland and France. His work owes more to Caravaggio's way of seeing than to that of any other artist; sometimes his palette becomes almost monochrome, so uniform is the luminosity bathing his vibrant nudes and all but immaterial landscapes in shimmering golden air. But this romantic quality of his art was more a matter of intention than of actual realization, and he tended to lose himself in a dreamworld of vague aspirations and literary allusions. All the same Carnovali supplied a healthy corrective to the static linear precision of academicism, with his emphasis on the mobility of forms steeped in light and the vibrancy of atmosphere.

All the ingredients of Romanticism—a vague yearning for an infinite known to be inaccessible, the melancholy evoked by the sight of nature's superb indifference to man, and poetic intensity of feeling—can be found in the work of the landscape-painter Antonio Fontanesi (1818-1882). His life, too, was typically that of the 'high romantic,' clouded with disappointments, devoted to one long quest, for the most part unavailing, of a congenial, understanding *milieu*, and he ended up by taking a professorial post in Japan. Imbued with the new political ideas that were stirring in Italy, he left (for the first time) his native town, Reggio Emilia, to join in Garibaldi's 1848 campaign, after which he took refuge abroad. Eleven years later he re-enlisted in the army, for the second War of Independence.

Throughout his career Fontanesi kept in touch with the chief art movements of the day, Italian, French and English. At Geneva, where in 1848 he settled for a long sojourn (broken however by numerous journeys outside Switzerland), he painted a number of landscapes to order, following in the steps of Diday and Calame and adopting their conventional manner, and he also produced lithographs and etchings. But, while in Geneva, he made the acquaintance of the French artist Daubigny, and his admiration for the naturalistic tendencies of the School of 1830 was heightened when in 1855 he went to Paris for the *Exposition Universelle* and met Corot, though it was Troyon's painting that impressed him most. Some years later, when in Dauphiné, he became intimate with the Lyonese artist Ravier and was strongly influenced by him. Fontanesi's contacts with the group of painters known as the "Macchiaioli," then coming to the fore in Florence, began in 1861, on the occasion of the first Italian exhibition and he came in touch with them again five years later (after a trip to London) when he settled in Florence in the hope of obtaining a professorial post at the Academy. But his art was neither advanced enough to please the new generation nor classical enough wholly to satisfy the old brigade. Finally, however, he was appointed teacher of figure-painting at Lucca. When a year later he was given a professorship of landscape art at Turin (the post being specially created for his benefit) he encountered nothing but misunderstanding and even frank hostility, and was so discouraged that in 1875 he accepted the offer of a similar post in Tokyo. Falling ill, he returned to Turin three years later and lived there until his death.

GIOACCHINO TOMA (1836-1891). LUISA SANFELICE IN PRISON, 1877. (24¾×31½")
NATIONAL GALLERY OF MODERN ART, ROME.

Fontanesi's art at once runs the gamut of romantic sentiment and also shows tendencies in line with French naturalism. He seeks to make his pictures the expression of a state of mind and uses nature as the vehicle of his personal emotion ; indeed he treats the elements of his composition in such a way that trees, figures and even rocks seem vibrant with poetic overtones. This twilight world, in painting which the artist seems to have dipped his brush in liquid darkness, with its trees eaten away as it were by corrosive shadows, and its lowering skies, reflects the vague, atavistic anguish of Man confronted by the Infinite. Yet, like Daubigny and Troyon, Fontanesi tries to impart a certain objectivity to his vision of nature, and to approximate to certain aspects of reality. For all its somberness the atmosphere is not storm-bound, but softly tremulous, and sheep and shepherdesses do not seem out of place in it. (We must admit, however, that Fontanesi's female figures, no longer nymphs and not yet ordinary peasants, sometimes have a rather tiresome sentimentality.) Yet when, happily inspired, he depicts trees and figures spellbound in one of those rare moments when everything seems charged with intimations of eternity, he composes with his brush a melodious ' Pastoral Symphony,' couched in a key of gentle melancholy.

Generally speaking, the Italian painters of the first half of the XIXth century fell short of a fully coherent artistic expression, nor were they able to found a movement of lasting importance. True, some of them were genuinely eager to discover a new way of seeing light and color, and also felt the need to keep in touch with the life around them. But their efforts were spasmodic and the driving force behind them was inadequate. The fact is that the realist revolution championed by Courbet in France met with little or no response from the Italian artists, who then were engaged heart and soul in an uphill struggle for national independence. With the French Revolution of 1789 behind him, Delacroix was free to voice the feelings aroused in him by the massacres of Scio and the ordeal of Greece at Missolonghi, and to body forth his vision of the ' Barricades ' of July, 1830. At the same time he was in a position to stand objectively back from his emotional participation in these events and translate his sympathy into great painting. But the Italian artists, busy throwing off an oppressive foreign yoke and unifying their country, had no breathing-space in which to take stock of themselves; committed to an active struggle for freedom and independence, they were debarred from that tranquillity of mind and detachment in which great works of art are created. Fontanesi, for example, who was born one year before Courbet and took part in the Wars of Independence, sought in his art no more than a poetic vision of nature.

It was the painters who arose in the second half of the XIXth century who achieved a richer harmony between their means of expression and the new values of the century. Thus at Milan, at Naples and especially at Florence, attempts were made, with a varying measure of success, to strike out in new directions and enlarge the scope of art. Two North Italian painters, Tranquillo Cremona (1837-1878) and Daniele Ranzoni (1843-1889), taking their cue from the painting of Carnovali, applied color in vigorous, separate brushstrokes, with a view to giving an illusion, as it were, of form. But their art was still a compromise with psychological illustration. Ranzoni could never keep the exalted status of the high-born ladies who sat for him out of his mind, while Cremona lingered too fondly over the charm of a woman's smile, often lapsing into mawkishness.

The personality of Giovanni Segantini (1858-1899) may justly claim our attention, though he cannot be said to have made an entire success of his art. Using a ' divisionist ' technique, he attempted to body forth his feeling, excessive perhaps but heartfelt and sincere, for peasant life in the countryside and the Alps, but the naturalism of his art was cloyed with literary allusions and conveyed a sentimental or social message. Moreover, despite the fact that he practiced the division of colors, Segantini never broke with academic conceptions of form. Indeed he was careful to stress the solidity of bodies by varying degrees of light, while his handling of chiaroscuro creates but an artificial luminosity. Thus, although nature was his constant theme, he could neither get down to nature as she really is nor implement that quasi-mystical ideal of the eternal grandeur of the earth which haunted him more and more throughout his career.

SILVESTRO LEGA (1826-1895). THE VISIT, 1868. (12¼ × 23½")
NATIONAL GALLERY OF MODERN ART, ROME.

At Naples, too, conscious of the need to adjust their vision to the new trends in art, painters were tending to shake off the thrall of the Academies. While Domenico Morelli, a highly successful artist in his day, was so much obsessed with the 'dramatic subject' that he actually set up against the Academies a new academicism of his own, the art of Gioacchino Toma (1836-1891), limited, isolated and provincial as it is, calls for special mention. In some of his pictures—notably his *Luisa Sanfelice in Prison*—he handles light in such a way as to bring poignantly home to us the sadness of the theme. In this picture, whose subject in the hands of an inferior artist might have given rise to the cheapest sentimentalism, Toma has expressed the poetic melancholy of the Neapolitan people, and with his delicate greys, his sober range of colors and the utter simplicity of his drawing, has imparted real beauty to a hackneyed theme. A simple-minded, unassuming artist, Toma could endow a mere work-basket with a singular poetic charm whose source was the purity of his own emotion. " Toma's merit lies chiefly in his mysterious gift for creating an atmosphere, and peopling it with dim, half-forgotten memories " (Emilio Cecchi). In the enormous output of pictures in Italy during the XIXth century, a favored few, which have something of the inspiration behind the *Sanfelice*, owe their exceptional appeal to the appropriateness of the ' tone ' in which the anecdote is rendered. Their mood is one of intimacy, spontaneity, simplicity; all action is suspended in an enchanted moment of solitude and silence. A case in point is Silvestro Lega's *Visit*, to which we shall refer later.

In Michele Cammarano (1835-1920) we have an artist of a very different stamp. High-spirited and passionate, he imparts a remarkable vitality to much of his work by violent contrasts of deep blacks and whites, and by his richly worked pigment. His favorite subjects were crowds, groups of people, military patrols and, in his landscapes, forest interiors. His work has analogies with some aspects of Courbet's art, which, as a matter of fact, Cammarano had an opportunity of seeing during a stay he made in Paris in 1870, when he was also much impressed by Delacroix and Géricault. In his famous picture of the *Piazza di San Marco*, painted at Venice in 1869, he has transformed what might have been just another " View of Venice " into an admirable picture, in which the rapid brushstrokes have 'fixed' the sudden bursts of light, and so rich are the varying intensities of the blacks that they seem almost to acquire color values. Here the freedom with which the forms are rendered gives the picture a spontaneous vitality admirably evoking the mood of gay Venetian gatherings.

Though it may seem that some of the figures are handled *à la Daumier*, this picture has more in common with the art tendencies of the second half of the XIXth century. Has it not, indeed, a modernity and realism reminding us of Manet's *Concert at the Tuileries Gardens*, painted in 1861 ?

ADRIANO CECIONI (1836-1886). THE CAFÉ MICHELANGELO, 1861. (32¼×20¾″)
ENRICO SOMARÉ COLLECTION, MILAN.

It was at Florence, however, that the new sensibility first found adequate expression. A small group of painters, known as ' I Macchiaioli '—whose procedure, as their name implies, was to paint in 'patches' or 'blobs' of color—used pure colors and a new technique to express a vision warmly human and almost primitive in its deep-felt sincerity. All these men were born between 1825 and 1838 ; some took part in the movement of 1848 and they all fought in the war of 1859. The ardor that led them to fight for freedom and a new order was reflected in their art by their love of familiar things, positive values and ideals within reach. They delighted in painting the green radiance of trees, changing with the changing hours of the day, and the countryside : villages drenched in sunlight and the workaday existence of the people, whose laborious lives leave so little trace on history. They, too, were of the working class and, with one exception, poor and destined to lives of hardship, even tragedy. Though they had something of a *succès de scandale* and were much talked of, they gained neither recognition nor reward during their lifetime and indeed were violently attacked. Yet these men were the pioneers of a new art. They knew this and put up a fight for their ideal, but the tradition they combated was too powerful and they met with little appreciation. When we remember how prevalent, even in the Italy of today, is anti-modern prejudice regarding all kinds of art, we can well imagine how hard their struggle must have been. The effect of this was to throw them back too much on themselves and limit them to a provincialism that cramped the full expansion of their talents. Even so, some of their works are of a very high order. One of the group, Telemaco Signorini, wrote : " After the 1848 revolution, a great many young artists turned their backs on the academies and academic rules. They accepted one teacher only : nature, just as she is, untrammelled by scholastic formulas. Thus they began that new art venture which for fifteen years was frowned upon, but which today has won through, and will hold its own, since it is justified by the march of history."

GIOVANNI FATTORI (1825-1908). FRENCH SOLDIERS, 1859. (6 × 12¾")
DR PAOLO STRAMEZZI COLLECTION, CREMA.

It was not in an academy that the young painters congregated to air their theories and discoveries, but at a café, the ' Michelangelo ' at Florence. Even today the name of this Café conjures up for the initiated memories of a whole art epoch. That witty artist Adriano Cecioni (1836-1886) for whom Carducci had such affection made an amusing sketch (in tempera on cardboard) of one of the ' epoch-making ' gatherings there. The ' Michelangelo ' was a rendez-vous for foreigners as well as Italians, who met there to discuss the art problems of the day—excitedly but good-humoredly. For some years, however, the new movement was more prolific of words and theories than of pictures. This was the period of gestation, during which they were studying Quattrocento art. " In the works of Filippo Lippi, Carpaccio and many others," wrote Signorini, " modern art may find a noble expression of our own ideals: complete sincerity of feeling and a love of nature under all her aspects." They looked not only to the past but also to contemporaries, Delacroix, Decamps and the Barbizon School, whose works they saw in the collection of the Princes Demidoff at the Villa San Donato, near Florence. And by 1855, when the painter De Tivoli returned from Paris where he had been in touch with Decamps and Troyon, the group were on the point of making good their new way of seeing by the use of that technique of painting in color-patches to which they owe their name. It was round about 1855, too, that Vincenzo Cabianca painted a black pig in front of a white wall, a work that has its niche in art history as the first demonstration of the ' macchia ' in practice. Actually, however, it was only after their spell of soldiering in the War of Independence of 1859 that they hit their stride and produced their best work. In 1862 at the Florence Exhibition—roughly equivalent to the Paris Salon—a critic mockingly referred to them in an article as the ' Macchiaioli,' an appellation which Signorini, who was by way of being the theoretician of the group, was so far from resenting that he used it as a slogan. (It is curious how many of the names of art movements that have made their mark—of the Impressionists and Fauves, for instance—originated in this manner.) Amongst the prominent members of the movement the following call for mention: Fattori—its most powerful personality who, like De Tivoli, came from Leghorn —De Modigliana, Abbati (born at Naples), Lega, Sernesi and Signorini who hailed from Florence. Others joined them later; even Boldini and De Nittis, who made their names as painters of the fashionable world of Paris, dallied for a time with Macchiaioli procedures.

The Macchiaioli themselves have explained in their writings what their program was. Nor were the problems of painting in patches mooted in Florence only. At Naples, too, the new theories were eagerly discussed, and in answer to the question, What exactly is the ' patch ' ? the art critic Vittorio Imbriani gave a reply which, for perspicacity and precision, could hardly be bettered. " It renders the artist's *first, distant impression* of an object or a scene: the initial, strongly characterized image that grips him, whether he actually has the object or the scene before him or visualizes it from memory, in his imagination. This dim and distant impression, which the painter records with the color-patch, may be followed by another impression, distinct and detailed. But, I repeat, if this first, fundamental, harmonic balance is not achieved by the artist, the execution and finish of a picture, however perfect, will never succeed in arousing any emotion in the spectator. On the other hand, even a bare patch of color, standing alone, without defining the object in any way, may quite well evoke an emotional response." In short, the Macchiaiolo artist aimed at simplification and expressed himself in a kind of shorthand intended to produce the feeling of nature taken on the wing as it were, seized in a fleeting moment of light and vibrancy. He attempted to render the atmosphere of day in terms of pure, contrasting colors which, applied in patches, had the effect of a " dialectic of light and shadow." To those who thought to see in pictures of this kind no more than hastily dashed off sketches, the painter and sculptor Adriano Cecioni replied indignantly : " The word ' patch ' has given rise to a misunderstanding among the Macchiaioli themselves. Several of them take it to mean a mere sketch, and imagine that the subsequent study of gradations and details—all that makes a ' finished ' picture—means that the patch is done away with. They are wrong ; the patch is the *basis*, and as such stays in the painting. This kind of painting is not a sketch, but based on a scientific *datum*, which is why it has revolutionized all art procedures, previous or subsequent to it. Above all it has taught us that nature must be *taken by surprise*..." This description of their theories makes it obvious that the young Florentine painters were following a line of

GIOVANNI FATTORI (1825-1908). LA SARDIGNA. (9 × 15″)
TERNI COLLECTION, FLORENCE.

GIOVANNI FATTORI (1825-1908). LA ROTONDA DEI PALMIERI, 1866. (5½ × 14½")
NATIONAL GALLERY OF MODERN ART, FLORENCE.

research remarkably like that of their contemporaries, the French Impressionists. We may note one difference, however : that they set much store on the architecture of the picture. For though the Impressionists discovered and employed color-light, the Macchiaioli, by using pure colors arranged in a kind of patchwork, clearly indicated the different planes and delineated forms in space without dissolving them into an all-enveloping luminosity. They were perhaps less venturesome and less brilliant than the Impressionists; nevertheless of all Italian artists it was the Macchiaioli who made the most vital and original contribution to XIXth-century art.

As so often happens when life and movement are to be depicted and the artist's creative impulse is at once profound and vigorous, the Macchiaioli did not blindly follow their theories but adjusted these to their personalities. In fact they produced their best work when they forgot that the patch was " a scientific *datum* " and the painter followed the promptings of his individual sensibility.

Giovanni Fattori (1825-1908) is generally held to be the leading figure of the group and indeed of all XIXth-century Italian painting. Born at Leghorn, he came of a family of humble artisans. His half-brother, several years older than he, wanted him to become a business man, but from his earliest years Fattori had set his heart on being a painter. After some preliminary studies at Leghorn he went, in 1846, to Florence where he began by working in Bezzuoli's studio, before enrolling at the Academy. From now on he made a practice, wherever he went, of jotting down sketches of everything that caught his eye, in the little sketchbooks he always carried about with him. These he used as memoranda or as starting-off points for pictures to be 'worked up' in his studio. Some have seen in this habit of Fattori's a consequence of his very real poverty at the time ; but more likely it was due to his constant wish to record without a moment's delay his first, fleeting impressions of the living world around him. Much later in life he made a great number of etchings, in which that delicate, clean-cut linework which had always characterized his drawing found a congenial medium; indeed these etchings are amongst the works in which his artistic personality shows itself to best effect.

What strikes us most, perhaps, about Fattori's character is its simplicity and ingrained diffidence. Throughout his long career he gives the impression of being a scrupulously observant, indefatigable worker, but also of lacking confidence in his very real ability. But for this timidity, he was temperamentally akin to such painters as Chardin and Corot. Painfully conscious of his lack of culture, he always felt at a disadvantage in social contacts and perhaps it was this sense of inferiority that made him hesitate so often in deciding what path to follow in his art.

In 1848-1849 he participated in the revolutionary movement, doing liaison work for the Leghorn group of insurgents. In 1850 he returned to Florence and took to attending regularly the artists' gatherings at the ' Michelangelo.' But though he liked hearing the other young artists airing their theories of art and boasting of their discoveries, Fattori showed some reluctance about accepting their ideas. The truth was that, though tempted by the new ways of handling color championed by his friends, he remained strongly attached to the romantico-academic tradition and convinced of the importance of line and subject in the picture. Again and again he looked back to the early Italian painters and he made drawings after Filippo Lippi and Ghirlandaio, the purity and serenity of whose compositions, no less than their harmonious rhythms and colors, delighted him. As for the work of his foreign contemporaries, though he had an opportunity of seeing the Demidoff Collection, he does not seem to have been particularly impressed by it. It is significant that, unlike so many of his fellow-artists, he felt no great desire to visit foreign countries and when at last, in 1875, he went to Paris, he was not influenced in the least by what he saw there. In any case he had the countryman's mistrust of ' foreign parts ' and whenever he needed advice sought it from an Italian artist, Giovanni Costa (1826-1903), with whom he struck up a friendship in or about 1861. Almost exactly the same age as Fattori, Costa refused to let himself be called a *macchiaiolo* ; his renderings of pastoral life were still imbued with the poetic romanticism of an earlier day and his pictures have a delicate appeal. Moreover, he had the artistic culture that his friend lacked, and their friendly relations greatly benefited Fattori who needed encouragement and was often all too conscious of " vacillating between Macchiaioli realism and romanticism," as he himself puts it in a letter. From 1860 onwards several of his small pictures display the sureness of his vision as regards pure colors arranged in an almost geometrical pattern sharply defining form. But though he follows this method in his *French Soldiers* and *A Patrol on the Seacoast*—immediate ' impressions ' he seems to have recorded for his own satisfaction—he obviously was pandering to the taste of the contemporary public when he painted pictures with frankly romantic subjects such as *Mary Stuart at the Crookstone Camp* (1861). In 1862 he was winner in a competition sponsored by the Government with his *Italian Camp after the Battle of Magenta* ; he personally rated this and three other pictures on similar subjects as his most successful works. Nevertheless it is not in these big compositions so much admired in their day, but usually in the smaller pictures, in which the painter has given spontaneous expression to his visual response, that we see him at his best and most original. An example is *La Rotonda dei Palmieri* (1866), a vivid, almost dramatic evocation

GIOVANNI FATTORI (1825-1908). WOMAN WITH A PARASOL AT THE SEASIDE, 1866-1868. (4¾ × 10¼″)
PRIVATE COLLECTION, MILAN.

of an effect of contrasting lights. The dazzling effulgence of the sunlit sea and the subdued half-light under the tent are rendered in light colors, in which whites, blacks and blues acquire a quite amazing sheen, due to the juxtaposition of color-patches in clean-cut, geometrically precise forms. The whole scene is built up in terms of color alone, and, owing to the intensity of the light combined with the deliberate economy of means here practiced by the painter, creates a feeling of stability and calm. Even when, dispensing with strong contrasts, Fattori limits himself to various shades of grey and beige, the colors have still a wonderful luminosity, an example being his *Woman with a Parasol* (also painted in 1866). In some of his very small pictures (Fattori and his friends often painted on the lids or bottoms of cigar-boxes) we can see how he deliberately ruled out " picturesque details " in favor of the leading motif. He does not disseminate the color patches into spots of varying tonalities scattered or in groups, but employs them in broad passages of color bringing out the essential structure of the object represented, this being exposed to the strongest light, to the exclusion of all secondary accents, and thus imparting to the color its richest intensity. We see the use of this procedure in such works as *Diego Martelli at Castiglioncello* and *Lady in the Open Air*, in which the planes are so arranged as to emphasize the colorations of the various forms, reduced to their most distinctive aspects. Figures, too, are often greatly simplified; fond of painting peasants though he is, Fattori does not aim at any psychological interpretation, any more than he tries to impart a social or philosophical significance to his subjects. Thus in *The Stone Breaker*—a theme which Courbet had employed some years before in one of his most famous pictures—while Fattori does not give us a precise depiction of the man at work, the figure is much more than a mere silhouette; rather it seems integrated into the luminous masses of the trees and heap of stones. In fact the artist's feeling of communion with Nature herself is so intense that his figures become at one with, and part of, her. It was during his long excursions in the neighborhood of Florence and in the Roman countryside (between 1873 and 1880) and, later, when he roamed the Tuscan Maremma (between 1880 and 1895 approximately), that Fattori found his richest source of inspiration, in direct contacts with the soil.

In Fattori's pictures of the countryside near Rome or of areas depopulated by the ravages of malaria we do not find that atmosphere of serene delight which pervades *La Rotonda dei Palmieri* and his other works of that period; on the contrary, he strikes a note of poignant emotion, and these pictures are imbued with a sense of utter desolation, of irremediable poverty and solitude. Luminous as is the air, it seems to weigh heavily on the white or night-black horses harnessed to those queer-shaped carts used in the Roman Campagna. In these compositions he often features rough-cast, lusterless walls which, placed transversely, give the composition the depth appropriate to it and, at the same time, bare as they are of any ornamental details, seem to act as barriers against the harsh indifference of nature. An instance is *The Halt* (National Gallery of Modern Art, Florence) of which it has been said perceptively: " Here life is no longer merely hard, but weary unto death. "

What he liked best were vast, very slightly undulating expanses of sun-scorched earth ; deserted beaches where the only trace of man's presence is here and there the dark cube of a hut rising from the sand ; horses and oxen, massive and motionless, drowsing in the noonday heat. These scenes convey a curiously haunting sense of solitude and the primaeval, while the crystalline quality of the air and the black lines with which he sometimes binds the forms to give them weight and substance emphasize their mournful, poetic appeal. When he paints scenes of military life, the composition is quite simple, determined by the artist's immediate overall impression. The figures of soldiers in camp or dispersed in the countryside, with the blue of the French uniforms or the black patches of men on horseback telling out against the chalky whiteness of a wall, all bathed in vivid, vibrant light, create a feeling of impermanence, of strangely dramatic suspense. Fattori also painted some portraits, and they too convey the feeling of actual physical presence that characterizes his landscapes. This emotivity of a very special kind in Fattori's work (it has been likened to certain tendencies in the poetry of the period) and the conciseness of his statements (which

SILVESTRO LEGA (1826-1895). WOMAN READING, 1875. (15×8¾″)
DR PAOLO STRAMEZZI COLLECTION, CREMA.

exactitude are quite in keeping with the naïvety of the subject. The exquisitely rendered light stresses the deliberate simplification of the drawing and brings out the full value of the colors, bluish blacks and greens harmonized to a range of muted tones. Here the spontaneity of the artist's response to the agreeable homeliness of the scene depicted imparts to it a poetic quality, at once candid and serene. During this period the painter was having a

TELEMACO SIGNORINI (1835-1901). A SUNNY DAY AT LA SPEZIA, 1860. (11¼ × 10¼")
ANTONIO LA ROCCA COLLECTION, ROME.

relatively easy life ; he was poor no doubt, but he was happy. He spent much of his time in the house of friends of his who lived near Florence, and the amenities and tranquillity of their home life are reflected in his work. But the years following 1870 brought a change : not only the death of his much-loved friends but the failure of a venture of his—a gallery specializing in Macchiaioli art—, and he was soon in great straits. His earlier, clean-cut and well-balanced style now gave place to a hastier, feverish method of execution ; the strongly vibrant brushstrokes slashed on to the canvas imparted a sense of tragedy, entirely absent hitherto, to his compositions. It was now that Lega definitely adopted the technique of the Macchiaioli; forms are swamped by the violence of the colors and tend towards abstraction. Though some of the themes he favored before 1870 recur, the linework is more stylized and the subject has ceased to matter; all he is interested in is the color-patch, which is given an almost excessive emphasis. In 1880 he developed an eye disease and by 1892 was almost totally blind. After depending for many years on the hospitality of friends, he died in 1895 of cancer, in a hospital at Florence.

Unlike Fattori and Lega, Telemaco Signorini (1835-1901), born at Florence, came of a cultured, well-to-do family with liberal, broad-minded views. To please his father, himself a painter, young Signorini dutifully studied painting, though literature was his first love and he never lost his taste for it. He studied for a time at the 'Academy of the Nude,' but soon became one of the most enthusiastic champions of open-air painting, as well as being a prominent figure at the artists' gatherings at the Café Michelangelo. Throughout his life, he was interested above all in ideas—this is apparent in his painting—and it was only natural that he should be the chief exponent of the new discoveries and doctrines of the Macchiaioli. Indeed his writings are not only interesting in themselves but throw much light on the movement. As much an intellectual as an artist, he was less sensitive than some of his friends to the beauties of nature, nor had he their gift of representing these in a direct, simple manner. Lacking both the rugged strength of Fattori and the poetic insight of Lega, Signorini stands out chiefly as a shrewd observer and brilliant experimenter. Of all the Macchiaioli, it was he who best realized how much there was to be learnt from foreign painting ; hence his desire to broaden his mind by frequent journeys to France and England as well as to various parts of Italy. And though he sometimes painted too much with an eye to demonstrating his theories, in several of his works we find accomplished draftsmanship combined with a sense of composition at once vibrant and finely balanced, seldom found in the work of his contemporaries.

He volunteered for service in the 1859 war, and his *Cemetery of Solferino* dates from this year. Built up with patches of intense darkness and with forms that all but disintegrate in a blaze of colors telling out against a welter of storm-clouds, this picture has an emotive drive rare in art of this period. For in this early phase, his temperamental vehemence, not to say pugnacity, led him to indulge in violent contrasts and harsh light effects. Signorini's " frenetic chiaroscuro " as it has been called is particularly noticeable in the small, spontaneous sketch *A Sunny Day at La Spezia* (1860), where the composition and colors bring to mind some of those abstract interiors which Vuillard painted shortly before 1900. After his return to Italy from a trip to Paris in 1861, where he met Troyon and Corot, Signorini formed the habit of joining his friends on long outings in the Florentine countryside. They usually ended up at Castiglioncello, a name that often appears in the titles of the canvases of several members of the group. But although he shared their fondness for depicting small villages drowsing in the languid hours of siesta and stacks of yellow hay dotting the fields, Signorini was always mindful of the literary and social message he wished his painting to convey, and this was also the period when he turned out his ' realist ' pictures such as *La Sala delle Agitate*, which involved him in much heated controversy. Though one of the first to champion the innovations of the Macchiaioli, he was also the first to break with the strict practice of their methods. And as a result of his frequent travels after 1868 and the widening of his outlook, a change came over his first manner ; his violent contrasts gave place to a softer, more varied range of colors, while his line became more clearly indicated and incisive. It

(7¾×9¾″)

MODERN ART, FLORENCE.

has been said that, of all the Macchiaioli, Signorini is the one whose art is least Italian in spirit, stress being laid on his frequent trips to Paris where he was on friendly terms with Manet, Zola and Degas. Yet it is far from certain that his contacts with foreign art had any very great effect on his development. Always eager to try out new procedures and versatile to the point of flightiness, he sometimes tended to let his painterly verve get the better of his very real sensibility. And, in fact, his art shows a concern for elegance that isolates it from that main stream of direct participation in the life of the people which constitutes the greatness of Fattori and Lega.

Amongst the painters of the Macchiaioli group, Signorini was the most popular with the general public. In Italy he was often called upon to be a jury member at various exhibitions ; also he was invited to join the teaching staff of the Academies of Naples and Florence and in 1892 was appointed an honorary member of the latter. In 1881 he made his first trip to England, where his work met with such success that he revisited that country several times in the course of his career.

It has been remarked that his painting shows "more character than style." However this may be, who can forget such pictures as that of the little piazza at Settignano, for example, with its shaded gardens, in which the brushstrokes are so light and sensitive that the very air seems dancing to their rhythm ? Indeed such is his delightful spontaneity and elegance, that had he been endowed with more tenacity of purpose, Signorini might well have blossomed out into the first Italian Impressionist.

relatively easy life ; he was poor no doubt, but he was happy. He spent much of his time in the house of friends of his who lived near Florence, and the amenities and tranquillity of their home life are reflected in his work. But the years following 1870 brought a change : not only the death of his much-loved friends but the failure of a venture of his—a gallery specializing in Macchiaioli art—, and he was soon in great straits. His earlier, clean-cut and well-balanced style now gave place to a hastier, feverish method of execution ; the strongly vibrant brushstrokes slashed on to the canvas imparted a sense of tragedy, entirely absent hitherto, to his compositions. It was now that Lega definitely adopted the technique of the Macchiaioli; forms are swamped by the violence of the colors and tend towards abstraction. Though some of the themes he favored before 1870 recur, the linework is more stylized and the subject has ceased to matter; all he is interested in is the color-patch, which is given an almost excessive emphasis. In 1880 he developed an eye disease and by 1892 was almost totally blind. After depending for many years on the hospitality of friends, he died in 1895 of cancer, in a hospital at Florence.

Unlike Fattori and Lega, Telemaco Signorini (1835-1901), born at Florence, came of a cultured, well-to-do family with liberal, broad-minded views. To please his father, himself a painter, young Signorini dutifully studied painting, though literature was his first love and he never lost his taste for it. He studied for a time at the 'Academy of the Nude,' but soon became one of the most enthusiastic champions of open-air painting, as well as being a prominent figure at the artists' gatherings at the Café Michelangelo. Throughout his life, he was interested above all in ideas—this is apparent in his painting—and it was only natural that he should be the chief exponent of the new discoveries and doctrines of the Macchiaioli. Indeed his writings are not only interesting in themselves but throw much light on the movement. As much an intellectual as an artist, he was less sensitive than some of his friends to the beauties of nature, nor had he their gift of representing these in a direct, simple manner. Lacking both the rugged strength of Fattori and the poetic insight of Lega, Signorini stands out chiefly as a shrewd observer and brilliant experimenter. Of all the Macchiaioli, it was he who best realized how much there was to be learnt from foreign painting ; hence his desire to broaden his mind by frequent journeys to France and England as well as to various parts of Italy. And though he sometimes painted too much with an eye to demonstrating his theories, in several of his works we find accomplished draftsmanship combined with a sense of composition at once vibrant and finely balanced, seldom found in the work of his contemporaries.

He volunteered for service in the 1859 war, and his *Cemetery of Solferino* dates from this year. Built up with patches of intense darkness and with forms that all but disintegrate in a blaze of colors telling out against a welter of storm-clouds, this picture has an emotive drive rare in art of this period. For in this early phase, his temperamental vehemence, not to say pugnacity, led him to indulge in violent contrasts and harsh light effects. Signorini's " frenetic chiaroscuro " as it has been called is particularly noticeable in the small, spontaneous sketch *A Sunny Day at La Spezia* (1860), where the composition and colors bring to mind some of those abstract interiors which Vuillard painted shortly before 1900. After his return to Italy from a trip to Paris in 1861, where he met Troyon and Corot, Signorini formed the habit of joining his friends on long outings in the Florentine countryside. They usually ended up at Castiglioncello, a name that often appears in the titles of the canvases of several members of the group. But although he shared their fondness for depicting small villages drowsing in the languid hours of siesta and stacks of yellow hay dotting the fields, Signorini was always mindful of the literary and social message he wished his painting to convey, and this was also the period when he turned out his 'realist' pictures such as *La Sala delle Agitate*, which involved him in much heated controversy. Though one of the first to champion the innovations of the Macchiaioli, he was also the first to break with the strict practice of their methods. And as a result of his frequent travels after 1868 and the widening of his outlook, a change came over his first manner ; his violent contrasts gave place to a softer, more varied range of colors, while his line became more clearly indicated and incisive. It

GIUSEPPE ABBATI (1836-1868). THE CLOISTER, CA. 1862. (7¾×9¾″)
NATIONAL GALLERY OF MODERN ART, FLORENCE.

has been said that, of all the Macchiaioli, Signorini is the one whose art is least Italian in spirit, stress being laid on his frequent trips to Paris where he was on friendly terms with Manet, Zola and Degas. Yet it is far from certain that his contacts with foreign art had any very great effect on his development. Always eager to try out new procedures and versatile to the point of flightiness, he sometimes tended to let his painterly verve get the better of his very real sensibility. And, in fact, his art shows a concern for elegance that isolates it from that main stream of direct participation in the life of the people which constitutes the greatness of Fattori and Lega.

Amongst the painters of the Macchiaioli group, Signorini was the most popular with the general public. In Italy he was often called upon to be a jury member at various exhibitions ; also he was invited to join the teaching staff of the Academies of Naples and Florence and in 1892 was appointed an honorary member of the latter. In 1881 he made his first trip to England, where his work met with such success that he revisited that country several times in the course of his career.

It has been remarked that his painting shows "more character than style." However this may be, who can forget such pictures as that of the little piazza at Settignano, for example, with its shaded gardens, in which the brushstrokes are so light and sensitive that the very air seems dancing to their rhythm ? Indeed such is his delightful spontaneity and elegance, that had he been endowed with more tenacity of purpose, Signorini might well have blossomed out into the first Italian Impressionist.

For a time the Macchiaioli acted as the nucleus of the most vital forces in Italian painting. But presently the artists drew apart, each taking his own path, as was the case notably with De Nittis and Boldini. Enthusiastic members of the group in its inception, Raffaello Sernesi and Giuseppe Abbati never made so great a name for themselves as did such men as Fattori and Lega; both of them died young, before their art had time to reach maturity. Nevertheless, some of their pictures rank as outstanding examples of Macchiaioli art at its best.

Born at Florence in 1838, Raffaello Sernesi died at the age of twenty-eight in hospital at Bolzano as a result of wounds received in the war, during which he had been taken prisoner by the Austrians. A restless, idealistic artist, and quite exceptionally sensitive to the luminosity of colors, Sernesi has been described as " the finest eye and the most creative colorist of all the Macchiaioli." His compositions display a deliberate, sometimes stylized simplicity ; the bright, limpid colors are saturated in a special kind of light, of which he alone had the secret, and which invests roofs, lanes and sunny wheatfields with a mysterious poetic glamour. While Fattori interpreted so faithfully the stolid, ageless life of the soil and Sernesi's color magic made of nature an enchanted wonderland, both alike brought to their vision the same purity of heart.

Like several of his friends, Sernesi loved Quattrocento art and made many sketches after Filippo Lippi and Botticelli. It has often been said of the Macchiaioli that their art is reminiscent of the past, and while some of the group link up with Fra Angelico, others hark as far back as the Etruscans. But we need hardly go to such lengths to explain their way of seeing. Sernesi's translucent colors, applied like a kind of enamel inlay, speak for his very modern outlook and the goal he set himself : a greater freedom of expression through direct

RAFFAELLO SERNESI (1838-1866). TUSCAN HOUSES, CA. 1863. (6¾ × 10″)
DR PAOLO STRAMEZZI COLLECTION, CREMA.

contact with nature, that never-failing fountainhead of rare emotions for those who know how to look at her in the right way.

Giuseppe Abbati (whose output was limited) had a special gift for conjuring up evocations of green meadows dotted with white oxen, softly waving trees, and slumbrous waters spellbound as it were in a mood of gentle, pensive melancholy. On friendly terms with the Macchiaioli, he often joined in their excursions into the country. Though occasionally Abbati had recourse to garish colors, we must admire his skill in rendering the vibrancy of air and water in a silvery haze of broken lights that sing out even in the shadows.

Abbati was born at Naples in 1836 and before coming into contact with the Macchiaioli at Florence he encountered other art movements, both at Venice, where he lived as a boy, and at Naples after 1856. Four years later he lost an eye in the war and in 1866, while serving in the war against Austria, was taken prisoner. On his release he settled down not far from Castiglioncello and devoted himself entirely to painting. Bitten by his dog, he died at Florence in 1868.

Many other names might well have found a place in this rapid survey of the vital forces in Italian painting during a century too often regarded as all but sterile in the field of art. During that period of intense activity, which ran from 1860 to round about 1880, there were other painters among the Macchiaioli who created works of much charm and sensitivity. In his *Woman with a Parasol* D'Ancona records in fluent brushstrokes the dramatic massing of contrasted lights on the form of a fashionably attired lady, and Cabianca and De Tivoli, to name but these, painted scenes sometimes tinged with melancholy, sometimes of nature in her smiling moods, that testify to the wonderful clarity, at once poetic and constructive, of their vision. All the same they lack the vital originality of artists like Fattori, Lega and Signorini.

RAFFAELLO SERNESI (1838-1866). ROOFS IN SUNLIGHT, 1862-1866. (5 × 7 ½″)
NATIONAL GALLERY OF MODERN ART, ROME.

2

TWENTIETH CENTURY

★

FUTURISM

BOCCIONI CARRA BALLA SEVERINI

METAPHYSICAL PAINTING

CHIRICO CARRA MORANDI

AMEDEO MODIGLIANI

FUTURISM

UMBERTO BOCCIONI   CARLO CARRÁ   GIACOMO BALLA   GINO SEVERINI

HARMONIES of pure colors, simplified construction, sobriety combined with spontaneity in the brushwork give the art of such painters as Fattori, Lega and others of their group its wonderfully poetic quality. Generally speaking, the Macchiaioli gave little thought to abstract theories of art; all they wanted was to body forth their visual sensations with simplicity, even a certain austerity, and this had a twofold advantage: not only did it prevent their lapsing into the illustration of romantic literary themes, but it preserved them from any taint of academicism. So far so good—but there was another side to the picture. Too little venturesome and too much wrapped up in themselves, the Macchiaioli were handicapped by a sort of provincialism. They failed to play any part in the great international art movements of the day, and though Fontanesi, and indeed most of the group, had had contacts with France, they did not benefit by these, nor did they contribute to improving the artistic taste of Italy as a whole. So much so that when the first generation of XXth-century painters came on the scene, the younger men agreed whole-heartedly with Severini in declaring that " the prevailing atmosphere (of Italian art) was too horrible for words, it was like living in a fog ! " True, the academic art of France was hardly less depressing, but the revolt of the Impressionists and the new spirit then prevailing in both art and literature were by way of creating an atmosphere far livelier than the Italian " fog." Of this the Futurists were well aware, however strenuously they paraded the nationalistic elements of their program. Anyhow it was they who enabled Italian art to cast off the shackles of tradition and come into line with the great new art ventures of the Western World.

Unlike the Fauve and Cubist movements, which owed their names to the witticisms of journalists and were limited to the field of pictorial art, that of the Futurists was thus baptized by a poet and man of letters Filippo Tommaso Marinetti, and *sub hoc signo* made war on all the forms of the past. The Futurists glorified what to their mind were the triumphs of the modern world: machinery, the conquest of space by the automobile and the airplane, all the new victories over the forces of nature which were filling Man with a sense of his boundless power. Born at Alexandria in Egypt in 1876, Marinetti studied in Paris, took his degree at the Sorbonne and wrote a play in French, *Le Roi Bombance*, which was put on at the Théâtre de l'Oeuvre in 1909. In the same year, on February 20, he published the Futurist Manifesto in the ' Figaro.' " Hitherto, literature has glorified immobility, ecstasy and somnolence ; we wish to exalt aggressive movement, feverish insomnia, gymnastic quick-steps, somersaults, slaps in the face and fisticuffs." And, in conclusion: " Standing on the summit of the world, we hurl once more a challenge to the stars ! " Here we have more than mere grandiloquent pugnacity ; a new note was struck and one which electrified the young Italians. Some painters, the pioneers of futurist art, made haste to join the movement. Marinetti was both the moving spirit of the group and its publicity man—sometimes indeed almost too vociferous in proclaiming the lofty aims of Futurism.

On February 11, 1910, was published (at Milan) the *Manifesto of the Futurist Painters* signed by Carrà, Russolo, Balla and Severini, the most famous members of the movement. Balla (born 1871) was the oldest ; he was living in Rome in the early years of the present century and imparted their first notions of modern painting to Boccioni (born 1882) and Severini (born 1883). The former had come to Rome from Calabria, the latter from Cortona, in about 1900 and both were casting about for a path to follow when Balla, who had just returned from a stay in Paris, told them about the recent developments, Impressionist and Post-Impressionist, in France. And he fired their enthusiasm to such good effect that in 1902 Boccioni set out for Paris, whence he traveled East to Berlin and as far as Petrograd. When on his return to Italy in 1904 he and Severini tried to launch their work, they encountered nothing but hostility, and meanwhile both were in severe financial straits. In 1906 Severini went to Paris, where he settled, while Boccioni moved to Milan. Boccioni's meeting with Marinetti had a decisive effect on the subsequent careers of these young painters. While keeping in touch with the latest art developments in Paris, Severini followed on the whole the directives given him by Boccioni. Other signatories of the first (1910) Manifesto were Carrà (born 1881) who had studied at Milan in the Brera Academy, and Russolo (born 1885) who came from Venice.

Nothing if not energetic, the Futurists were extremely active in propagating their doctrines, both by the written word (for example the *Technical Manifesto of Futurist Painting*, one of many publications of this order, issued on April 11, 1910) and by lecture tours covering the chief towns of Italy. Their audiences were often far from appreciative and we are told that they often bombarded the lecturer and his friends on the platform with missiles of all sorts, " mostly of an edible order," the result being that the " Futurist Evenings " usually broke up in extreme confusion. Few in the audience had the faintest notion what these wild young men were driving at and when on one occasion the lecturer declaimed some lines from Dante they were loudly hissed—under the impression that Dante was a Futurist poet ! The most exciting and uproarious of these meetings took place in 1900 at the Lyric Theater in Milan, the Chiarella Theater in Turin and La Fenice in Venice.

Early in 1911 the Futurist painters gave two shows at Milan, one at the La Intima Gallery, the other at the Ricordi Pavilion. The last-named exhibition was violently criticized by the painter Soffici in a Florence newspaper, *La Voce*. Soffici, who had lived in Paris and was familiar with the latest developments, could not stomach the pretensions of the Futurists and their claim to be world leaders of the *avant-garde* of art. The Futurists were quick to make reprisals; with Boccioni for their ringleader they invaded a café where Soffici and other members of the staff of *La Voce* were seated and soundly boxed their ears; the result being a free fight of epic quality which, after a temporary lull while the belligerents were at the police-station, started again with renewed violence at the Florence railroad station. It is amusing to record that two years later Soffici joined up with the Futurists.

Eager to exhibit at Paris, the young Italians spent the year 1911 preparing for the show which on February 5, 1912, opened at the Bernheim Gallery. This is an important date in the history of the movement ; the canvases exhibited were amongst its most significant productions and their influence on the course of modern painting is unquestionable. But what exactly was their " message " ?

In their manifestos and public meetings the Futurists deliberately took an aggressive attitude, at once calculated to shock the public and, in the last analysis, of an intellectual order. " Art is an intellectual activity " was one of Severini's *dicta*, and from his discursions on this theme we gather that the group looked for guidance to Nietzsche's philosophy and Dostoevski's novels. As for their aims in the field of pictorial art, these are explained at much length in their manifestos, in newspaper articles and in elucidations and memoirs written by members of the group. As a matter of fact the two 1910 manifestos are rather vague so far as painting is concerned. They declare that " Italy is not just a land of the dead, one vast Pompeii, white with sepulchres," and declaim against " the tyranny of the Museum, the servile adulation of old canvases, old statues, old moth-eaten, musty, moldering bric-à-brac." Modernity at all costs was their watchword. " The only vital art is one which draws its sustenance from its contemporary environment... Can we afford to disregard the frenzied activities of the great cities, the new psychology of night life, the ravaged faces of the pleasure-seeker, the prostitute, the apache and the dipsomaniac ? " Impressive no doubt, but *au fond* less a painterly than a literary tirade.

The directive ideas of Futurist painting are clearly stated in the preface to the Catalog of the 1912 Paris Exhibition and expounded at greater length in Boccioni's *Futurist Painting and Sculpture*, published in 1914. He held that it was the Impressionists who broke most effectively with the past, when they sponsored " the view that sensation and creation are identical. But," he adds, " a new combination of complementary colors or tonal contrasts implementing a new expressionist distortion of forms completely fails to move us, if these new procedures are not associated with objects as new as they." The notions of ' simultaneity ' and ' interpretation ' which the Impressionists restricted to color should, to Boccioni's mind, affect form no less. In fact the theory here enounced by him was put into practice by the Cubists. But, for the Futurists, the *object* was never static ; it was a sort of nucleus of energies issuing as forms. Thus it had to be rendered in terms of its lines of force ; and only thus could the artist give his work " a new power of objective poetry." In other words, he was called on to interpret the dynamic expansion of bodies in Space—thus creating " an emotive field of Space," a synthesis of the various abstract rhythms of each object present

UMBERTO BOCCIONI (1882-1916). STATES OF MIND I : THE FAREWELLS, 1911. (27 ¼ × 37 ¾")
NELSON A. ROCKEFELLER COLLECTION, NEW YORK.

P.I. III 62

UMBERTO BOCCIONI (1882-1916). THE FORCES OF A STREET, 1911. (39½ × 31½")
MRS NELL URECH-WALDEN COLLECTION, SCHINZNACH (SWITZERLAND).

in it. Dynamism, in fact, was to be the painter's aim. " Dynamism is the essential life element
in the forms that the vital force creates *ad infinitum*." But this dynamism is not merely a
sum-total of movements. " A horse in motion is not just a stationary horse that happens to
be moving, but something different in kind—and should be expressed as something of a
completely different order." What was wanted was a new form built up from the successive
states of movement that constituted, so to speak, its ' potential '; this potential being
termed by Boccioni " state of mind."

Thus Boccioni and his group asked of painting that it should body forth all the confused
but strongly felt sensations produced in us by the visible world, whose individual elements
are always changing, in perpetual flux. It was impossible, they said, to interpret the modern
world in terms of the old conventions, that is in limiting the picture to appearances, to what
our eyes are used to seeing. Rather, it was the painter's duty to evoke that inner life which
is the very essence, the latent ' power ' in every object. It was once thought that only human
pains and pleasures mattered ; on the contrary, it was those of so-called inorganic matter
that had the prior claim. Boccioni goes so far as to say that he is quite as much interested

in " the sufferings of an electric light bulb " as in those of a human being ! Obviously there is something of the extravagant emotionalism of the High Romantics in all this, but what perhaps strikes us most is that these theories are more of a literary than of an artistic order. As far as painting is concerned, the obvious danger of the Futurist doctrines lay in their pointing the way to a sort of esoteric symbolism. Still, though these young Italians did not always escape this pitfall, they produced some works of indisputable merit. Boccioni was also greatly interested in the problems of sculpture and published several interesting works on the subject. He applied to the domain of plastic art properly so called the same ideas that he had formulated regarding painting and proposed opening new fields for sculpture by the use in it of materials other than those traditionally regarded as " noble "—i. e. marble and bronze. Thus in his *Technical Manifesto of Futurist Sculpture*, published April 11, 1912, he wrote that " the sculptor can employ twenty or more different kinds of material in a single work, provided this does not impair the plastic emotion it is intended to convey." Though Boccioni sometimes expressed himself over-dogmatically and stridently there

UMBERTO BOCCIONI (1882-1916). THE DRINKER, 1914. (33¾ × 34¼")
PRIVATE COLLECTION, MILAN.

can be no question that the welcome he accorded to the theories of the " new art " and his revolt against all that savored of academicism were intensely sincere.

While in some of the pictures painted in 1909 Boccioni still kept closely to post-impressionist procedures, he also painted in that year a *Female Figure* which clearly shows his intention of representing form by an arrangement of planes projected on to the picture surface. (The Cubists were proceeding on the same lines in France.) But some of the works shown subsequently at the Bernheim Gallery also display that new dynamism at which the Futurists aimed. Thus in *The City Rises* (1910) the forms of men and horses, swept aside as it were by a great rushing wind, disclose in the background a forest of factory chimneys. The idea was a new one, but the literary symbolism is all too obvious and the technique is still basically *pointilliste*. In 1911 he painted " States of Mind " : *The Farewells, Those who go, Those who stay*, after making a number of preliminary drawings and studies for the three pictures, which rank amongst his most significant works. Here Boccioni, discarding any polemical intentions, displays a true painterly *élan*, and his abstract patterns with their wave-like lines of force, blue-black undulations and glints of the eerie light of the sea-depths, evoke to wonderful effect a world of the imagination given material form. We seem to see blind forces at play, writhing dementedly, and man vainly struggling to withstand their destructive onslaught by constructing machines, factories and cities, which in their turn crush him out of existence. However, in the three definitive versions of the *States of Mind* the artist makes us perhaps too conscious of his insistence on the contrasts in these visions of seething chaos; the calculated juxtapositions of realistic elements and abstract forms are too obvious. In fact the general effect is rather that of a representation of physical movement than of a real dynamism stemming from elemental forces.

In *The Street Enters the House* the structure of the composition is based on interpenetrating planes, traversed by shafts of light and aerial vibrations, and by contrast, the old-

UMBERTO BOCCIONI (1882-1916). CHARGE OF LANCERS, 1915. TEMPERA AND COLLAGE ON CARDBOARD. (20 × 13″)
PRIVATE COLLECTION, MILAN.

—

P.I. III 65

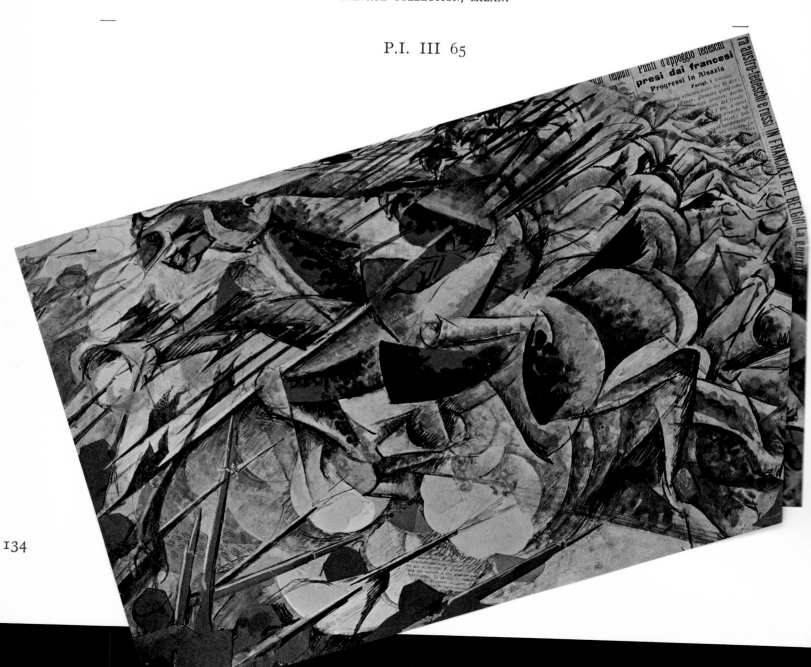

UMBERTO BOCCIONI (1882-1916). THE DRINKER, 1914. (33¾ × 34¼")
PRIVATE COLLECTION, MILAN.

in " the sufferings of an electric light bulb " as in those of a human being ! Obviously there is something of the extravagant emotionalism of the High Romantics in all this, but what perhaps strikes us most is that these theories are more of a literary than of an artistic order. As far as painting is concerned, the obvious danger of the Futurist doctrines lay in their pointing the way to a sort of esoteric symbolism. Still, though these young Italians did not always escape this pitfall, they produced some works of indisputable merit. Boccioni was also greatly interested in the problems of sculpture and published several interesting works on the subject. He applied to the domain of plastic art properly so called the same ideas that he had formulated regarding painting and proposed opening new fields for sculpture by the use in it of materials other than those traditionally regarded as " noble "—i. e. marble and bronze. Thus in his *Technical Manifesto of Futurist Sculpture*, published April 11, 1912, he wrote that " the sculptor can employ twenty or more different kinds of material in a single work, provided this does not impair the plastic emotion it is intended to convey." Though Boccioni sometimes expressed himself over-dogmatically and stridently there

UMBERTO BOCCIONI (1882-1916). CHARGE OF LANCERS, 1915, TEMPERA AND COLLAGE ON CARDBOARD. (20 × 13")
PRIVATE COLLECTION, MILAN.

can be no question that the welcome he accorded to the theories of the " new art " and his revolt against all that savored of academicism were intensely sincere.

While in some of the pictures painted in 1909 Boccioni still kept closely to post-impressionist procedures, he also painted in that year a *Female Figure* which clearly shows his intention of representing form by an arrangement of planes projected on to the picture surface. (The Cubists were proceeding on the same lines in France.) But some of the works shown subsequently at the Bernheim Gallery also display that new dynamism at which the Futurists aimed. Thus in *The City Rises* (1910) the forms of men and horses, swept aside as it were by a great rushing wind, disclose in the background a forest of factory chimneys. The idea was a new one, but the literary symbolism is all too obvious and the technique is still basically *pointilliste*. In 1911 he painted '' States of Mind '' : *The Farewells, Those who go, Those who stay,* after making a number of preliminary drawings and studies for the three pictures, which rank amongst his most significant works. Here Boccioni, discarding any polemical intentions, displays a true painterly *élan,* and his abstract patterns with their wave-like lines of force, blue-black undulations and glints of the eerie light of the sea-depths, evoke to wonderful effect a world of the imagination given material form. We seem to see blind forces at play, writhing dementedly, and man vainly struggling to withstand their destructive onslaught by constructing machines, factories and cities, which in their turn crush him out of existence. However, in the three definitive versions of the *States of Mind* the artist makes us perhaps too conscious of his insistence on the contrasts in these visions of seething chaos; the calculated juxtapositions of realistic elements and abstract forms are too obvious. In fact the general effect is rather that of a representation of physical movement than of a real dynamism stemming from elemental forces.

In *The Street Enters the House* the structure of the composition is based on interpenetrating planes, traversed by shafts of light and aerial vibrations, and by contrast, the old-

CARLO CARRÀ (1881). JOLTS OF A CAB, 1911. (20½ × 26¼")
H. WALDEN COLLECTION, KUNSTMUSEUM, BASEL.

fashioned horse-carriage in the center strikes an anecdotal note. In *The Forces of the Street*
beams of light and projected shadows build up an harmonious overall rhythm, the facets of
bodies in movement absorbing or reflecting the erratic play of light. Later Boccioni showed
a tendency to move away from abstraction towards a more expressionist procedure : thus
in *Elasticity* and *Dynamism of a Woman's Head* (1912) the forms, constructed on simultaneous planes, are more fully delineated and more static. In the large picture named *Materia*,
on which he worked for a long time, he sought to embody all his theories. This is a portrait
of his mother, symbolically placed in the center of the canvas, with all the elements radiating
out from her in planes of light. However, it is in such pictures as *The Drinker* that he conveys
most effectively the direct sensation of an object visualized as a simultaneous conjunction
of the planes which give it individuality. Finally, though Boccioni may not always quite
bring off the effect he is aiming at, his work must be ranked among the most representative
productions of the period. Another notable contribution to Futurist art was made by Carrà,
though perhaps he had a less intense feeling than Boccioni's for construction in terms of
movement. His *Milan Galleria*, painted in 1912, is one of the most significant works of the
movement and even the titles of his pictures—e.g. *What the Streetcar said to me* (1910) and
Jolts of a Cab (1911)—tell of his zest for the discovery of new, essentially 'modern' themes.
    Another of the young men who signed the Futurist Manifestos was Gino Severini, an
artist of a very different stamp from Boccioni and Carrà. His work is gay, imaginative,
full of new inventions ; his color-forms fall asunder, re-shape themselves, plunge and slither

CARLO CARRÀ (1881).
THE MILAN GALLERIA, 1912. (35 ¼ × 23 ½″)
GIANNI MATTIOLI COLLECTION, MILAN.

CARLO CARRÀ (1881). SIMULTANEITY: WOMAN AND BALCONY, 1912. (57¾ × 52¼″)
PRIVATE COLLECTION, MILAN.

through an eye-bewildering maze of planes and tonalities, and the artist's high spirits and exuberance, playful if sometimes tinged with irony, make themselves felt in every inch of the canvas. While keeping to the principles enacted by Boccioni, Severini did not adopt the intellectual or aggressive attitude of his friends. He lived in Paris and delighted in painting the night life of the Montmartre cafés and the colorful crowds at the Bal Tabarin. In his art, too, Post-Impressionism was the starting-off point, but he juggles with forms built up of pointillist dots and a kaleidoscopic medley of glittering flakes of color to such happy effect that his best canvases are vibrant with an inner life of their own. There is nothing in the least ' philosophical ' in his view of dynamism ; for Severini that somewhat overworked term meant simply the vital energy of the cabaret dancer and the shimmering play of artificial light on faces, dresses and bodies in movement. He liked bright colors, blues and whites, but delicate transitions no less than strong contrasts. In his *Pan Pan at the Monico* bodies, heads and limbs are broken up, reconstructed, multiplied in a giddy whirl that reminds one of a merry-go-round. Even when we know that the painter spent two years on the making of this picture, we are none the less carried away by its amazing spontaneity and the sheer physical excitement pervading it. Severini played an important part in the development of Futurism. While Boccioni was the theoretician of the movement, Severini acted as a connecting link between Italy and the new art developments in Paris. He counted Picasso and Braque no less than Matisse and Dufy amongst his friends and always regretted that his colleagues in Milan did not keep more in touch with what was happening in Paris. The intransigent nationalism of the Futurists and still more their claim to be the sole originators of " the new modern art " irritated even Severini, and was still more resented, naturally enough, by the painters who then were making art-history in Paris.

In his preface to the Catalog of the Paris Exhibition Boccioni, after voicing his admiration of and respect for the art of the Cubist painters, added : " But the Cubists persist in painting the immobile, the frozen, the static aspects of nature... It is quite obvious that in the aesthetic doctrines of our Paris friends there is a lurking *penchant* towards academicism." The Futurist Exhibition had a *succès de scandale* ; several newspapers jeered at it, openly or by innuendo. In the *Petit Bleu* of February 9, Apollinaire wrote : " It is the most dangerous painting imaginable. So far the new art which is being built up in France seemed to have kept to the nature of a melody ; now the Futurists are showing us, by the titles of their pictures anyhow, if not by the pictures themselves, that it could be stepped up to a sort of symphony." These remarks, slightly garbled, were often quoted by the

CARLO CARRÀ (1881). THE RED RIDER, 1914. WATERCOLOR AND INK. (10¼ × 14¼")
PRIVATE COLLECTION, MILAN.

GIACOMO BALLA (1871). LEASH IN MOTION, 1912. (35¾ × 43½")
A. CONGER GOODYEAR COLLECTION, NEW YORK.

Futurists, who read into Apollinaire's article an acknowledgment of the triumph of their art. After Paris the Exhibition went on tour—to London, Brussels, Berlin and other cities—usually accompanied by Boccioni himself. Meanwhile he launched the *Manifesto of Futurist Sculpture* and henceforth he practiced sculpture as well as painting.

In his account of the Paris Salon des Indépendants of 1913 Apollinaire welcomed the advent of the " Orphic School "—whose principal exponent was Delaunay—, observing that " it marks the introduction into painting of the literary method of ' Simultaneism.' " This was borne out by the title of one of Delaunay's 1913 exhibits, *Simultaneous Windows*, in connection with which Madame Delaunay observes that " for the first time pure colors, by becoming planes and clashing in simultaneous contrasts, create a new kind of form, built up not by light-and-shade but by the basic relations between colors themselves." Exactly these ideas had been promulgated by the Futurists some time before and they were not slow to bring the charge of plagiarism in an article in the new Italian review *Lacerba*. Similarly, when Fernand Léger published his " Notes for a Lecture " in *Montjoie*, voicing theories patently resembling those of the Italians, Boccioni pointed out indignantly that the " discovery of dynamism " was his.

Severini has maintained that both Apollinaire and Léger would have liked to associate themselves closely with the Futurist movement, but were put off by the attitude of Boccioni

GINO SEVERINI (1883). DANCER AT THE BAL TABARIN, 1913. (24 × 18″)
PRIVATE COLLECTION, MILAN.

and Marinetti. However this may be, it is certain that Futurism stood for a tendency in keeping with all that was most vital in the art of this period. Making its appearance shortly after Cubism and almost at the same time as French Orphism (and other similar movements), Futurism unquestionably embodied the basic elements of contemporary art. In this same year, 1913, Boccioni exhibited his sculpture in Paris and Severini gave a one-man show in London. When the first World War broke out, Boccioni and Marinetti played an active part in the movement in favor of Italy's joining up with the Allies. Wounded in the war, Boccioni died in 1916 as the result of a riding accident. Sant-Elia, the architect, who had published the *Manifesto of Futurist Architecture*, also was killed in the war. By the time the war ended the movement had petered out ; Carrà had turned to Metaphysical Painting and Severini to other forms of art.

GINO SEVERINI (1883). SPHERICAL EXPANSION OF LIGHT (CENTRIFUGAL), 1914. (24 × 19½")
PRIVATE COLLECTION, MILAN.

GIORGIO DE CHIRICO (1888). THE SEER, 1915. (35¼ × 27½″)
PRIVATE COLLECTION, NEW YORK.

METAPHYSICAL PAINTING

GIORGIO DE CHIRICO   CARLO CARRÀ   GIORGIO MORANDI

THE term Metaphysical Painting is usually applied to the painting of a quite special nature produced from 1915 onwards by de Chirico and Carrà ; subsequently, though for only a short while, by De Pisis, and still later by Morandi. It should be noted, however, that several years before 1915 Chirico's painting had already begun to display characteristics which would justify its being described as " metaphysical." In fact there was no real break between de Chirico's Italian period and his earlier productions, especially those of the years he spent in Paris.

" One never discovers reality once for all," wrote Guillaume Apollinaire, " for the truth is ever new." Though Apollinaire was a fervent champion of the Cubists and did so much to make their work understood and appreciated, he was also one of the first (as also was Picasso) to express admiration for de Chirico's art.

In *The Cubist Painters* (1912) Apollinaire writes, referring to the young artists with whom we are about to deal : " They are moving farther and farther from the old art of optical illusion and natural proportions, in order to express the grandeur of metaphysical forms." On the face of it there seems little justification for drawing a parallel between the work of such men as Picasso or Braque during this period and the kind of art which came to be known as "metaphysical." None the less their aim was, in the last analysis, identical ; both Cubists and Metaphysicals sought to plumb the mystery of the visible world and to construct a plastic system that was an ordered expression of its inner meaning. But whereas Picasso examined objects " like a surgeon dissecting a corpse " and disintegrated their normal aspects with a view to reconstructing them in terms of a creative synthesis, de Chirico, while creating with forms that are in some ways abstract, retained more or less the familiar aspects of the objects themselves, and painted *situations*. Thus the enigmatic quality of his art stems from his depiction of reality under a form which seemingly tallies with our visual experience, but actually is unreal since it is located in a Space different from ours and is composed of incongruous, indeed uncanny, juxtapositions of objects. Hence the curious, almost nightmarish effects produced by de Chirico's paintings ; the world he shows us is a world we know—but only in our dreams. Metaphysical as is de Chirico's art (and such it was even before it was given that name), its tensely poetic atmosphere is one transcending reality—surrealist, in short.

De Chirico was born in 1888 at Volo, in Greece, of Italian parents. He studied for a time in Athens ; then on his father's death, settled in Munich, where he enrolled in the Royal Academy of Fine Arts. It was during his three years' stay in Munich that he came under two influences which were to have a decisive effect on his career as an artist, a fact of which de Chirico himself makes no secret. One of these was the philosophy of Nietzsche and

GIORGIO DE CHIRICO (1888). THE ENIGMA OF THE HOUR, 1911. (21½ × 27¾")
GIANNI MATTIOLI COLLECTION, MILAN.

Schopenhauer, the other Böcklin's painting. The most striking feature of Böcklin's paintings is their somewhat grandiloquent romanticism combined with a vague symbolism based on the artist's reactions to Death and the Infinite, which he expresses with seemingly realistic forms and in colors steeped in a pale, ghostly sheen resembling moonlight.

De Chirico was fascinated by this strange, exotic art, with its intimations of a reality that is not real and an unreal world that somehow appears real. When in 1908 the young painter made his self-portrait, showing himself in a romantic posture, in front of a background stretching out into illimitable distance, he inscribed at the foot of the canvas his confession of faith : *Et quid amabo nisi quod aenigma est ?* In 1908 he left Germany and went to Italy where, after a stay at Milan, he settled in Florence.

The exact dating of his early works is none too easy, but it would seem that de Chirico's true, highly original personality did not make itself apparent until 1910. It is well in evidence in the pictures of cities—facetiously lumped together under the name of " Chirico City " —which he made in the following year. This was also the year when he went to Paris to join his brother Alberto Savinio, a writer and musician, who subsequently took to painting.

" Who can deny the strangely suggestive relationship between perspective and metaphysics ? "—thus de Chirico himself. And indeed it would be hard to name any other artist who has de Chirico's mysterious power of evoking a world of utter silence and bright arcades whose long architectural recessions repeat themselves *ad infinitum,* cutting the picture space into sharply demarcated zones of light and shadow, whose only denizen is some enigmatic statue, the fabric of a dream.

The painter does not merely express the romantic nostalgia of the expatriate ; he also conveys that aspect of eternity which the works of men assume in certain contexts and that sense of desolation emanating from the relics of some vanished civilization, whose emblem is a statue bearing the name of "Melancholia," rising in forlorn eminence in some public square. In de Chirico's canvases lingering memories of his youth in Greece are mingled with reminiscences of Italy, and he has not forgotten that queer impression we all have in childhood of a mysterious power lurking in certain objects : a window, a black patch of shadow, an expanse of garishly blue sea. He constantly uses the same elements, but each time re-arranges them in Space in a new, carefully composed pattern, charged with faintly sinister suggestions. Sometimes he assigns a leading place to buildings, as in the set of pictures depicting *Towers* ; sometimes he splits a vast illusionist perspective into tracts of light and dark. The architectural features are built up in diagonals extending to a vanishing point outside the canvas. In the distance a clearly indicated horizon line (the sea, a passing train), instead of acting as a backdrop, conjures up vistas of infinity. De Chirico paints in contrasts of bright and dark tones, allotting a much larger place to the empty spaces on the canvas than to the full ones. Shadows function as new elements ; indeed they construct forms even more intriguing than those on which the light falls, and they bear no real relation to

GIORGIO DE CHIRICO (1888). MORNING MEDITATION, 1912. (27 ½ × 20 ½")
PRIVATE COLLECTION, MILAN.

GIORGIO DE CHIRICO (1888). METAPHYSICAL INTERIOR WITH A SMALL FACTORY, 1917. (18 × 14¼″)
GIANNI MATTIOLI COLLECTION, MILAN.

CARLO CARRÀ (1881). PENELOPE, 1917. (37¼ × 21¼")
CARLO FRUA DE ANGELI COLLECTION, MILAN.

the incidence of the light—hence the disturbing atmosphere they induce, suggesting some impending, unspecified catastrophe. All seems natural enough, yet everything is ominous in this queer, *unheimlich* world. The shadow falling from a statue we do not see seems charged with some dark presage for the little girl bowling her hoop in *The Melancholy and Mystery of a Street*. The black shadow of an unseen building strikes, darkly menacing, across a row of houses which, though drawn with geometrical precision, seem to have no weight or substance.

In 1913 de Chirico began to place everyday objects, such as bananas or artichokes, in the foreground of his perspectives, thus giving more explicitness to the nightmare atmosphere of his compositions. The drawing became more emphatic, the pigment brighter and more richly worked. Various theories have been advanced to give a logical explanation of these evocations of an imaginary world, but really they seem uncalled for; all that matters is the painter's amazing power of giving poetic reality to his private dreamworld. The events of 1914 seemed to justify de Chirico's dark forebodings, and he now took to using mannequins as his models. Though he began by merely draping them in Greek peplums like lay figures, they soon developed into full-fledged automata.

The 1914 Salon des Indépendants had brought notoriety to de Chirico, whose work had hitherto been appreciated only by a small group of friends. But in the summer of 1915 he had to go to Italy to join the army, and was posted to Ferrara where before long, as the result of a nervous breakdown, he was sent to hospital. He has described the effect this Italian town produced on him. The impulse to " a truly metaphysical conception of art " was given him, he says, by his glimpses of certain interiors, " certain window displays and shops, and certain quarters of the town, for example the old ghetto where cakes and candies of exceedingly strange, metaphysical shapes were to be seen." Crackers and cookies figure in some of his pictures, where their frankly realistic depiction in the midst of geometric structures and abstract forms has a singular ambivalence. In fact de Chirico stressed that feeling of irrationality induced by the " meetings " of unlikely objects—the characteristic climate of the subconscious—and rather to his surprise he was enthusiastically taken up by the Surrealists, who saw in his art the illustration of a passage in their favorite author, Lautréamont : " Beautiful as the unlooked-for meeting of an umbrella and a sewing machine on an operating table."

In 1916 he painted his most famous mannequin pictures : *The Disquieting Muses*, *Hector and Andromache* (of which there are several versions) and *The Troubadour*. There are hints here of the influence of Cubism in its first phase ; while keeping a certain semblance of reality, these mannequins lend themselves to the reconstruction of objects in geometric forms upon which the composition is centered without regard to normal spatial relations. While in hospital at Ferrara de Chirico made the acquaintance of Carlo Carrà (in January, 1917). It was Carrà who applied the term " metaphysical " to the kind of painting they both were engaged on at this time.

Some years older than de Chirico, Carrà came to metaphysical painting by paths quite other than his friend's. Until about 1918 de Chirico's painting showed a more or less steady evolution, unmarked by any drastic change ; ever eager though he was to reveal new aspects of the world, it was always the same world that he portrayed. Carrà, however, took an active part in the Futurist movement until 1916 and contributed to its development. When he broke with ' dynamism,' it was to rally to the great Italian tradition ; thus in 1916 he published two appreciative articles on Giotto and Paolo Uccello respectively. As for de Chirico, he had fallen under the spell of Böcklin before he came to Italy for his first long stay there and much as he admired the great Italian Masters, Böcklin meant more to him. However, Carrà and de Chirico had this in common : that they both had come in contact with the Paris *avant-garde* artists, though each took something different from them ; thus, while de Chirico seems to have seen in Cubist procedures a means of rendering his vision of space on more or less abstract lines, Carrà was influenced by the Douanier Rousseau and the more formal aspects of Cubism as found in Derain's art. (In his *Metaphysical Painting*, published in 1919, Carrà devotes two chapters to these artists.) Lastly, the two painters had a different

GIORGIO MORANDI (1890). METAPHYSICAL STILL LIFE, 1920. (26¾ × 24¼")
PRIVATE COLLECTION, MILAN.

cultural background ; whereas de Chirico had been a devotee of Nietzsche and Schopenhauer, Carrà was drawn to the philosophy of Vico and Benedetto Croce. In their writings he discerned a ' spiritual ' outlook that much appealed to him and it was partly this that led him away from Futurism to what he called metaphysical art.

When Carrà met de Chirico in January, 1917, he found in the themes that he freely borrowed from his friend a crystallization as it were of his tendencies towards a ' return to the subject,' combined with that spiritualization of form which had already been suggested to him by the Italian Masters of the XIVth and XVth centuries. " What we wish to paint," he wrote, " is not plastic reality in its raw state but that essential form which has so great a clarity that it reveals reality itself. Without this constructive premise it is impossible to achieve spiritual freedom, and any claim to our independence of the physical world is but a vain pretense. Thus the painter should always direct his attention to the very essence of things ; there is no other way of achieving true architectonic austerity. And this is what we mean by ' the new reality ' and ' metaphysical painting.' " Carrà also points out that *ordinary things* are the only true intermediaries between the essence of the world of reality and ourselves, and that if the artist is to bring out " the secret magnificence " of that world it is these ordinary things that he must scrutinize. Both in his writings and his painting Carrà's attitude is far more intellectual and less instinctual than de Chirico's. It is perhaps significant in this connection that his whole metaphysical output amounted to remarkably few, barely twenty, canvases, though his interest in this form of art lasted from 1916 to 1921 approximately. This was because he worked over his compositions again and again, to such effect that the successive layers of paint are visible, and these pictures came to have the tactile quality which doubtless he was aiming at. Most striking of the compositions built up in this way is perhaps *The Drunken Gentleman* in which the big white head conveys a quite remarkable impression of a solid mass existing in space. Above all Carrà stresses the 'quiddity' of objects; he simplifies and crystallizes them to the extreme limit of recognizability. While taking over from de Chirico his favorite motifs, mannequins, geometrical instruments and so forth, he presents them in tranquil, unalarming contexts, whereas de Chirico uses them to evoke an ambiance of eerie magic.

The intimate association of de Chirico and Carrà, of no small importance to this period of Italian painting, was short-lived; beginning in January, 1917, it ended in 1919-1920. Meanwhile De Pisis showed leanings towards this form of art, but only incidentally, and from 1918 Morandi followed up similar lines of research which, though this phase was not of long duration, certainly affected his subsequent development.

GIORGIO MORANDI (1890). STILL LIFE, 1948. (13 ¼ × 10 ¼ ")
PRIVATE COLLECTION, MILAN.

Giorgio Morandi, who was born in 1890 at Bologna, where he still lives, is regarded today as one of the leading contemporary painters. His art cannot be assigned to any specific movement, though in some respects it is the most vital interpretation of those esoteric tendencies whose origins are traceable in Metaphysical Painting. Morandi has always worked in self-imposed isolation, developing and broadening his vision by patient, comprehensive study of certain great works of the past and also of some modern developments. He had a deep devotion to Cézanne but for many years was acquainted with the Aix master's work by way of reproductions only. Though he figured in a Futurist Exhibition (in 1914), he was never connected with that movement. In 1918 he pursued the same lines of research as de Chirico and Carrà, but here again he knew the latter's work through photographs. We may perhaps add that Morandi has never published any expositions of his aesthetic theories and has never been to Paris, but has devoted his whole life to the practice of his art.

Alberto Savinio once wrote that Metaphysical Painting constituted not so much a real " school " as a special way of seeing, and it is from this angle that we can best perceive the link between Morandi's art and that of de Chirico and Carrà. In the landscapes Morandi painted between 1911 and 1914 he depicts trees and houses with broad, apparent brush-strokes and the composition is unified by an overall use of color-light. Later, about 1916, when he was painting chiefly still lifes, he showed more concern for individualizing the forms of objects. The bright, flat colors of these pictures foreshadow Morandi's recent compositions, in which objects, released as it were from the pull of gravity, live and have their being under their most essential aspects. From 1916 on Morandi showed a particular fondness for those groupings of long-necked bottles, salad-bowls and goblets which have become a sort of *leitmotiv* constantly recurring, if always modified, in all his work up to date. However, during those early years this quasi-abstract handling of forms had a descriptive bias ; there was a decorative quality in these still lifes which was subsequently superseded by a very different type of composition. In his latest works the orchestration of the various elements in a limited space, usually unified by a pastel-grey tonality, creates an atmosphere of profound serenity in which the ' souls ' of objects are made visible rather than their material selves.

In 1918 Morandi entered on what is known as his " metaphysical period." However, he did not employ the themes favored by de Chirico and Carrà ; there are no mannequins or baleful apparitions in his pictures, nor does he try to create that queer, hallucinative aura we find in the works of the first metaphysical painters. On the contrary he seems bent on evoking an ambiance of the most complete clarity, in which volumes are precisely circumscribed and objects defined with almost meticulous exactitude. The colors are frank, with a smooth enamel finish. One might almost describe his pictures of this period as exercises of the plastic sensibility with a view to reducing the artist's visual experience to a mathematical schema. " I like the set rule which corrects emotion," Braque once wrote and Morandi, too, seems to keep his expression under rigorous control. Even when, in a later phase, he allowed himself a wider emotional freedom he continued to avoid any overstatement and practiced a deliberate economy of means. Thus Metaphysical Painting served Morandi as a sort of discipline which he imposed on himself during a period ending in, approximately, 1920. A discipline that he did not discard in the years that followed, but which he modified, indeed, intensified in his quest of an ever subtler expression of the secret life of objects.

By the use of an original, ever-changing palette of soft, translucent colors and the spacious tranquillity he gives his compositions Morandi, too, creates an atmosphere of magic; but, while never allowing reality to enter into them unless it has a poetic quality, neither does he let imagination override the *data* of reality.

AMEDEO MODIGLIANI (1884-1920). ELVIRE, 1919. (36 × 23½")
PROF. W. HADORN COLLECTION, BERN.

152

AMEDEO MODIGLIANI

BORN at Leghorn in 1884, Amedeo Modigliani went to Paris at the age of twenty-two and remained there almost continuously until his death in 1920. Thus his life in Paris spanned those fourteen years from 1906 to 1920 which, when we look back on them today, seem almost fabulous, so numerous were the front-rank artists who made good their personalities and so great was the number of memorable works produced during that supremely exciting period. One of its most impressive revelations was assuredly the art of Modigliani. Yet his art was wholly personal and owed nothing to any of the many 'movements' of the day ; indeed some have seen in it a XXth-century revival of the great Italian tradition. This view is certainly far-fetched ; the genius of the Sienese and Botticelli did not miraculously find a second blossoming in the work of this modern Italian of the School of Paris. True, Modigliani was Italian through and through, not merely by the accident of birth but temperamentally ; that instinctive cult of an ideal of beauty, his natural flow of sympathy towards the world around him and the streak of sentimentality running through his work— all were typically Italian. But above all he was bent on realizing his artistic personality as an individual. In early youth, before coming to Paris, he wrote to a friend : " We artists have different rights from other people's because we have different needs which — and this we must believe in and proclaim—set us above the morality of the world at large." We are told that Modigliani had read Nietzsche, but the attitude he expresses here is that of a man passionately and uniquely conscious of his mission as an artist. "Beauty," he says, writing to the same friend, " imposes painful duties but by the same token they call forth all that is most beautiful in the human soul." In Paris Modigliani found exactly the atmosphere needed to bring his lofty aspirations to fruition and to get the best out of himself. Thus the roots of his art, we might say, were in Italy, but it flowered in Paris, whose cosmopolitan life had then a freedom greater, perhaps, than that enjoyed at any other period of the city's history. Modigliani's art stemmed from the fusion of an innate, essentially Italian yearning for beauty with the stimulating ferment of early XXth-century Paris, and his originality is due to the fact that its foundations in the past were solid enough to withstand the violent tensions of his brief but brilliant career and to enable tradition to achieve a form in keeping with our times. In the course of its evolution the art of Modigliani showed no abrupt or drastic change at any point ; all we find are gradual, if profound, modifications, and, despite the feverish intensity of his quest, he never once lost sight of the goal he had set himself.

The year when Modigliani came to Paris, 1906, was that of the death of Cézanne and also that of the famous Salon des Indépendants at which the ' Fauves ' acquired their name. This was the time when Derain and Picasso were investigating Negro sculpture and primitive art of the so-called ' high periods ' ; and also when in the *bateau-lavoir*, that epoch-making

AMEDEO MODIGLIANI (1884-1920). PORTRAIT OF THE PAINTER KISLING, 1918-1919. (32×18″)
PRIVATE COLLECTION, PARIS.

AMEDEO MODIGLIANI (1884-1920). PORTRAIT OF THE PAINTER HENRI LAURENS, 1917-1918. (21½ × 18″)
PRIVATE COLLECTION, PARIS.

Montmartre studio, Picasso was starting work on *Les Demoiselles d'Avignon*, key-picture so
to speak of the new movement that was soon to change the whole tenor of modern art under
the name of Cubism. A legendary glamour still clings about the *vie de Bohème* of Montmartre

AMEDEO MODIGLIANI (1884-1920). LEOPOLD ZBOROWSKI, 1917. (42 × 26")
MUSEUM OF ART, SAO PAULO, BRAZIL.

AMEDEO MODIGLIANI (1884-1920). SEATED WOMAN.
PRIVATE COLLECTION, PARIS.

and Montparnasse in those colorful years ; Modigliani lived at various times in both those districts of Paris, where he soon became one of the most striking, and also most tragic, figures of the artist colony. His friends—poets and writers—have spoken of his drinking bouts, his drug-taking, his violent, tangled love-affairs ; but all agree in stressing the innate good breeding, and the aristocratic bearing which despite a quarrelsome, restless disposition he never lost even in his worst moral lapses and in the direst financial straits.

In 1907 the great Cézanne Memorial Exhibition took place at the Salon d'Automne and Modigliani's output of the next two years shows how closely he must have studied Cézanne's works, especially those of his last period. *The Italian Peasant* and *The 'Cellist*, for instance, are studies in the Cézannian technique; in them Modigliani, too, seeks to render volumes by means of color harmonies. He achieved his true artistic personality only when he succeeded in giving line and color in combination the power of expressing volumes. For he constantly aspired towards a world of beauty neither abstract nor built up of forms alone, but created by a harmony of line wedded to color : a line that does not merely state the incidental aspects of the subject but envelops it throughout, thus rendering volume in its intrinsic wholeness, stripped of all non-essentials. Though Modigliani briefly dallied with Lautrec's brisk, incisive drawing, and in another canvas followed the ' Fauve ' practice of giving color extreme emphasis by the use of color accents, it was not long before he lit on that special style which is basic to his *œuvre*. In this his line follows without break the contour of the body extended to its maximum on the flat surface of the canvas ; hence those long swan-like necks and the exaggerated ovals of some of the faces—distortions characteristic of Modigliani's art. But this line is not decorative, nor does it merely delineate bodies, on the contrary it brings out the inner harmony of the subject ; while the colors, too, with their broad, well-balanced harmonies combine expressive power with formal lay-out.

In 1909, at the suggestion of Brancusi, with whom he then was sharing a studio in Montmartre, Modigliani took up sculpture. Negro carving was still in fashion and he looked to it for guidance. By now Cubism has opened our eyes to the abstract volumes and hieratic synthesism of Negro sculpture; Modigliani, however, discerned in it hints of the possibility of regaining the power of expressing volumes by the use of a long, unbroken line, sinuous, fluent and carried to its ultimate extension.

So far as is known, Modigliani never painted a still life and only very few landscapes; he confined himself almost entirely to portraits and nudes. His models were casual acquaintances, lifelong friends, or children as poor as himself whom chance threw in his way. All are literally models, that is to say he posed them for the picture. Sitting motionless, usually with their arms crossed, in relaxed attitudes, and day-dreaming, their minds void for the moment of the petty anxieties of daily life, they gaze towards the painter. Or, rather, it is the painter who is gazing at them with tender feeling, a sense of intimate communion with beings as forlorn as himself—more so indeed since they have not his consolation, his hope of creating supreme beauty through the medium of his art. The strange thing is that somehow Modigliani seems to communicate that hope to those he painted ; their eyes may appear vacant, but in them is a glimmer, a dim reflection as it were, of the artist's secret dream. It has been said that all Modigliani's portraits are alike; the truth is that in one sense they all are portraits of himself. In any case, as the years went by, he simplified the expressions of faces, making them less individual, more universal.

Modigliani's nudes have something of the poignancy of his portraits, though imbued with a serene repose that lifts them above the level of mere naked bodies. (This was not the view taken by the police authorities, who in 1918 closed down the Berthe Weill Gallery in which an exhibition of Modigliani's nudes was being held, on the grounds of their alleged indecency.) There is no denying that this art is sensual—in fact there was no need of the nudes to prove this—but the harmonies of Modigliani's smooth flexible lines, those long sweeping curves that seem to have been dashed off in a sudden gust of inspiration, impart to the women's bodies figuring in so many of his works an intensity of emotion far indeed from being of a merely sensual order.

During the first years of the 1914 war Modigliani met Leopold Zborowski who, by sheer pertinacity, backed by his faith in the artist, succeeded in selling some of his canvases ; this enabled him to lead a life somewhat less hard than when he was selling his sketches in the Paris cafés. Another bright spot in his life was the devotion of Jeanne Hébuterne, by whom in 1918 he had a daughter. In the picture named *Maternity* he has marvellously conveyed, in all its essential purity, the beauty of a young mother with her child on her knee. Here the simplicity of the drawing and the superb harmony of the undulating colors with the line produce a curious effect—almost one of intrusion—on the spectator, as though the painter were giving access to the most secret places of his heart. This serene inspiration, welling up from a profound understanding of life and the pathos of the human situation, led Modigliani during the last two years of his life to paint what are his most powerfully emotive pictures. In the midst of the tragedy of the war and the hardly less tragic vicissitudes of his own life, Modigliani seems to voice a message of hope ; we must never lose faith, he tells us, either in mankind or in beauty. Thus it is that, far from being as some have thought the final phase of a special kind of mannerism, his last works are an anticipation of the future. For he gave expression to the desire for a reversion to certain ' constants ' of art that has been felt by many modern artists and has been given so many names, such as " neo-plasticism " and " the return to nature." Thus his art can be regarded under two aspects : as an art of the free imagination in so far as his poetic vision leads him to transmute natural forms, but also as a very human art that bodies forth a world in which the life of men is depicted in its essential purity and grandeur and there is nothing of that fierce revolt against the human that we find in, for example, Soutine's work.

In 1918, suffering from consumption, Modigliani had to go to the South of France. On his return to Paris he exhibited (in 1919) at the Salon d'Automne and also in London. He died of a haemoptysis in hospital, on January 25, 1920.

BIBLIOGRAPHY

Specially compiled by Dr Eugenio Battisti, Assistant at the University of Rome, for this third and concluding volume in our series devoted to Italian Painting—THE CREATORS OF THE RENAISSANCE, THE RENAISSANCE, FROM CARAVAGGIO TO MODIGLIANI—, the following bibliography comprises a selected list, in chronological order, of the chief publications relating to the art periods covered in our three volumes.

GENERAL

G. B. CAVALCASELLE and J. A. CROWE, *A New History of Painting in Italy from the Second to the Sixteenth Century*, London 1864 etc. ; *Storia della pittura italiana*, Italian edition, Florence 1886-1908 ; *A History of Painting in North Italy*, London 1912. A. VENTURI, *Storia dell'arte italiana*, Milan 1901 etc. B. CROCE, *Estetica come scienza dell'espressione*, Bari 1902. A. MICHEL, *Histoire de l'art*, Paris 1905 etc. B. BERENSON, *The Story and Criticism of Italian Art*, 3 vol. London 1912-1916. R. VAN MARLE, *The Development of Italian schools of Painting*, The Hague 1922 etc. (Italian edition of the first two volumes, Milan 1932 etc.). L. VENTURI, *Pittura italiana in America*, Milan 1931. B. CROCE, *La critica e la storia delle arti figurative*, Bari 1934. J. SCHLOSSER, *La letteratura artistica*, Florence 1935. L. VENTURI, *History of Art Criticism*, New York 1936 ; *Histoire de la critique*, Brussels 1938, Italian edition, Florence 1945 and 1948. M. MARANGONI, *Saper vedere*, Milan 1938. M. PITTALUGA, *Storia dell'arte italiana*, Florence 1937-1938. L. VENTURI, *Art Criticism Now*, Baltimore 1941. L. VENTURI, *Painting and Painters, How to look at a Picture, Giotto to Chagall*, 1945 (Italian edition Rome 1947, French edition Paris 1950). B. BERENSON, *Metodo e attribuzione*, Florence 1947. M. SALMI, *Storia dell'arte italiana*, 3 vol. Florence 1948. A. LEROY, *Histoire de la peinture italienne*, Paris 1948. L. VENTURI, *Gli studi di storia dell'arte medioevale e moderna*, Cinquant'anni di vita intellettuale italiana, Naples 1950. J. ALAZARD, *L'Art italien*, Paris 1950 etc.

For individual painters, see the *Enciclopedia italiana* ; for more detailed information, lists of works and virtually complete bibliographies, see the *Allgemeines Künstler Lexikon*, by Thieme-Becker, Leipzig 1907 etc.

MIDDLE AGES AND HIGH RENAISSANCE

EARLY WRITERS

F. VILLANI, *Liber de origine civitatis Florentinae et eiusdem famosis civibus* (1381-1382), Florence 1847. C. CENNINI, *Il libro dell'arte* (ca. 1390), Florence 1859, New Haven 1932. L. GHIBERTI, *I commentari* (ca. 1450), Berlin 1912, Florence 1951. B. FACIO, *De viris illustribus* (ca. 1457), Florence 1745. Cr. LANDINO, *Commento alla Divina Commedia di Dante*, Florence 1481. ANONYMUS, *I XIV uomini singolarj in Firenze dal 1400 innanzi* (1482-1488), Florence 1887. G. SANTI *Cronaca rimata delle imprese del duca Federigo d'Urbino* (after 1482), Stuttgart 1897. L. B. ALBERTI, *De re aedificatoria*, Florence 1485 ; *De Pictura*, Basel 1540, Florence 1950 ; *De Statua*, Venice 1568. Antonio MANETTI (?), *Vita del Brunelleschi*, Florence 1887, Florence 1927. P. DELLA FRANCESCA, *De prospectiva pingendi* (before 1492), Strasbourg 1899, Florence 1942 ; *Trattato sui cinque corpi regolari*, Rome 1915. L. PACIOLI, *De divina proportione*, Venice 1509, Vienna 1889.

STANDARD WORKS

F. v. RUMOHR, *Italienische Forschungen*, Berlin 1827. G. VOIGT, *Die Wiederbelebung des Klassischen Alterthums oder das erste Jahrhundert des Humanismus*, Berlin 1859. E. MUNTZ, *L'art à la cour des papes pendant le XVe et le XVIe siècle*, Paris 1878. E. GEBHART, *Les origines de la Renaissance en Italie*, Paris 1879. L. COURAJOD, *Les véritables origines de la Renaissance*, Gazette des Beaux-Arts, I, 1881. L. GEIGER, *Renaissance und Humanismus in Italien und Deutschland*, Berlin 1882. B. BERENSON, *The Venetian Painters of the Renaissance*, London 1894 ; *The

Florentine Painters of the Renaissance, London 1896. F. X. KRAUS, *Geschichte d. christl. Kunst*, Freiburg-im-B. 1896-1900. B. BERENSON, *The Central Italian Painters of the Renaissance*, New York, London 1897. J. SCHLOSSER, *Quellenbuch zur Kunstgeschichte des abendländischen Mittelalters*, Vienna 1897 etc. M. G. ZIMMERMANN, *Giotto und die Kunst Italiens im Mittelalter*, Leipzig 1899. B. BERENSON, *The Drawings of the Florentine Painters*, London 1903, Chicago 1938. C. NEUMANN, *Byzantinische Kultur und Renaissance-Kultur*, Historische Zeitschrift, XCI, 1903. P. MOLMENTI, *La Peinture vénitienne*, Florence 1904. H. THODE, *Franz von Assisi und die Anfänge der Kunst der Renaissance in Italien*, Berlin 1904. L. VENTURI, *Le origini della Pittura veneziana*, Venice 1907. W. GOETZ, *Mittelalter und Renaissance*, Historische Zeitschrift, XCVIII, 1907. B. BERENSON, *The North Italian Painters of the Renaissance*, 1907. Ph. MINNER, *Le Quattrocento*, Paris 1908. E. JACOBSEN, *Das Quattrocento in Siena*, Strasbourg 1908. W. BOMBE, *Geschichte der Peruginer Malerei*, Berlin 1912. P. TOESCA, *Pittura e miniatura in Lombardia*, Milan 1912. G. DEHIO, *Ueber die Grenzen der Renaissance gegen die Gotik*, Kunsthistorische Aufsätze, Munich, Berlin 1914. A. PELLIZZARI, *I trattati attorno le arti figurative in Italia*, Naples 1915. L. TESTI, *Storia della pittura veneziana*, Bergamo 1915. B. BERENSON, *Venetian Paintings in America*, New York 1916. L. VENTURI, *La Critica d'arte in Italia durante i secoli XIV e XV*, L'Arte XX, 1917. A. VENTURI, *L'ambiente artistico urbinate nella seconda metà del 400*, L'Arte 1917, p. 278 etc. J. WILPERT, *Die römischen Mosaiken und Malereien der kirchlichen Bauten vom IV. bis XIII. Jahrhundert*, Freiburg 1917. K. BORINSCKI, *Die Weltwiedergeburtsidee in der neueren Zeit*, Sitzungsberichte der bayerischen Akademie der Wissenschaft, 1919. E. MÜNZ, *Precursori e propugnatori del Rinascimento*, Florence 1920. G. TOFFANIN, *La fine dell'Umanesimo*, Turin 1920. R. v. MARLE, *La peinture romaine au Moyen Age*, Strasbourg 1921. A. GOLDSCHMIDT, *Das Nachleben der antiken Formen im Mittelalter*, Vorträge d. Biblioteca Warburg, I, 1921-1922. P. MOLMENTI, *La Storia di Venezia nella vita privata dalle origini alla caduta della Repubblica*, Bergamo 1921-1925. L. VENTURI, *La critica d'arte e Francesco Petrarca*, L'Arte XXV, 1922. U. GNOLI, *Pittori e miniatori dell'Umbria*, Spoleto 1923. D. v. HADELN, *Venezianische Zeichnungen des Quattrocento*, Berlin 1924. E. PANOFSKY, *Idea*, Leipzig, Berlin 1924. M. DVORAK, *Idealismus und Naturalismus in der gotischen Skulptur und Malerei*, Munich 1924. G. SOULIER, *Les influences orientales dans la peinture toscane*, Paris 1924. P. TOESCA, *Storia dell'Arte Italiana*, I, Turin 1927. A. MONTEVERDI, *Medioevo*, La Cultura, VI, 1927. M. W. BUNDY, *The Theory of Imagination in Classical and Mediaeval Thought*, Urbana 1927. D. FREY, *Gotik und Renaissance*, Augsburg 1928. Ch. H. HASKINS, *The Renaissance of the Twelfth Century*, Cambridge, Mass., 1928. A. DYROFF, *Ueber die Entwicklung und Wert der Aesthetik des Thomas von Aquino*, Archiv für systematische Philosophie und Soziologie, XXXIII, 1929. A. VENTURI, *La pittura del Quattrocento nell'Alta Italia*, Bologna 1930. J. HUIZINGA, *Das Problem der Renaissance*, Munich 1930. L. SORRENTO, *Medioevo, il termine e il concetto*, Annuario dell'Università Cattolica del S. Cuore, Milan 1930-1931. A. VENTURI, *La Pittura del Quattrocento nell'Emilia*, Verona 1931. R. VAN MARLE, *Iconographie de l'Art profane*, The Hague 1931-1932. B. BERENSON, *Il Quattrocento senese*, Dedalo, March-April 1931 ; *Il Quattrocento fiorentino*, Dedalo, July, September, November 1932 ; *Italian Pictures of the Renaissance, a list of the principal artists and their works and index of places*, Oxford 1932. G. v. SCHLOSSER,

Sull'antica storiografia italiana dell'arte, Palermo 1932. E. GILSON, *Humanisme médiéval et Renaissance*, Paris 1932. I. B. SUPINO, *La pittura italiana del Quattrocento*, Perugia 1932. C. NEUMANN, *Ende des Mittelalters. Legende von der Ablösung des Mittelalters durch die Renaissance*, Deutsche Vierteljahrschrift für Literatur, Wissenschaft und Geistesgeschichte, XI, 1933. G. TOFFANIN, *Storia dell'Umanesimo*, Naples 1933. J. NORDSTROM, *Moyen âge et Renaissance*, Paris 1933. G. FALCO, *Il problema del Medioevo*, Turin 1933. I. SICILIANO, *Medio Evo e Rinascimento*, Rome 1936. E. LAVAGNINO, *Storia dell'Arte Mediovale*, Turin 1936. F. Y. MATHER Jr., *Venetian Painters*, London 1937. M. BRION, *Laurent le Magnifique*, Paris 1937. B. BERENSON, *Les peintres italiens de la Renaissance*, Paris 1937. E. PANOFSKY, *Studies in Iconology*, New York 1939. G. WEISE, *Die geistige Welt der Gotik und ihre Bedeutung für Italien*, Halle 1939. R. MORGHEN, *Rinascita romanica e Rinascimento*, Religio, XV, 1939. F. SIMONE, *La coscienza della rinascita negli umanisti*, La Rinascita, II and III, 1939 and 1940. P. d'ANCONA and M. L. GENGARO, *Umanesimo e Rinascimento*, Turin 1940, Turin 1948. J. HUIZINGA, *Autunno del Medioevo*, Florence 1940. G. F. FIOCCO, *La Pittura Toscana del Quattrocento*, Novara 1941. M. SALMI, *Firenze, Milano, e il primo Rinascimento*, Milan 1941. J. LAUTS, *Venezianische Malerei des Quattrocento*, Zeitschrift f. Kunstgeschichte, 1941. G. TOFFANIN, *Storia dell'Umanesimo*, 1942. E. ARSLAN, *La Pittura e la Scultura veronese dal sec. VIII al sec. XVII*, Milan 1943. H. TIETZE, E. TIETZE CONRAT, *The Drawings of the Venetian Painters in the 15th and 16th Centuries*, New York 1944. F. HERMANIN, *L'arte in Roma dal secolo VIII al XIV*, Bologna 1945. R. PALLUCCHINI, *Cinque secoli di pittura veneta*, Venice 1945. J. HUIZINGA, *Das Problem der Renaissance*, Parerga, Basel 1945. D. VALERI, *Cinque secoli di pittura veneta*, Padua 1945. R. PALLUCCHINI, *I capolavori dei musei veneti*, Venice 1946. R. LONGHI, *Viatico per cinque secoli di pittura veneziana*, Venice 1946. L. BARFUCCI, *Lorenzo dei Medici e la società artistica del suo tempo*, Florence 1946. R. LONGHI, *Calepino Veneziano*, Arte Veneta, April/September 1947. F. ANTAL, *Florentine Painting and its Social Background*, London 1947. P. TOESCA, *Storia dell'Arte Italiana II*, Il Trecento, Turin 1951.

XIIIth Century: In addition to P. TOESCA, *Storia dell'arte italiana I*, Turin 1927, see : O. SIREN, *Toscanische Malerei im XIII. Jahrhundert*, Berlin 1922. Ch. DIEHL, *Manuel d'art byzantin*, Paris 1925-1926. P. MURATOFF, *La Pittura bizantina*, Rome 1929. E. VAVALA, *La Croce dipinta italiana*, Verona 1929. B. BERENSON, *Studies in Medieval Painting*, New Haven 1930. W. ARSLAN, *Su alcune croci pisane*, Rivista d'arte 1936, pp. 217 etc. V. LAZAREFF, *New Light on the Problems of the Pisan School*, Burlington Magazine, LXVIII, 1936, pp. 68-73. G. SINIBALDI and G. BRUNETTI, *Catalogo della mostra giottesca*, Florence 1943. R. LONGHI, *Giudizio sul Duecento*, Proporzioni 1948. E. GARRISON, *Italian Romanesque Panel Painting*, Florence 1949. G. COOR-ACHENBACH, *Some Unknown Representations by the Magdalen Master* Burlington Magazine, March 1951.

Giovanni Cimabue: J. STRZYGOWSKI, *Cimabue und Rom*, Vienna 1888. A. AUBERT, *Die Malerische Dekoration der San Francesco Kirche in Assisi, Cimabue Frage*, Leipzig 1907. E. BENKARD, *Das literarische Porträt des Giovanni Cimabue*, Munich 1917. R. OFFNER, *Cimabue*, The Arts, 1924. A. CHIAPPELLI, *Nuovi studi su Cimabue*, Nuova Antologia CCCXII, 1924, p. 321 etc. C. H. WEIGELT, *The Madonna Rucellai*, Art in America XVIII, 1929. A. NICHOLSON, *Cimabue*, Princeton 1934. R. SALVINI, *Cimabue*, Rome 1946 ; *Postilla a Cimabue*, Rivista d'arte 1950, vol. 26 pp. 43-60.

Pietro Cavallini: F. HERMANIN, *Un affresco di Pietro Cavallini in S. Cecilia in Trastevere*, Archivio della Società romana di storia patria, vol. XXIII, 1900, p. 397 ; *Nuovi affreschi di Pietro Cavallini in S. Cecilia in Trastevere*, L'Arte 1901, vol. IV, p. 239 etc. ; *Gli affreschi di P. Cavallini in S. Cecilia in Trastevere*, Gallerie nazionali italiane 1902, vol. V, p. 61. P. TOESCA, *Gli antichi affreschi di S. Maria Maggiore*, L'Arte 1904, vol. VII, p. 312 etc. A. VENTURI, *Pietro Cavallini a Napoli*, L'Arte 1906, p. 117. F. HERMANIN, *Pietro Cavallini e Arnolfo di Cambio a S. Cecilia in Trastevere*, Congresso nazionale di studi romani, vol. I, pp. 569-574. E. LAVAGNINO, *Pietro Cavallini*, Roma, vol. III, 1925, pp. 305-313 and 337-385. A. BUSUIOCEANU, *Pietro Cavallini e la pittura romana del Duecento e del Trecento*, Ephemeris Daco-Romana, Rome 1925.

Duccio di Boninsegna: C. H. WEIGELT, *Duccio di Boninsegna*, Leipzig 1911. G. DE NICOLA, *Mostra di opere di Duccio da Boninsegna e della sua scuola*, Siena 1912. W. DE GRUENEISEN, *Studi su Duccio di Boninsegna*, Siena 1913. R. VAN MARLE, *Recherches snr l'iconographie de Giotto et de Duccio*, Strasbourg 1920. E. CARLI, *Vetrata duccesca*, Florence 1946. C. BRANDI, *Carmine o della pittura*, with 2 essays on Duccio and Picasso, Florence 1947 ; *Duccio*, Florence 1951.

XIVth Century: A. BRACH, *Giotto's Schule in der Romagna*, Strasbourg 1902. O. WULFF, *Zur Stilbildung der Trecentomalerei*, Repertorium f. Kunstwiss. XXVII, 1904. O. SIREN, *Giottino*, Leipzig 1908. P. TOESCA, *La pittura e miniatura in Lombardia*, Milan 1912. KHVOSHINSKY and SALMI, *I pittori Toscani*, Rome 1912. O. SIREN, *Giotto and Some of his Followers*, Cambridge 1917. L. VENTURI, *La critica d'arte alla fine del Trecento*, L'Arte XXVIII, 1925. E. VAVALA, *La pittura veronese del Trecento*, 1926. P. TOESCA, *La pittura fiorentina del Trecento*, Bologna 1929. L. COLETTI, *Studi sulla pittura del Trecento a Padova*, Rivista d'Arte, 1930-1931 ; *L'arte di Tommaso da Modena*, Bologna 1933. C. BRANDI, *Catalogo della Mostra dei pittori Riminesi*, 1935 ; *Giotto*, L'Arte, 1938. L. COLETTI, *I Primitivi*, vol. III, Novara 1941. S. BETTINI, *Giusto de Menabuoi e l'arte del Trecento*, Padua 1944. M. MARABOTTINI, *Giovanni da Milano*, Florence 1950. W. SUIDA, *Studien zur Trecentomalerei*, Repertorium für Kunstwissenschaft XXIX. R. LONGHI, *Mostra della Pittura bolognese del Trecento*, Bologna 1950, idem Paragone V.

Standard work : P. TOESCA, *Il Trecento*, Turin 1951.

Giotto: R. SALVINI, *Giotto, Bibliografia*, Rome 1938. J. RUSKIN, *Giotto and his Work at Padua*, London 1854. H. JANITSCHEK, *Dantes Kunstlehre und Giottos Kunst*, Leipzig 1892. H. THODE, *Giotto*, Leipzig 1899. M. PERKINS, *Giotto*, London 1902. O. SIREN, *Giotto*, Stockholm 1906. F. RINTELEN, *Giotto und die Giotto Apokryphen*, Munich 1912-1923. A. SCHMARSOW, *Kompositionsgesetze der Franz Legende*, Leipzig 1918. L. VENTURI, *Introduzione all'arte di Giotto*, L'Arte vol. XXII, 1919, pp. 49-56. I. B. SUPINO, *Giotto*, Florence 1920. C. CARRÀ, *Giotto*, Rome 1924. E. ROSENTHAL, *Giotto in der mittelalt. Geistesentwicklung*, 1924. C. WEIGELT, *Giotto*, Leipzig 1925. G. L. LUZZATTO, *L'arte di Giotto*, 1927. R. OFFNER, *Studies in Florentine Paintings*, New York 1927. P. TOESCA, *Giotto*, Bologna 1927. B. KLEINSCHMIDT, *Die Basilika San Francesco in Assisi*, Berlin 1928. E. MOLTESEN, *Giotto und die Meister der Franz-Legende*, Copenhagen 1930. J. ALAZARD, *Giotto*, Paris 1937. G. FIOCCO, *Giotto e Arnolfo*, Florence 1937. C. BRANDI, *Giotto*, L'Arte I, 1938. R. OFFNER, *Giotto-non Giotto*, The Burlington Magazine, LXXIV and LXXV, pp. 259-96 etc., 1939. Th. HETZER, *Giotto*, Frankfort 1941. P. TOESCA, *Giotto*, Turin 1941. R. OERTEL, *Wende der Giotto-Forschung*, Zeitschrift f. Kunstgesch. XI 1941-1942. M. SALMI, *Giotto*, Paris 1942. A. SOFFICI, *Selva*, Arte, Florence 1943. R. OERTEL, *Werke des Giotto*, Zeitschr. f. Kunstgesch. 1943-1944, pp. 1-27. P. TOESCA, *Gli affreschi della Vita di S. Francesco*, Florence 1946 ; *Gli affreschi dell'antico e nuovo Testamento nel Santuario di Assisi*, Florence 1947. A. BUSCH-BROWN, *Giotto, two problems in the origin of his style*, Art Bulletin XXXIV, 1952, pp. 42-46.

Sienese Painting: G. MILANESI, *Documenti per la storia dell'arte Senese*, Siena 1854. B. BERENSON, *Essays in the Study of Sienese Painting*, New York 1918. E. CECCHI, *Trecentisti senesi*, Rome 1928

(French edition, Paris 1928). C. K. WEIGELT, *La pittura senese del Trecento*, Bologna 1930. B. BERENSON, *Missing Pictures of the Sienese Trecento*, International Studio, 1930, p. 31 etc. ; *Quadri senza casa, il Trecento senese*, Dedalo, 1930-31, p. 263. G. H. EDGELL, *A History of Sienese Painting*, New York 1932. F. M. PERKINS, *Pittura senese*, Siena 1933 ; *Capolavori dell'arte senese*, Florence 1946.

Simone Martini: E. MUNZ, *Les peintures de Simone Martini à Avignon*, Paris 1885. R. VAN MARLE, *Simone Martini et les peintres de son école*, Strasbourg 1920. C. BRANDI, *Die Stilentwicklung des Simone Martini*, Pantheon Jahrj. 1934 pp. 225-230. A. PETER, *Quand Simone Martini est-il venu à Avignon ?* Gazette des Beaux-Arts I, 1939 p. 153 etc. A. DE RINALDIS, *Simone Martini*, Rome 1936. P. BACCI, *Fonti e commenti per la storia degli artisti senesi*, Siena 1944. L. COLETTI, *The Early Works of Simone Martini*, The Art Quarterly XII, 1949, pp. 295-308.

Pietro Lorenzetti: E. T. DE WALD, *Pietro Lorenzetti*, Art Studies VII, Cambridge 1929-1930, pp. 131-166. P. BACCI, *Dipinti inediti di P. Lorenzetti in Siena e nel contado*, Siena 1930. E. CECCHI, *Pietro Lorenzetti*, Milan 1930. G. SINIBALDI, *Lorenzetti*, Siena 1933. C. BRANDI, *Ricomposizione e restauro della Pala del Carmine di Pietro Lorenzetti*, Bollettino d'Arte I, 1948, pp. 68-77. C. VOLPE, *Proposte per il problema di Pietro Lorenzetti*, Paragone II Nº 23 1951, pp. 13-26.

Ambrogio Lorenzetti: W. ROTHES : *Die Blütezeit der Sienischen Malerei und ihre Bedeutung für die Entwicklung der Italienischen Kunst*, Strasbourg 1904. G. SINIBALDI, *I Lorenzetti*, Siena 1933. C. BRANDI, *Lo stile di A. Lorenzetti*, Critica d'arte 1935-1936, pp. 61-68. C. VOLPE, *Ambrogio Lorenzetti e le congiunzioni fiorentine-senesi del quarto decennio del Trecento*, Paragone 1951 Nº XIII.

Lorenzo Monaco: O. SIREN, *Don Lorenzo Monaco*, Strasbourg 1905. V. GOLZIO, *Lorenzo Monaco*, Rome 1931. A. M. CIARANFI, *Lorenzo Monaco miniatore*, L'Arte 1932 III and IV, pp. 285-317, V pp. 379-399. G. PUDELKO, *The Stylistic Development of Lorenzo Monaco*, The Burlington Magazine, December 1938. H. D. GRONAU, *The Earliest Work of Lorenzo Monaco*, I-II, Burlington Magazine, July-August 1950.

Gentile da Fabriano: B. MOLAIOLI, *Bibliografia di Gentile da Fabriano*, Bollettino dell'Istituto di Archeologia e Storia dell'Arte, 1929. A. COLASANTI, *Gentile da Fabriano*, Bergamo 1909. B. MOLAIOLI, *Gentile da Fabriano*, Fabriano 1927. A. L. MAYER, *Zum Problem Gentile da Fabriano*, Pantheon 1933 II, pp. 41-46. L. GRASSI, *Considerazioni intorno al " Polittico Quaratesi "*, Paragone 1951 Nº 15.

Pisanello: G. F. HILL, *Pisanello*, London 1903. K. ZOEGE, V. MANTEUFFEL, *Die Bilder und Zeichnungen des A. Pisanello*, Halle 1909. G. BIADEGO, *Pisanus Pictor*, Venice 1909-1910. A. CALABI, G. CORNAGGIA, *Pisanello, L'opera medaglistica paragonata a quella pittorica*, Milan 1928. G. F. HILL, *Dessins de Pisanello choisis et reproduits*, Paris, Brussels 1929. G. M. RICHTER, *Pisanello Studies*, The Burlington Magazine, August-September 1929. A. H. MARTINIC, *Pisanello*, Paris 1930. A. DE HEVESY, *Zur Pariser Pisanello Ausstellung*, Pantheon, May 1932. A. VENTURI, *Orme del Pisanello a Ferrara*, L'Arte, November 1933. A. E. POPHAM, *Antonio Pisano, called Pisanello*, Old Master Drawings, March 1937. A. VENTURI, *Pisanello*, Rome 1939. B. DEGENHART, *Pisanello*, Vienna 1940. J. THIIS, *Pisanello*, Oslo 1941. B. DEGENHART, *L'opera pittorica di Pisanello*, Turin 1945 ; *Le quattro tavole della leggenda di S. Benedetto*, Arte Veneta III, 1949, fasc. 9/12, pp. 7-22.

Sassetta: B. BERENSON, *A Sienese Painter of the Franciscan Legend*, London 1909, Strasbourg 1914, Florence 1946. E. K. WATERHOUSE, *Sassetta and the Legend of St. Antony Abbot*, The Burlington Magazine, September 1931. J. POPE-HENNESSY, *Sassetta*, London 1939 ; *La peinture siennoise du Quattrocento*, Paris 1947. C. BRANDI, *Quattrocentisti senesi*, Milan 1949. E. CARLI, *Sassetta's Borgo San Sepolcro Altarpiece*, The Burlington Magazine, May 1951, pp. 145-152.

Fra Angelico: D. LANGTON, *Fra Angelico*, London 1902. I. B. SUPINO, *Fra Angelico*, Florence 1909. F. SCHOTTMÜLLER, *Fra Angelico da Fiesole*, Stuttgart 1911. A. PICHON, *Fra Angelico*, Paris 1912. J. M. STRUNK, *Beato Angelico*, Munich 1913. W. HAUSENSTEIN, *Fra Angelico*, Munich 1923. M. WINGENROTH, *Angelico da Fiesole*, Leipzig 1926. P. MURATOFF, *Frate Angelico*, Rome 1928. E. SCHNEIDER, *Fra Angelico*, Paris 1938. Pio O. P. CINTI, *Il beato Angelico*, Florence 1940. G. BAZIN, *Fra Angelico*, Paris 1941. A. M. CIARANFI, *Gli affreschi di S. Marco a Firenze*, Milan 1947. P. BARGELLINI, *Le Couvent de S. Marco*, Florence 1949. M. SALMI, *Problemi dell'Angelico*, Commentari, April-June, July-September, 1950, pp. 75-81 and 146-156.

Masaccio: A. SCHMARSOW, *Masaccio-Studien*, Kassel 1895-1899. P. TOESCA, *Masolino da Panicale*, Bergamo 1907. E. SOMARÉ, *Masaccio*, Milan 1924. J. MESNIL, *Masaccio et les débuts de la Renaissance*, The Hague 1927. A. SCHMARSOW, *Masolino-Masaccio*, Leipzig 1928. H. O. GIGLIOLI, *Masaccio*, Florence 1928, Rome 1939 ; *Bibliografia Masaccesca*, Bollettino dell'Istituto di Archeologia e Storia dell'Arte 1929, pp. 55-101. H. LINDBERG, *To the Problem of Masolino and Masaccio*, Stockholm 1931. M. PITTALUGA, *Masaccio*, Florence 1935. U. PROCACCI, *Documenti e ricerche sopra Masaccio e la sua famiglia*, Rivista d'Arte 1935, p. 489 etc. R. LONGHI, *Fatti di Masolino e di Masaccio*, Critica d'Arte XXV et XXVI 1940. E. LAVAGNINO, *Masaccio " dicesi è morto a Roma "*, Emporium III, 1943. M. SALMI, *Masaccio*, Rome 1948. K. STEINBART, *Masaccio*, Vienna 1948. R. LONGHI, *Recupero di un Masaccio*, Paragone I, 1950, pp. 3-5. K. CLARK, *An Early Quattrocento Trittico from S. Maria Maggiore*, The Burlington Magazine, XCIII, 1951, pp. 339-347. R. LONGHI, *Presenza di Masaccio nel Trittico della Neve*, Paragone XXV, 1952, pp. 8-16. M. SALMI, *Gli scomparti della Pala di Santa Maria Maggiore acquistati dalla " National Gallery "*, Commentari III, I, pp. 14-21 ; *La Cappella Brancacci a Firenze*, Milan n. d.

Paolo Uccello: Ph. SOUPAULT, *Paolo Uccello*, Paris 1929. L. VENTURI, *Paolo Uccello*, L'Arte I 1930 pp. 52-87. M. SALMI, *Paolo Uccello, Andrea del Castagno, Domenico Veneziano*, Rome 1938. W. BOECK, *Paolo Uccello*, Berlin 1939. M. PITTALUGA, *Paolo Uccello*, Rome 1946 ; *Gli affreschi del Chiostro verde*, Milan 1946. M. SALMI, *Riflessioni su Paolo Uccello*, Commentari I, 1950, pp. 22-33. J. POPE HENNESSY, *The Complete Work of Paolo Uccello*, London 1950.

Filippo Lippi: I. B. SUPINO, *Fra Filippo Lippi*, Florence 1902. H. MENDELSOHN, *F. Lippi*, Berlin 1909. B. BERENSON, *Fra Angelico, Fra Filippo e la cronologia*, Bollettino d'Arte, July-August 1932. R. OERTEL, *Fra Filippo Lippi*, Vienna 1942. M. SALMI, *Filippo Lippi, gli affreschi del Duomo di Prato*, Bergamo 1944. M. PITTALUGA, *Filippo Lippi*, Florence 1948.

Domenico Veneziano: A. SCHMARSOW, *Domenico Veneziano*, L'Arte 1912, pp. 9-20, 81-97. R. LONGHI, *Un frammento della pala di Domenico Veneziano per S. Lucia dei Magnoli*, L'Arte XXVIII, 1925, pp. 31-35. W. BOECK, *Domenico Veneziano*, Pantheon 1934, pp. 79-85. G. PUDELKO, *Studien über Domenico Veneziano*, Mitteilungen des Kunsthistorischen Instituts, Florence, January 1934. M. SALMI, *Paolo Uccello, Andrea del Castagno, Domenico Veneziano*, Rome 1938. J. POPE HENNESSY, *The Early Style of Domenico Veneziano*, The Burlington Magazine 1951, July, pp. 216-223.

Piero della Francesca: R. LONGHI, *Piero dei Franceschi e lo sviluppo dell'arte veneziana*, L'Arte XVII, 1914, pp. 198-221. A. VENTURI, *Piero della Francesca*, Florence 1922. R. LONGHI, *Piero della Francesca*, Rome 1927. M. SALMI, *Piero della Francesca e il palazzo ducale di Urbino*, Florence 1945 ; *Un ipotesi su Piero della Francesca*, Arti figurative III, 1947. J. ALAZARD, *Piero della Francesca*, Paris 1948.

V. GILARDON, *Piero della Francesca*, Geneva, Paris 1948. J. L. VAUDOYER, *Piero della Francesca*, Paris 1949. P. BORRA, *Piero della Francesca*, Milan 1950. B. BERENSON, *Piero della Francesca o dell'arte non eloquente*, Florence 1950. R. LONGHI, *Piero in Arezzo*, Paragone 11, 1950. K. CLARK, *Piero della Francesca*, London 1951. R. LONGHI, *La leggenda della croce*, Milan 1951. H. FOCILLON, *Piero della Francesca*, Paris 1952.

Andrea Mantegna: H. THODE, *Mantegna*, Leipzig 1897. P. KRISTELLER, *A. Mantegna*, Berlin, Leipzig 1902. A. BLUM, *A. Mantegna*, Paris n. d. F. KNAPP, *Mantegna*, Berlin n. d. G. FIOCCO, *L'arte di A. Mantegna*, Bologna 1927. H. G. HEYDEN, *A. Mantegna*, The Hague 1931. G. FIOCCO, *Andrea Mantegna*, Milan 1937 ; *La Cappella Ovetari*, Milan 1947.

Cosimo Tura and Ferrarese Art in the XVth Century: G. BARUFFALDI, *Vite de' pittori e scultori ferraresi*, 2 vol., Ferrara 1844. L. N. CITTADELLA, *Ricordi e documenti intorno alla vita di Cosimo Tura, detto Cosme*, Ferrara 1866. A. VENTURI, *L'arte a Ferrara nel periodo di Borso d'Este*, Rivista Storica Italiana II, 1885, p. 591 etc. ; *Cosme Tura*, Jahrb. der preuss. Kunstsamml. 1888 ; *Ercole dei Roberti*, Archivio storico dell'arte, 1889. F. HARCK, *Gli affreschi del palazzo di Schifanoia in Ferrara*, Ferrara 1886. G. GRUYER, *L'art ferrarais à l'époque des princes d'Este*, 2 vol., Paris 1897. E. G. GARDNER, *The Painters of the School of Ferrara*, London 1911. — *Catalogo dell'esposizione della pittura ferrarese del Rinascimento*, Ferrara 1933. R. LONGHI, *Officina ferrarese*, Rome 1934 ; *Ampliamenti all'Officina ferrarese*, Critica d'arte, supplement to N° IV 1940. O. HATZCH, *Cosimo Tura*, Pantheon Jahrg. VII, 1940, pp. 152-165. S. ORTOLANI, *Cosme Tura, Francesco del Cossa, Ercole de Roberti*, Milan 1941.

Antonello da Messina: G. DI MARZO, *Di Antonello da Messina e dei suoi congiunti*, Palermo 1903 ; *Nuovi studi e appunti su Antonello da Messina*, Palermo 1905. L. VENTURI, *Studi Antonelliani*, L'Arte V, 1908, pp. 443-450. S. BOTTARI, *Antonello da Messina (1430-1479)*, Messina 1939. Jan LAUTS, *Antonello da Messina*, Vienna 1940. C. BRANDI, *Catalogo della Mostra dei Dipinti di Antonello da Messina*, Rome 1942. G. FIOCCO, *Colantonio e Antonello*, Emporium 1950, vol. CXI, pp. 51-66.

Giovanni Bellini: P. MOLMENTI, *I pittori Bellini, ricerche e documenti*, Studi e ricerche di storia e d'arte, Turin 1892. G. GRONAU, *Die Künstlerfamilie Bellini*, Leipzig 1909 ; *Giovanni Bellini*, Stuttgart 1930. L. DUSSLER, *Giovanni Bellini*, Frankfort 1935. E. CAMMAERTS, *Les Bellini*, Paris n. d. C. GAMBA, *Giovanni Bellini*, Milan 1937. V. MOSCHINI, *Giambellino*, Bergamo 1943. F. WITTGENS, *Pietà e Madonne di Giovanni Bellini*, Milan 1949. R. PALLUCCHINI, *Giovanni Bellini*, Catalogo illustrato, della Mostra, Venice 1949. G. FIOCCO, *I disegni di Giambellino*, Arte 9/12, pp. 40-54, Venice 1949. R. GALLO, *I polittici già nelle cappelle del coro di S. Maria della Carità*, Arte Veneta 9/12, pp. 136-140, Venice 1949.

Vittore Carpaccio: E. LUDWIG and P. MOLMENTI, *Vittore Carpaccio*, Milan 1906, Paris 1910. G. FIOCCO, *Vittore Carpaccio*, Rome 1930, Milan 1942. L. G. ROSENTHAL, *Vittore Carpaccio*, Paris n. d. L. VITALI, *Vittore Carpaccio*, Bergamo 1935. V. MOSCHINI, *Vittore Carpaccio, La leggenda di S. Orsola*, Milan n. d.

Andrea del Castagno: G. FIOCCO, *Andrea del Castagno a Venezia*, L'Arte XXIV, 1921. G. SINIBALDI, *Andrea del Castagno*, L'Arte IV, 1933. W. R. DEUTSCH, *Zur Entwicklung Andrea del Castagno*, Pantheon 1934, pp. 355-365. M. SALMI, *Paolo Uccello, Andrea del Castagno, Domenico Veneziano*, Rome 1938. G. M. RICHTER, *Andrea del Castagno*, Chicago 1943. M. SALMI, *Gli affreschi di Andrea del Castagno ritrovati*, Bollettino d'Arte, Rome 1950, pp. 295-308.

The Pollaiuolo Brothers: M. CRUTTWELL, *A. Pollaiolo*, London 1907. C. L. RAGGHIANTI, *A. Pollaiolo e l'arte fiorentina del Quattrocento*, Critica d'Arte 1935-1936. A. SABATINI, *Antonio e Pietro Pollaiolo*, Florence 1944. S. ORTOLANI, *I Pollajolo*, Milan 1948.

Andrea del Verrocchio: M. MACKOWSKI, *Verrocchio*, Leipzig 1901. M. CRUTTWELL, *Il Verrocchio*, London 1904. M. REYMOND, *Verrocchio*, Paris 1905. A. BERTINI, *L'arte del Verrocchio*, L'Arte XXXVIII, 1936, pp. 433-473. P. GROTEMEYER, *Andrea del Verrocchio*, Pantheon Jahrg. III, 1936, pp. 109-115. L. PLANISCIG, *Verrocchio*, Vienna 1941.

Sandro Botticelli: P. H. HORNE, *Alessandro Filipepi called S. Botticelli, Painter of Florence*, London 1908. W. BODE, *S. Botticelli*, Berlin 1921. A. SCHMARSOW, *S. del Botticello*, Dresden 1923. Y. YASHIRO, *S. Botticelli and the Florentine Renaissance*, London 1923 ; *S. Botticelli*, London, Boston 1925, 3 vol. A. VENTURI, *Botticelli*, Rome 1925. E. STEINMANN, *Botticelli*, Leipzig 1925. C. GAMBA, *Botticelli*, Milan n. d. L. VENTURI, *S. Botticelli*, Vienna 1937. I. MESNIL. *Botticelli*, Paris 1938. R. SALVINI, *Botticelli*, Novara 1942. S. BETTINI, *Botticelli*, Bergamo 1942.

Luca Signorelli: G. MANCINI, *Vita di L. Signorelli*, Florence 1903. M. CRUTTWELL, *Luca Signorelli*, London 1911. M. SALMI, *Luca Signorelli*, Florence 1922. A. VENTURI, *Luca Signorelli*, Florence 1922. L. DUSSLER, *Luca Signorelli*, Berlin, Leipzig 1926. E. CARLI, *Luca Signorelli. Gli affreschi del Duomo di Orvieto*, Bergamo 1946.

THE RENAISSANCE

EARLY WRITERS

L. DA VINCI, *Trattato della Pittura*, edited by Ludwig, Vienna 1882. P. GIOVIO, *De viris illustribus* (before 1524), ed. by Tiraboschi, Storia della Letteratura italiana, Modena 1781, p. 286 etc. Antonio BILLI, *Libro* (1481-1530), ed. by Frey, Berlin 1892. ANONIMO GADDIANO (ca. 1537-1542), *Vite*, ed. by Frey, Berlin 1892. G. B. GELLI, *Vite*, ed. by Mancini, Archivio Storico Italiano, 1896. F. DE HOLLANDA, *Tractado de pintura antiqua*, 1538, ed. by J. de Vasconcellos, Vienna 1890, ed. by Pellizzari, Naples 1914. ARETINO, *Lettere*, Paris 1609. M. A. MICHIEL, *Notizie d'opere di disegno* (1521-1534), Vienna 1888. B. VARCHI, *Due Lezioni sopra la pittura e scultura*, Florence 1546. P. PINO, *Dialogo di Pittura*, Venice 1548, Venice 1946. M. BIONDO, *Della nobilissima pittura*, Venice 1549. A. F. DONI, *Disegno partito in più ragionamenti*, Venice 1549. G. VASARI, *Le vite dei più eccellenti Architetti, Pittori e Scultori italiani da Cimabue insino a' tempi nostri*, Florence 1550, Rome 1927. L. DOLCE, *Dialogo intitolato l'Aretino*, Venice 1557. B. CELLINI, *La vita scritta da lui medesimo* (1558-1566), Florence 1901. A. A. GILIO, *Due Dialoghi*, Camerino 1564. V. DANTI, *Il primo libro del trattato delle perfette proporzioni*, Florence 1567. G. VASARI, *Le vite de' più eccellenti Pittori, Scultori e Architettori di nuovo ampliate, ... con l'aggiunta delle Vite de' vivi e de' morti da l'anno 1550 insino al 1567*, Florence 1568, ed. by Milanesi, Florence 1873-1885. G. PALEOTTI, *Discorso intorno alle immagini sacre e profane*, Bologna 1582. R. BORGHINI, *Il Riposo*, Florence 1584. G. ARMENINI, *De' veri precetti della pittura*, Ravenna 1587. P. LOMAZZO, *Trattato dell'arte della Pittura*, Milan 1584 ; *Idea del Tempio della Pittura*, Milan 1590.

GENERAL

In addition to the general works on Humanism and the Renaissance mentioned above in the Bibliography of the Middle Ages and High Renaissance, see :

J. MICHELET, *La Renaissance*, Paris 1855. J. BURCKHARDT, *Die Kultur der Renaissance in Italien*, Stuttgart 1860. W. PATER, *The Renaissance*, London 1878. E. MÜNTZ, *Histoire de l'Art pendant la Renaissance*, Paris 1889. J. BURCKHARDT, *Geschichte der Renaissance in Italien*, Stuttgart 1891. R. HILDEBRANDT, *Zur sogenannten Renaissance*, Leipzig 1897. K. BRANDI, *Das Werden der Renaissance*, Göttingen 1910. J. MESNIL, *L'art au Nord et au Sud des Alpes à l'époque de la Renaissance, Etudes comparatives*, Paris, Brussels 1911. W. GOETZ, *Renaissance and Antike*, Historische

Zeitschrift CXIII, 1914. H. Voss, *Malerei der Spätrenaissance*, Berlin 1920. G. Volpe, *La Rinascenza in Italia e le sue origini*, Florence 1925. M. Dvorak, *Geschichte der italienischen Kunst im Zeitalter der Renaissance*, Munich 1927. H. Baron, *Renaissance in Italien*, Archiv für Kulturgeschichte, XVII and XXI 1927-1931. W. Dilthey, *L'analisi dell'uomo e l'intuizione della natura dal Rinascimento al secolo XVIII*, Venice 1927. E. Cassirer, *Individuo e cosmo nella filosofia del Rinascimento*, Leipzig 1927, Florence 1945. L. Venturi, *La critique d'art en Italie à l'époque de la Renaissance*, Rieti 1928. C. Ricci, *La Pittura del Cinquecento nell'Alta Italia*, Verona 1928. B. Spaventa, *Rinascimento, Riforma, Controriforma*, Venice 1928. H. Hefele, *Zum Begriff der Renaissance*, Historisches Jahrbuch, XL, 1929. A. Haseloff, *Begriff und Wesen der Renaissance-Kunst*, Mitteilungen des Kunsthistorischen Instituts in Florenz, III, 1930. L. Venturi, *Arte e pensiero nel Rinascimento*, L'Arte I, 1930, pp. 519-531. H. Hauser, *La modernité du XVIe siècle*, Paris 1930. G. de Ruggero, *Storia della Filosofia, Rinascimento, Riforma e Controriforma*, Bari 1930. E. Kaufmann, *Renaissancebegriff in der deutschen Kunstgeschichteschreibung*, Winterthur 1932. D. Cantimori, *Sulla storia del concetto di Rinascimento*, Annali della R. Scuola Normale Superiore di Pisa, Series II, I, 1932. E. Mâle, *L'Art religieux après le Concile de Trente*, Paris 1932. G. Weise, *Der Doppelte Begriff der Renaissance*, Deutsche Vierteljahrschrift für Literatur, Wissenschaft und Geistesgeschichte XI, 1933. K. Burdach, *Riforma, Rinascimento, Umanesimo*, Florence 1935. G. Gentile, *Studi sul Rinascimento*, Florence 1936 ; *Il pensiero italiano nel Rinascimento*, Florence 1940. E. Garin, *Il Rinascimento italiano*, Milan 1941. E. Walser, *Umanità ed Arte nel Rinascimento italiano*, Florence 1942. L. Becherucci, *Manieristi Toscani*, Bergamo 1944. R. Pallucchini, *La Pittura veneziana del 1500*, Novara 1944. A. Marcu, *Il valore dell'arte del Rinascimento*, Florence 1945. F. Chabod, *Il Rinascimento* in Rota, *Questioni di Storia Moderna*, Milan 1948.

Leonardo da Vinci: E. Verga, *Bibliografia Vinciana 1493-1930*, by Zanichelli, Bologna 1930 (subsequently brought up to date with articles appearing in the Raccolta Vinciana). L. Beltrami, *Documenti e memorie riguardanti la vita e le opere di Leonardo da Vinci*, Milan 1916. G. Calvi, *Vita di Leonardo*, Brescia 1936. J. P. Richter, *The Literary Works of Leonardo da Vinci*, London, New York 1939. E. Solmi, *Le fonti dei manoscritti di Leonardo da Vinci*, Turin 1928. A. Marinoni, *L. da Vinci, gli scritti letterari*, Milan 1952 (with a bibliography of the published manuscripts). A. Venturi, *I disegni di Leonardo da Vinci*, Rome 1923-1941. A. E. Popp, *Leonardo da Vinci Zeichnungen*, Munich 1928. A. E. Popham, *The Drawings of Leonardo da Vinci*, New York 1945. A. de Rinaldis, *Storia dell'opera pittorica di Leonardo da Vinci*, Bologna 1926. L. Venturi, *La critica e l'arte di Leonardo da Vinci*, Bologna 1919. F. M. Bongioanni, *Leonardo da Vinci Pensatore*, Piacenza 1935. R. Marcolongo, *Leonardo da Vinci artista e scienziato*, Milan 1939. T. Beck, *Leonardo da Vinci*, Berlin 1896 etc. G. Gronau, *Leonardo*, London 1903, Chicago 1915. W. von Seidlitz, *Leonardo da Vinci, der Wendepunkt der Renaissance*, Berlin 1909. J. Thiis, *Leonardo da Vinci*, Oslo 1909 etc. O. Siren, *Leonardo da Vinci*, Stockholm 1911, London 1916, Paris 1928. A. Venturi, *Leonardo pittore*, Bologna 1920. W. Bode, *Studien über Leonardo da Vinci*, Berlin 1920. E. Hildebrandt, *Leonardo da Vinci, der Künstler und sein Werk*, Berlin 1927. W. Suida, *Leonardo und sein Kreis*, Munich 1929. T. Klingsor, *Leonardo da Vinci*, Paris 1930. H. Bodmer, *Leonardo*, Stuttgart 1931. R. Bayer, *Leonardo da Vinci*, Paris 1933. *Catalogo della Mostra di Leonardo*, Milan 1939. S. Bottari, *Leonardo*, Bergamo 1942. L. H. V. Heydenreich, *Leonardo*, Berlin 1943. R. Langton Douglas, *Leonardo da Vinci, his Life and his Pictures*, Chicago 1944. O. H. Giglioli, *Leonardo, Introduzione alla conoscenza di lui*, Florence 1944. L. Goldschieder, *Leonardo da Vinci*, Paris 1948.

Piero di Cosimo: F. Knapp, *Piero di Cosimo*, Halle 1899. R. Langton Douglas, *Piero di Cosimo*, Chicago 1946.

Andrea del Sarto: F. Knapp, *Andrea del Sarto*, Leipzig 1928. J. Fraenkel, *Andrea del Sarto, Gemälde und Zeichnungen*, Strasbourg 1935. A. J. Rusconi, *Andrea del Sarto*, Bergamo 1935.

Michelangelo: E. Steinmann, *Michelangelo. Bibliographie 1510-1926*, Leipzig 1927. K. Frey, *Die Dichtungen des Michelagniolo Buonarroti*, Berlin 1897 ; *Sammlung ausgewählter Briefe an Michelagniolo*, Berlin 1899 ; *Die Handzeichnungen Michelagniolos Buonarroti*, Berlin 1909-1925. A. E. Brinckmann, *Michelangelo's Zeichnungen*, Munich 1925. V. Colonna, *Rime e lettere*, Florence 1860 ; *Carteggio pubblicato da Ferrero e Müller*, Turin 1892. A. Condivi, *Vita di Michelagniolo Buonarroti*, ed. by C. Frey, Berlin 1887. D. Giannotti, *Dialoghi*, ed. by D. Redig de Campos, Florence 1939. H. Wölfflin, *Die Sixtinische Decke*, Rep. f. Kw. XIII, 1890, p. 264 etc. C. Justi, *Michelangelo*, Leipzig 1900. E. Steinmann, *Die Sixtinische Kapelle*, Munich 1901-1905. R. Rolland, *La vie de Michel-Ange*, Paris 1906 etc. K. Frey, *Michelagniolo Buonarroti*, Berlin 1907. H. Thode, *Michelangelo und das Ende der Renaissance*, 3 vol., Berlin 1908-1913 ; *Michelangelo, Kritische Untersuchungen*, Berlin 1908-1913. C. Justi, *Michelangelo, Neue Beiträge zur Erklärung seiner Werke*, Berlin 1909. K. Frey, *Michelangelo Studien*, Vienna 1920. E. Steinmann, *Michelangelo im Spiegel seiner Zeit*, Leipzig 1930. Baumgart-Biagetti, *Gli affreschi di Michelangiolo nella Cappella Paolina*, Vatican 1934. R. Huyghe, *Michel-Ange*, Paris 1937. C. de Tolnay, *La théorie de l'Art et Michel-Ange*, Le Congrès International d'Esthétique et de Science de l'Art, Paris 1937, pp. 25 etc. M. Brion, *Michel-Ange*, Paris 1939. H. Mackowsky, *Michelangelo*, Stuttgart 1939-1940. E. Panofsky, *Studies in Iconology*, New York 1939. E. Carli, *Michelangelo*, Bergamo 1941. A. Bertini, *Michelangelo fino alla Sistina*, Turin 1942. C. de Tolnay, *Michelangelo* : 1st vol. *The Youth of Michelangelo*, Princeton University Press 1943 ; 2nd vol. *The Sistine Ceiling*, idem 1945 ; 3rd vol. *The Medici Chapel*, idem 1948. C. Gamba, *La pittura di Michelangelo*, Novara 1945. D. R. de Campos - B. Biagetti, *Il Giudizio Universale di Michelangelo*, Vatican 1944. C. de Tolnay, *Werk und Weltbild des Michelangelo*, Zurich 1949. G. Papini, *Vita di Michelangelo nel suo tempo*, Florence 1949. G. Fiocco, *Primizie di Michelangelo*, Rivista d'Arte XXVI, 1950, pp. 149-155. C. de Tolnay, *Michelangelo*, Rome 1951. Goldschneider, *Michelangelo's Drawings*, London 1951.

Pontormo: F. Goldschmidt, *Pontormo, Rosso und Bronzino*, Leipzig 1911. F. Mortimer Clapp, *Jacopo Carucci da Pontormo, His Life and Works*, Yale University, New Haven 1916. C. Gamba, *Il Pontormo*, Florence 1921. K. Steinbart, *The Gothic Painter Iacopo Carucci of Pontormo*, Pantheon, January 1939. E. Toesca, *Pontormo*, Rome 1943. L. Becherucci, *Disegni del Pontormo*, Bergamo 1943. G. Nicco Fasola, *Pontormo o del Cinquecento*, Florence 1947. C. de Tolnay, *Les fresques de Pontormo dans le chœur de San Lorenzo à Florence*, Critica d'Arte XXXIII, 1950.

Bronzino: A. McComb, *Bronzino*, Cambridge 1928.

Raphael: V. Golzio, *Raffaello nei documenti, nelle testimonianze dei contemporanei e nella letteratura del suo secolo*, Vatican City 1936. E. Müntz, *Raphaël*, Paris 1886. O. Fischel, *Raphael's Zeichnungen*, Strasbourg 1898. A. Rosenberg, *Raphael*, Berlin 1923. H. Focillon, *Raphaël*, Paris 1926. L. Serra, *Raffaello*, Rome 1930, Turin 1941. A. Venturi, *Raffaello*, Rome 1920, Paris 1927, Rome 1931. C. Gamba, *Raphaël*, Paris 1932. F. Fosca, *Raphaël*, Paris 1937. W. E. Suida, *Raphael*, London 1941, Paris 1948. A. Bertini-Calosso, *Ritratti e Madonne di Raffaello*, Novara 1941. H. Grimm, *Raphaël*, Berlin 1941. S. Ortolani, *Raffaello*, Bergamo 1942. U. Nebbia, *Raffaello*, Novara 1945. R. Vischer, *Raffaello e Rubens*, Bari 1945. O. Fischel, *Raphael*,

London 1948. U. MIDDELDORF, *Raphael's Drawings*, New York 1949. C. GAMBA, *Pittura Umbra del Rinascimento, Raffaello*, Novara 1949.

Correggio: S. DE VITO-BATTAGLIA, *Correggio, Bibliografia*, Rome 1934. J. MAYER, *Correggio*, Leipzig 1871, London 1876. Q. BIAGI, *Della vite e delle opere certe e incerte di Antonio Allegri detto il Correggio*, Modena 1881. C. RICCI, *Antonio Allegri detto il Correggio*, London 1896. H. THODE, *Correggio*, Leipzig 1898. T. STURGE MOORE, *Correggio*, London 1906. G. GRONAU, *Correggio*, Stuttgart and Leipzig 1907. O. HAGEN, *Correggio Apokryphen*, Berlin 1915. A. VENTURI, *Il Correggio*, Rome 1927. P. DE STOECKLIN, *Le Corrège*, Paris 1928. C. RICCI, *Correggio*, Rome 1930. E. MOTTINI, *Correggio*, Bergamo 1934. A. O. QUINTAVALLE, *Il Correggio*, Turin 1934. E. BODMER, *Il Correggio e gli Emiliani*, Vienna 1942, Novara 1943.

Parmigianino: FRÖLICH-L. BUM, *Parmigianino und der Manierismus*, Vienna 1921. G. COPERTINI, *Il Parmigianino*, Parma 1932. A. O. QUINTAVALLE, *Il Parmigianino*, Milan 1948. G. COPERTINI, *Nuovi contributi di studi e di recerche sul Parmigianino*, Parma 1949. S. FREEDBERG, *Parmigianino*, Cambridge 1950.

Giorgione: Ludwig JUSTI, *Giorgione*, Berlin 1908. G. GRONAU, *Kritische Studien zu Giorgione*, Kunstwissenschaft XXXI, 1908, p. 403 etc., 503 etc. L. VENTURI, *Giorgione e il Giorgionismo*, Milan 1913. A. FERRIGUTO, *Almoro Barbaro*, Venice 1922 ; *Il significato della Tempesta di Giorgione*, Padua 1922. M. CONWAY, *Giorgione*, London 1929. L. HOURTICQ, *Le problème de Giorgione*, Paris 1931. H. POSSE, *Die Rekonstruktion der Venus mit dem Cupido von Giorgione*, Jahrbuch der Preussischen Kunstsamml. 1931. J. WILDE, *Röntgenaufnahmen der " Drei Philosophen " Giorgione's*, Jahrbuch der Kunsthist. Samml. Vienna VI, 1932. L. VENTURI, *Giorgione*, Enciclopedia italiana, vol. 17, 1933. A. FERRIGUTO, *Attraverso i misteri di Giorgione*, Castelfranco veneto 1933. G. GOMBOSI, *The Budapest Birth of Paris X-rayed*, Burlington Magazine, October 1935. Ph. DUNCAN, *The Leadership of Giorgione*, Washington 1937. G. M. RICHTER, *Giorgio da Castelfranco*, Chicago 1937. G. FIOCCO, *Giorgione*, Bergamo 1941. A. MORASSI, *Giorgione*, Milan 1941. V. MARIANI, *Giorgione*, Rome 1945. R. L. DOUGLAS, *Some Early Works of Giorgione*, The Art Quarterly XIII, 1950, pp. 23-24. F. M. GODFREY, *The Birth of Venetian Genre and Giorgione*, The Connoisseur CXXVIII, 1951, pp. 75-82. A. MORASSI, *The Ashmolean " Madonna Reading " and Giorgione's Chronology*, Burlington Magazine July 1951, pp. 212-216.

Titian: G. B. CAVALCASELLE and J. A. CROWE, *Tiziano*, Florence 1878. O. FISCHEL, *Tiziano*, Stuttgart, Berlin and Leipzig 1904. G. GRONAU, *Titian*, London 1904. E. WALDMANN, *Titian*, Berlin 1922. O. ZOFF, *Titian*, Munich 1922. V. BASCH, *Titien*, Paris 1927. W. SUIDA, *Titian*, Rome, Leipzig 1933, Paris 1935. E. VERGA, *Catalogo della Mostra di Tiziano*, Venice 1935. H. TIETZE, *Titian, Leben und Werk*, Vienna 1936. G. DELOGU, *Tiziano*, Bergamo 1940. H. KNACKFUSS, *Titian*, Leipzig 1940. C. GAMBA, *Tiziano*, Novara 1941. G. GRAPPE, *Titien*, Paris 1942. G. STEPANOW, *Titian*, Zurich, Leipzig 1943. L. GRASSI, *Tiziano*, Rome 1945.

Sebastiano del Piombo: L. DUSSLER, *Sebastiano del Piombo*, Basel 1942. R. PALLUCCHINI, *Sebastian Viniziano*, Milan 1944.

Lorenzo Lotto: B. BERENSON, *Lorenzo Lotto*, London 1901. L. COLETTI, *Lotto e Michelozzo*, Le Arti, April 1938. M. PUCCINI, *Lorenzo Lotto nelle Marche*, Emporium VIII 1939. A. BAUTI, *Il libro dei conti di Lorenzo Lotto*, Le tre Venezie VI, 1940. L. BIAGI, *Lorenzo Lotto*, Rome 1942. A. BAUTI, *Gli affreschi di Trescore*, Milan 1946.

Girolamo Savoldo: R. LONGHI, *Cose bresciane del Cinquecento*, L'Arte XX, 1917, p. 110 ; *Due Dipinti di G. G. Savoldo*, Vita Artistica 1927, pp. 72-75. W. SUIDA, *Savoldo*, Pantheon, February 1937. F. LOCHI, *Catalogo della Mostra della pittura Bres-*

ciana del Rinascimento, Brescia 1939. G. NICCO FASOLA, *Lineamenti del Savoldo*, L'Arte II, 1940, pp. 51-81. G. CREIGHTON, *Milan and Savoldo*, The Art Bulletin XXVII, June 1945, pp. 124-138 ; *Ritrattristica apocrifa Savoldesca*, Arte Veneta 1949, pp. 103-110. V. CAPELLI, *Nota al Savoldo Giovane*, Emporium VII 1951, pp. 13-24.

Jacopo Bassano: W. ARSLAN, *I Bassano*, Bologna 1931. S. BETTINI, *L'arte di Jacopo Bassano*, Bologna 1933. W. ARSLAN, *Nuovi dipinti dei Bassano*, Bolletino d'arte, 1938, pp. 462-474. R. LONGHI, *Suggerimenti per Jacopo Bassano*, Arte Veneta II, 1948.

G. B. Moroni: D. CUGINI, *Moroni Pittore*, Bergamo 1939. G. LANDORFF, *Giovan Battista Moroni*, Bergamo 1939.

Jacopo Tintoretto: H. THODE, *Tintoretto*, Bielefeld 1901. E. VON DER BERCKEN and A. L. MAYER, *Jacopo Tintoretto*, Munich 1923. M. PITTALUGA, *Tintoretto*, Bologna 1925. V. MOSCHINI, *Tintoretto*, Rome 1931. G. DELOGU, *Tintoretto. La Scuola di S. Rocco*, Bergamo 1937. R. PALLUCCHINI, *Tintoretto a S. Rocco*, Venice 1937. *Catalogo della Mostra del Tintoretto*, Venice 1937. L. COLETTI, *Tintoretto*, Bergamo 1940. E. VON DER BERCKEN, *Tintoretto*, Munich 1942. H. TIETZE, *Tintoretto*, London 1942. U. NEBBIA, *Tintoretto e la Scuola di S. Rocco*, Bergamo 1949. R. PALLUCCHINI, *La Giovinezza del Tintoretto*, Milan 1950. Eric NEWTON, *Tintoretto*, London 1952.

Paolo Veronese: A. M. BRIZIO, *Note per una definizione critica dello stile di P. Veronese*, L'Arte 1926, pp. 213-242 ; and 1928, pp. 1-10. P. H. OSMOND, *P. Veronese, his Career and Work*, London 1927. G. FIOCCO, *Paolo Veronese*, Bologna 1928, Rome 1934. A. VENTURI, *Paolo Veronese*, Milan 1928. U. OJETTI, *Paolo Veronese*, Milan 1928. G. DELOGU, *Paolo Veronese*, Bergamo 1936. A. ORLIAC, *Véronèse*, Paris 1939. R. PALLUCCHINI, *Catalogo della Mostra di Paolo Veronese*, Venice 1939. C. BRANDI, *Visione del Veronese*, Arcobaleno 1939. R. PALLUCCHINI, *Gli affreschi di Paolo Veronese a Maser*, Bergamo 1939-1943 ; *Paolo Veronese*, Bergamo 1940. L. COLETTI, *Paolo Veronese e la pittura a Verona nel suo tempo*, Pisa 1940. M. GOERING, *Paolo Veronese und das Settecento*, Jahrb. Preuss. Ksts. 1940. E. TEO, *Paolo Veronese*, Milan 1943. W. SUIDA, *Some New Aspects of Paolo Veronese's Work*, Art Quarterly, 1945. R. PALLUCCHINI, *Paolo Veronese*, Bergamo 1946.

XVIIth AND XVIIIth CENTURIES

EARLY WRITERS

K. VAN MANDER, *Het Leven der Moderne oft deetijsche doorluchtighe Italiaensche Schilders*, Alcmaer 1603. G. B. AGUCCHI, *Trattato* (1607-1615), in D. MAHON, *Studies in Seicento Art and Theory*, London 1947. C. GIGLI, *La Pittura trionfante*, Venice 1615. G. MANCINI, *Manoscritto della Biblioteca Marciana* (1619-1621) *e Viaggio di Roma per vedere la pittura* (ca. 1625) ed. by Schudt, Leipzig 1923. G. BAGLIONE, *Le vite de' pittori, scultori, architetti... dal 1572 fino a' tempi di Papa Urbano VIII*, Rome 1642 and 1935. C. RIDOLFI, *Le Meraviglie dell'Arte*, Venice 1648. P. BERRETTINI DA CORTONA, *Trattato della pittura*, Florence 1652. F. SCANELLI, *Il Microcosmo della Pittura*, Cesena 1657. M. BOSCHINI, *La carta del navegar pittoresco*, Venice 1660. CHANTELOU, *Journal de Voyage du Bernin en France*, Paris 1930. G. B. PASSERI, *Vite de Pittori, Scultori et Architetti* (1670-1680), ed. by J. Hess, Vienna 1934. G. P. BELLORI, *Le Vite de' pittori, scultori et architetti moderni*, Rome 1672 and 1931. L. SCARAMUCCIA, *Le finezze de' Pennelli Italiani*, Pavia 1674. M. BOSCHINI, *Le ricche miniere della pittura veneziana*, Venice 1674. J. VON SANDRART, *Teutsche Academie*, Nuremberg 1675. C.C. MALVASIA, *Felsina Pittrice*, Bologna 1678. F. BALDINUCCI, *Notizie dei professori del disegno da Cimabue in qua*, Florence 1681-1728. DE PILES, *Abrégé de la vie des Peintres*, Paris 1696. CIOCCHI, *La Pittura in Parnaso*, Florence 1725. L. PASCOLI, *Le vite dei Pittori, Scultori, ed Architetti Moderni*, Rome

1730-1736. B. DE DOMINICI, *Le vite dei Pittori, Scultori ed Architetti Napoletani*, Naples 1742. LESSING, *Laokoon*, Berlin 1766. J. B. BOYER, MARQUIS D'ARGENS, *Examen critique des différentes écoles de peinture*, Berlin 1768. ZANETTI, *Della Pittura Veneziana*, Venice 1771. MENGS, *Opere*, Parma 1786. L. LANZI, *Storia pittorica dell'Italia*, Bassano 1789. J. D. FIORILLO, *Geschichte der Künste*, Göttingen 1798. J. RUSKIN, *Modern Painters*, London 1843. J. BURCKHARDT, *Der Cicerone*, Leipzig 1855. J. MORELLI, *Notizie d'opere del disegno*, Bologna 1884.

GENERAL

H. WÖLFFLIN, *Renaissance und Barock*, Munich 1888. A. SCHMARSOW, *Barock und Rokoko*, Leipzig 1897. A. RIEGL, *Die Entstehung der Barockkunst in Rom*, Vienna 1908. K. ESCHER, *Barock und Klassizismus*, Leipzig 1910. J. A. F. ORBAAN, *Documenti sul Barocco in Roma*, Rome 1920. W. WEISBACH, *Der Barock als Kunst der Gegenreformation*, Berlin 1921. U. OJETTI, L. DAMI, N. TARCHIANI, *La pittura italiana del Seicento e del Settecento alla Mostra di Palazzo Pitti*, Milan 1924. H. VOSS, *Die Malerei des Barock in Rom*, Berlin 1924. W. WEISBACH, *Die Kunst des Barock in Italien, Frankreich, Deutschland und Spanien*, Berlin 1924. E. BERGNER, *Das Barock in Rom*, Leipzig 1925. I. HAUMANN, *Das oberitalienische Landschaftsbild des Settecento*, Strasbourg 1927. M. MARANGONI, *Arte barocca*, Florence 1927. N. PEVSNER, O. GRATULOFF, *Barock-Malerei in den romanischen Ländern*, Potsdam 1928. O. POLLAK, *Die Kunsttätigkeit unter Urban VIII*, Vienna 1928. B. CROCE, *Storia dell'età barocca in Italia*, Bari 1929. G. B. FIOCCO, *La pittura veneziana del Seicento e Settecento*, Bologna 1929. A. DE RINALDIS, *La pittura del Seicento nell'Italia Meridionale*, Florence 1929. G. DELOGU, *Pittori minori liguri, lombardi, piemontesi del Seicento e del Settecento*, Venice 1931; *La pittura italiana del Seicento*, Florence 1931. V. MOSCHINI, *La pittura italiana del Settecento*, Florence 1931. U. OJETTI, *Il Settecento italiano*, Milan 1932. N. PEVSNER, *Die Wandlung um 1650 in der italienischen Malerei*, Wiener Jahrbuch für Kunstgeschichte 1932, pp. 69-92. G. FOGOLARI, *La pittura del Settecente italiano*, Milan 1932. M. GOERING, *Italienische Malerei des Siebzehnten und Achtzehnten Jahrhunderts*, Berlin 1936. E. K. WATERHOUSE, *Baroque Painting in Rome*, London 1937. T. H. FOKKER, *Roman Baroque Art*, Oxford 1938. O. GROSSO, M. BONZI, C. MERCENARO, *Pittori genovesi del Seicento e del Settecento*, Genoa 1938. V. GOLZIO, *Documenti artistici sul Seicento nell'archivio Chigi*, Rome 1939. A. E. BRICKMANN, *Die Kunst der Rokoko*, Berlin 1940. G. LORENZETTI, *La pittura italiana del Settecento*, Novara 1942. E. D'ORS, *Del barocco*, Milan 1945. A. MORASSI, *Mostra della pittura del Seicento e Settecento in Liguria*, Milan 1947. A. DE RINALDIS, *L'arte in Roma del Seicento al Novecento*, Bologna 1948. V. GOLZIO, *Il Seicento e il Settecento*, Turin 1950. J. DUPONT and F. MATHEY, *The Seventeenth Century*, Geneva 1951. F. FOSCA, *The Eighteenth Century*, Geneva 1952.

Caravaggio: W. KALLAB, *Caravaggio*, Jahrb. d. Kunsthist. Samml., Vienna 1906-1907, pp. 272-292. L. VENTURI, *Studi su Michelangelo da Caravaggio*, L'Arte 1910, pp. 191-201; *idem*, Bollettino d'arte 1912. G. ROUCHÈS, *Le Caravage*, Paris 1920. L. VENTURI, *Il Caravaggio*, Rome 1921. M. MARANGONI, *Il Caravaggio*, Florence 1922; *Note sul Caravaggio alla Mostra del Seicento e Settecento*, Bollettino d'arte 1922-1923, pp. 217-229. H. VOSS, *Caravaggios Frühzeit*, Jahrbuch der Preuss. Ksts., Berlin 1923, pp. 73-98. R. LONGHI, *Precisioni nelle Gallerie italiane*, Vita Artistica 1927 and 1928. N. PEVSNER, *Eine Revision der Caravaggio-Daten*, Zeitschr. f. bild. Kunst 1927-1928, pp. 368-392; *Die Lehrjahre des Caravaggio*, Zeitschrift f. bild. Kunst 1928-1929, pp. 278-288. A. VON SCHNEIDER, *Caravaggio und die Niederländer*, Marburg-Lahn 1933. V. BLOCH, *I Pittori della realtà nel Seicento*, Rome 1935. A. VON SCHNEIDER, *Zur Stilbildung Caravaggio's*, Pantheon 1936, pp. 347-354. P. FRANCASTEL, *Le réalisme de Caravage*, Gazette des Beaux-Arts 1938, pp. 45-62. L. SCHUDT, *Caravaggio*, Vienna

1942. R. LONGHI, *Ultimi studi sul Caravaggio e la sua cerchia, ultimissime sul Caravaggio*, Proporzioni I, 1943, pp. 5-63 and 99-102 (with many notes on Caravaggio's followers). B. BERENSON, *Del Caravaggio, delle sue incongruenze e della sua fama*, Florence 1950. R. LONGHI, *Catalogo della Mostra del Caravaggio e dei Caravaggeschi*, Milan 1951; *Caravaggio*, Milan 1951. L. VENTURI, *Caravaggio*, Novara 1951. Articles by G. HESS and D. MAHON in Burlington Magazine 1951 June, July, September. Articles by R. LONGHI in Paragone 1951, Nos 15, 17, 19, 21. Articles by D. MAHON in Paragone 1952, No 25. Antologia di " Critica caravaggesca rara " in Paragone No 17, 23.

Orazio Gentileschi: R. LONGHI, *Gentileschi padre e figlia*, L'Arte No 19, 1916, fasc. 5/6, pp. 245-314. C. GAMBA, *Orazio Gentileschi*, Dedalo 1922-1923, pp. 245-266. N. PEVSNER, *Ein Altargemälde von Gentileschi in Turin*, Zeitschr. f. bild. Kunst No 63, 1929-1930, pp. 272-275. T. MEZZETTI, *L'attività di Orazio Gentileschi nelle Marche*, L'Arte 1930, I, fasc. VI, pp. 541-551. B. MOLAJOLI, *A proposito del Gentileschi nelle Marche*, Rassegna Marchigiana, Pesaro 1931. R. CARITÀ, *La data di nascita di Orazio Gentileschi*, Arti Figurative 1946, No 1-2.

Carlo Saraceni: A. PORCELLA, *Carlo Saraceni*, Rivista di Venezia 1928, pp. 369-412. E. P. RICHARDSON, *Ranieri, Saraceni and the Meaning of Caravaggio's Influence*, The Art Quarterly 1942.

Evaristo Baschenis: M. BIANCALE, *A proposito del Baschenis*, L'Arte XVI, 1913, pp. 77 etc. L. ANGELINI, *I Baschenis pittori bergamaschi*, Bergamo 1943.

Domenico Feti: R. OLDENBURG, *Domenico Feti*, Rome 1921. O. BENESCH, *Seicento Studien II*, Jahrb. d. Kunstinst. Samml. Vienna, pp. 245-268.

Bernardo Strozzi: G. FIOCCO, *Bernardo Strozzi*, Rome 1921. O. GROSSO, *Il quadro di Erminia fra i pastori e la pittura dello Strozzi nel decennio 1620-1630*, Genoa 1942. G. MIGONI, *Bernardo Strozzi*, Illustrazione italiana 1948, No 28, pp. 57-68. P. ZAMPETTI, *Lo Strozzi*, Emporium CIX, 1949, pp. 17-27.

Michelangelo Cerquozzi: G. BRIGANTI, *Catalogo della Mostra dei Bamboccianti*, Rome 1950; *Pieter van Laer e Michelangelo Cerquozzi*, Proporzioni III, 1950, pp. 183-198.

Bernardo Cavallino: A. DE RINALDIS, *Bernardo Cavallino*, Naples 1909. E. SESTIERI, *Cenni sullo svolgimento dell'arte di Bernardo Cavallino*, L'Arte 1920, vol. 23, pp. 245-269. S. ORTOLANI, *Cavalliniana*, L'Arte No 25, 1922, pp. 190-199. A. VENTURI, *Cavallino*, Bologna 1925. O. BENESCH, *Seicento Studien I*, Jahrb. Kunstinst. Samml. I, Vienna pp. 245-268. M. MASCIOTTA, *La bella maniera del Cavallino*, Primato VII, 1942. C. REFICE, *Ancora del pittore Bernardo Cavallino*, Emporium VI, 1951, pp. 259-270.

Annibale Carracci and the School of Bologna: G. C. MALVASIA, *Felsina pitrice*, Bologna 1678. A. BOLOGNINI-AMORINI, *Le vite di Ludovico, Agostino, Annibale ed altri di Carracci*, Bologna 1840. A. VENTURI, *I Carracci e la loro scuola*, Milan 1895. H. TIETZE, *Annibale Carracci's Galerie im Palazzo Farnese und seine römische Werkstätte*, Jahrb. d. Kunsth. Samml. d. Allerh. Kaiserh. XXVI, 1906-1907, pp. 49-182. L. VENTURI, *Il 1609 e la pittura italiana*, Rome 1909. G. ALBANI, *I Carracci*, Bologna 1909. G. ROUCHÈS, *Les Carraches*, Paris 1913. A. FORATTI, *I Carracci nella teoria e nella pratica*, Città di Castello 1913; *La controriforma a Bologna e i Carracci*, Archiginnasio IX, 1914, pp. 15-20; *Il paesaggio dei Carracci e della loro scuola*, Archiginnasio XVI, 1921, pp. 161-170; *Influssi del Correggio sui Carracci*, Il Correggio, pp. 78-82. G. ROUCHÈS, *Le paysage chez les peintres de l'école bolonaise*, Gazette des Beaux-Arts, 1921. H. DELABORDE, *Les Carraches et leur école*, Etudes sur les Beaux-Arts I, pp. 380-409. R. PEYRE, *Les Carraches*, Paris. H. BODMER, *Die Jugendwerke des Annibale Carracci*, Zeitschr. f. bild. Kunst LVIII, 1924-1925, pp. 104-113. C. L. RAGGHIANTI, *I Carracci e la critica d'Arte nell'età barocca*, La Critica III-V,

XXXI, 1933. H. BODMER, *The Aldobrandini Land-scapes in the Doria Pamphilj Gallery*, The Art Bulletin XVI, 1934, pp. 260-274. R. LONGHI, *Momenti della pittura bolognese*, L'Archiginnasio XXX, 1935, p. 132 etc. H. BODMER, *L'accademia dei Carracci*, Bologna N° 8, 1935; *Die Fresken des Annibale Carracci im Camerino des Palazzo Farnese in Rom*, Pantheon Jahrg. V, 1937, pp. 146-149. D. MAHON, *Studies in Seicento Art and Theory*, London 1947. L. VENTURI, *L'Ecclettismo e i Carracci*, Commentari N° I, 1950, pp. 163-171.

Domenichino: S. MURRI, *Notizie storiche di quattro insigni dipintori*, Bologna 1844. L. SERRA, *L'educazione artistica del Domenichino*, L'Arte X, 1907, pp. 346-358; *Domenico Zampieri*, Rome 1909. L. PARIGI, *Pittori musicali, il Domenichino*, La Rassegna Musicale III, 1930, pp. 54-62. J. POPE-HENNESSY, *The Drawings of Domenichino at Windsor Castle*, London 1948.

Guido Reni: M. V. BÖHN, *Guido Reni*, Leipzig 1910. V. COSTANTINI, *Guido Reni*, Milan 1928. F. MALAGUZZI VALERI, *Guido Reni*, Florence 1929. W. ARSLAN, *Guido Reni*, Bologna 1934. J. HESS, *Le fonti dell'arte di Guido Reni*, Il Comune di Bologna, March 1934. O. KURTZ, *Guido Reni*, Jahrbuch der Kunsthist. Samml. Vienna XI, 1937. G. P. BELLORI, *Le vite di Guido Reni, Andrea Sacchi e Carlo Maratti*, Rome 1942. G. GIONGO, *Guido Reni giovane*, Commentari N° 4, 1952, pp. 189-220.

Guercino: J. A. CALVI, *Notizie della vita e delle opere di G. F. Barbieri detto il Guercino*, Bologna 1808. G. ATTI, *Intorno alla vita e alle opere di G. Barbieri detto il Guercino*, Rome 1861. G. PACCHIONI, *Note sul Guercino*, L'Arte N° 14, 1911, pp. 29-35. G. CANTALAMESSA, *Per le future monografie del Guercino*, Rome 1914; *Lo stile del Guercino*, Rome 1915. R. LONGHI, *The Climax of Caravaggio's Influence on Guercino*, Art in America, June 1926. D. MAHON, *Notes on the Young Guercino. Cento and Bologna*, Burlington Magazine LXX, 1937, pp. 112-127. V. WEISBACH, *Et in arcadia ego*, Gazette des Beaux-Arts, December 1937, pp. 287-296. J. ROSENBERG, *Rembrandt and Guercino*, The Art Quarterly N° 2, 1944. D.MAHON, *Studies in Seicento Art and Theory*, London 1947. M. PRAZ, *Guercino e il classicismo del seicento*, La Rassegna d'Italia IV, 1949, pp. 535-540.

Mattia Preti: S. MITIDERI, *Mattia Preti detto il Cavalier Calabrese*, L'Arte XVI 1913, pp. 428-450. A. CHIMIRRI - A. FRANGIPANE, *Mattia Preti*, Milan 1914. L. MONTALTO, *Il passaggio di Mattia Preti a Napoli*, L'Arte XXIII, fasc. 3/5 1920, pp. 97-113, 205-225. A. VENTURI, *Grandi artisti italiani*, Bologna 1928, pp. 233-254. V. MARIANI, *Mattia Preti a Malta*, Rome 1929. A. FRANGIPANE, *Mattia Preti*, Milan 1929. G. GODDARD KING, *Mattia Preti*, The Art Bulletin XVIII, fasc. 3 1936, pp. 371-386. V. POSCETTI, *Mattia Preti il Cavalier Calabrese*, Bollettino dell'Unione Storica ed Arte, July-August 1943.

Pietro da Cortona: N. FABRINI, *Vita del Cavalier Pietro da Cortona*, Cortona 1896. H. GEISENHEIMER, *Pietro da Cortona e gli affreschi nel Palazzo Pitti*, Florence 1900. POLLAK, *Neue Regesten des Pietro da Cortona*, Kunstchronik XXIII, 1912. H. POSSE, *Das Deckenfresco des Pietro da Cortona in Palazzo Barberini*, Jahrbuch der Preuss. Kunsts. XL, 1919, pp. 93-126. A. MUÑOZ, *Pietro da Cortona*, Rome 1921. M. LENZI, *Pietro da Cortona e la galleria di Palazzo Pamphili*, Roma V, 1927, pp. 495-499. VON BELOW, *Beiträge zur Kenntnis Pietro's da Cortona*, Belvedere 1930, fasc. 12, pp. 181 etc. E. P. RICHARDSON, *Three Masters of the Roman Baroque*, Bulletin of the Detroit Institute of Art XXII, 1942-1943. S. LUDOVICI, *Le vite di Francesco Saverio Baldinucci, Pietro Berretini detto da Cortona*, Archivi d'Italia II, XVII 1950, pp. 77-91. V. BARBERINI, *Pietro da Cortona e l'Arazzeria Barberini*, Bollettino d'Arte XXXV, 1950, pp. 43-51, 145-152.

Baciccio: R. SOPRANI - C. G. RATTI, *Vite de' pittori, scultori ed architetti genovesi*, vol. II, pp. 74-90, Genoa 1768-1769. F. IMPARATO, *Documents relatifs à Baciccio*

in Archivio Storico dell'Arte II, 1889, pp. 153-155. M. PEROTTI, *L'arte di Giambattista Gaulli*, L'Arte XIX 1916, pp. 207-233. P. TACCHI VENTURI, *Le convenzioni tra G. B. Gaulli e il Generale dei Gesuiti Gian Paolo Oliva*, Roma IV, 1935; *Pitture nella cupola della volta del Tempio Farnesiano*, Atti del terzo Congresso nazionale di Studi Romani, vol. II. V. M. BRUGNOLI, *Disegni del Baciccio*, Arti figurative I, 1945; *Contributi a G. B. Gaulli*, Bollettino d'Arte XXXIV 1949, pp. 225-239.

Giuseppe Maria Crespi: M. MARANGONI, *Giuseppe Maria Crespi lo spagnolo*, Dedalo fasc. IX and X 1921. H. VOSS, *G. M. Crespi*, Rome 1921. C. MARCHESINI, *G. M. Crespi*, Il Comune di Bologna 1933-1934. G. ZUCCHINI, *Opere d'arte inedite*, I, Il Comune di Bologna N° 8, 1934. C. GNUDI, *Sebastiano Mazzoni e le origini del Crespi*, Il Comune di Bologna N° 1, 1935. G. CASINI, *Aggiunte al Crespi*, Archiginnasio fasc. 1-3 1941. A. MORANDOTTI, *Cinque pittori del Settecento*, Venice 1943. F. ARCANGELI and C. GNUDI, *Mostra celebrativa del Crespi*, Catalog with preface by R. LONGHI, Bologna 1948. A. PODESTÀ, *La Mostra di G. M. Crespi*, Emporium 1948 LIV, pp. 243-246. F. ARCANGELI, *Due inediti del Crespi*, Paragone I 1952, pp. 43-47.

Alessandro Magnasco: G. BELTRAMI, *A. Magnasco*, Milan 1913. B. GEIGER, *Magnasco*, Berlin 1914; *Beitrag zu Magnasco*, Pantheon Jahrg. 1938, pp. 283-285. A. MORANDOTTI, *Cinque Pittori del Settecento, Catalogo della Mostra a Palazzo Massimo a Roma*, Venice 1943. M. POSPISIL, *Antonio Magnasco*, Florence 1944. B. GEIGER, *Saggio d'un catalogo delle pitture di A. Magnasco, regesti e bibliografia*, Venice 1945. G. EVANS, *The Subtle Satire of Magnasco*, Gazette des Beaux-Arts, July-August 1947, pp. 37-44. B. GEIGER, *Magnasco affreschista a Brignano*, Emporium, May 1948, pp. 211-217; *Magnasco*, Bergamo 1949. A. MORASSI, *Catalogo della Mostra del Magnasco*, Bergamo 1949. *Come "vedere" il Magnasco*, Admirator, Florence 1949. W. ARSLAN, *Appunti su Magnasco, Sebastiano e Marco Ricci*. G. NICCO FASOLA, *Libertà e limiti del Magnasco*, Commentari I, V, 1950, pp. 229-237. F. ARCANGELI, *Fortuna di due mostre*, Paragone II, 1951, N° 23, pp. 73-76.

Giambattista Tiepolo: F. H. MEISSMER, *Tiepolo*, Leipzig 1897. P. MOLMENTI, *Gian Battista Tiepolo*, Milan 1909. SACK, *Gian Battista e Domenico Tiepolo*, Hamburg 1910. G. FIOCCO, *Gian Battista Tiepolo*, Florence 1921. D. V. HADELN, *Handzeichnungen von G. B. Tiepolo*, Florence 1927. P. MOLMENTI, *La Villa Valmarana*, Venice 1928. S. DE VITO BATTAGLIA, *Gianbattista Tiepolo*, Bergamo 1932. G. FIOCCO, *Tiepolo Giovane*, Art in America 1938. H. W. HEGEMANN, *Tiepolo*, Berlin 1940. G. FIOCCO, *Tiepolo in Spagna*, Le Arti 1942-1943. G. B. MORASSI, *Tiepolo*, Bergamo 1943. G. LORENZETTI, *Catalogo ufficiale della Mostra del Tiepolo*, Venice 1951.

Pietro Longhi: E. MASI, *Pietro Longhi e Carlo Goldoni*, Nuova Antologia VIII, Rome 1887. A. RAVA, *Pietro Longhi*, Bergamo 1900; *Pietro Longhi*, Florence. O. UZANNE, *Pietro Longhi*, Paris 1924. E. ARSLAN, *Inediti di Pietro e Alessandro Longhi*, Emporium II, 1946.

Venetian Painting in the XVIIIth Century: I. HAUMANN, *Das oberitalienische Landschaftsbild des Settecento*, Strasbourg 1927. G. FIOCCO, *La pittura veneziana del Seicento e Settecento*, Bologna 1929. G. DE LOGU, *Pittori veneti minori del Settecento*, Venice 1930. G. LORENZETTI, *La pittura veneziana del Settecento*, Novara 1942.

Antonio Canaletto: H. F. FINBERG, *Canaletto in England*, Walpole Society IX, 1920-1921, X 1921-1922. W. G. CONSTABLE, *Canaletto and Guardi*, Burlington Magazine XXXIX, 1921, pp. 298-304. T. BORENIUS, *A Canaletto Curiosity*, Burlington Magazine XXXIX, 1921, pp. 108-113. G. SIMONSON, *Antonio Canal*, Burlington Magazine XL, 1922, pp. 36-41. M. STUEBEL, *Canaletto*, Berlin 1923. H. VOSS, *Canaletto*, Rep. f. Kunstw. 1926, p. 8 etc. W. G. CONSTABLE, *Canaletto in England, some further Works*, Burlington

Magazine L, 1927, pp. 17-23. D. V. HADELN, *Die Zeichnungen von A. Canal genannt Canaletto*, Vienna 1930. M. PITTALUGA, *Le acqueforti del Canaletto*, L'Arte IV, 1934, pp. 308-340. R. PALLUCCHINI, *Francesco Guardi e Antonio Canaletto*, Novara 1941; *Canaletto e Guardi*, Primato XXII, 1941; *Canaletto et Guardi*, Paris 1942. G. F. GUARNATI, *Le acqueforti del Canaletto*, Venice 1945. E. ARSLAN, *New Findings on Canaletto*, The Art Bulletin XXX, 1948, pp. 225-227.

Bernardo Bellotto: R. MEYER, *Die beiden Canaletto, Antonio Canal und Bernardo Bellotto*, Dresden 1878. G. FERRARI, *I due Canaletto*, Turin 1914. O. UZANNE, *Les deux Canaletto*, Paris. H. A. FRITZSCHE, *Bernardo Bellotto genannt Canaletto*, Burg 1936.

Francesco Guardi: G. DAMERI, *L'arte di F. Guardi* Venice 1912. P. PANIZZA, *Francesco Guardi*, Trento 1912. G. FIOCCO, *Francesco Guardi*, Florence 1923 and 1937. M. TINTI, *Guardi*, Paris 1930. V. LASAREFF, *Francesco and Giannantonio Guardi*, Burlington Magazine LXV, 1934, pp. 53-72. W. ARSLAN, *Contributo a Francesco Guardi*, Bollettino del Ministero della Pubblica Istruzione X, 1936. R. PALLUCCHINI, *Visto da vicino, Le pitture di Francesco Guardi all'Angelo Raffaele di Venezia*, Emporium V, 1938. W. H. WILLIAMS, *Drawings and Related Paintings by Francesco Guardi*, The Art Quarterly II, 1939, pp. 265-273. R. PALLUCCHINI, *Guardis Zeichnungen im Museum Correr zu Venedig*, Florence 1943. M. GOERING, *F. Guardi*, Vienna 1944. M. MURARO, *Novità su Francesco Guardi*, Arte Veneta III, 1949, pp. 123-130. S. J. BYAM, *The Drawings of Francesco Guardi*, London 1949. A. PODESTA, *Il Guardi figurista alla mostra di Trento*, Emporium LV, 1949, pp. 117-120. F. DE MAFFEIS, *Antonio Guardi*, Verona 1951. T. PIGNATTI, *I documenti dell'organo dell'Angelo Raffaele*, Arte Veneta IV, 1950, pp. 144-145. A. MORASSI, *Conclusioni su Antonio e Francesco Guardi*, Emporium 1951, pp. 195-216.

XIXth CENTURY

GENERAL

E. PANZACCHI, *L'Arte nel secolo XIX*, Leghorn 1901. A. FRANCHI, *Arte e artisti toscani dal 1850 ad oggi*, Florence 1902. P. MOLMENTI, *La pittura veneziana*, Florence 1903. L. CALLARI, *Storia dell'arte contemporanea italiana*, Rome 1909. U. OJETTI, *Ritratti di artisti italiani*, Milan 1911 and 1923. D. MORELLI and E. DALBONO, *La scuola napoletana di pittura nel secolo XIX*, Bari 1915. A. SOFFICI, *Scoperte e massacri: scritti sull'arte*, Florence 1919. U. OJETTI, *Macchiaiuoli e Impressionisti*, Dedalo I 1920-1921, pp. 331 etc. F. SAPORI, *La peinture italienne depuis le milieu du XIXe siècle*, Revue de l'art ancien et moderne XLIII, 1923. P. PANCRAZI, *I Toscani dell'Ottocento*, Florence 1924. L. VENTURI, *Il gusto dei Primitivi*, Bologna 1925. E. CECCHI, *Pittura italiana dell'Ottocento*, Milan 1926 and 1946. E. SOMARÉ, *Storia dei pittori italiani dell'Ottocento*, Milan 1928. U. OJETTI, *La pittura italiana dell'Ottocento*, Milan 1929. L. VENTURI, *Pretesti di critica*, Milan 1929. R. FRANCHI, *La pittura italiana dall'Otto al Novecento*, Palermo 1929. C. CARRÀ, *Pittori romantici lombardi*, Rome, Bergamo 1932. L. VENTURI, *Les macchiaioli*, Gazette des Beaux-Arts X 1933, p. 238 etc. A. M. COMANDUCCI, *I pittori italiani dell'Ottocento*, Milan 1934. A. M. BRIZIO, *Ottocento e Novecento*, Turin 1935. L. BENITE, G. FOGOLARI, G. PISCHEL FRANCHINI, *La pittura dell'Ottocento*, Milan 1942. E. SOMARÉ, *La pittura italiana dell'Ottocento*, Novara 1944. A. FRANCHI, *I Macchiaioli toscani*, Milan 1945. A. M. COMANDUCCI, *Dizionario illustrato dei pittori e incisori italiani moderni*, Milan 1945. M. BERNARDI, *Ottocento piemontese*, Turin 1946. M. BORGIOTTI, *I Macchiaioli*, Florence 1946. A. DRAGONE - J. DRAGONE CONTI, *I paesisti piemontesi dell'Ottocento*, Milan 1947. M. BERNARDI, *Pitture italiane dell'Ottocento*, Turin 1948. M. PIERA CAZZULLO, *La scuola toscana dei Macchiaioli*, Florence 1948. R. CALZINI, *Pittori*

italiani dell'Ottocento, Catalog of the Exhibition at the Wildenstein Gallery, New York 1949. G. CASTELFRANCO, *Pittori italiani del secondo Ottocento*, Rome 1952. (With a bibliography of the catalogs of the chief private collections in Italy.)

Giovanni Fattori: F. PERA, *Bibliografie livornesi*, V, Leghorn 1895, p. 25 etc. R. PANTINI, *Artisti contemporanei: Giovanni Fattori*, Emporium XVII 1903, p. 3 etc. A. FRANCHI, *Giovanni Fattori*, Florence 1910. A. GHIGLIA, *L'opera di Giovanni Fattori*, Florence 1913. A. SOFFICI, *Giovanni Fattori*, Rome 1921. E. SOMARÉ, *L'opera di Giovanni Fattori*, L'esame IV 1925, p. 667 etc. E. CECCHI, *Giovanni Fattori e la pittura toscana intorno al 1860*, Il Convegno 1925, p. 378 etc. F. PAOLIERI, *Giovanni Fattori*, 1925. M. TINTI, *Giovanni Fattori*, Rome, Milan 1926. PAPINI, NOMELLINI, FOCARDI, *Giovanni Fattori*, Florence 1926. E. CECCHI, *Giovanni Fattori*, Rome 1933. A. M. FRANCINI CIARENFI, *Incisioni di Fattori*, Bergamo 1944. R. BALDACCINI, *Fattori*, Milan 1949.

Silvestro Lega: M. TINTI, *Silvestro Lega*, Rome, Milan. E. SOMARÉ, *Silvestro Lega*, Milan 1926. M. TINTI, *Silvestro Lega*, Bergamo 1931. M. VALSECCHI, *Lega*, Milan 1950.

Telemaco Signorini: T. SIGNORINI, *Caricaturisti e caricaturati al Caffè Michelangelo*, Florence 1895. H. ZIMMERN, *Telemaco Signorini*, The Art Journal, London 1895, p. 266 etc. V. PICA, *Artisti contemporanei, Telemaco Signorini*, Emporium VIII 1898, p. 323. T. SIGNORINI, *Riomaggiore*, Florence 1909, 1942. F. SAPORI, *Signorini*, Turin 1919. E. SOMARÉ, *Telemaco Signorini*, Milan 1926. U. OJETTI, *Telemaco Signorini*, Milan, Rome 1930. E. SOMARÉ, *Signorini*, Rome 1931.

Raffaello Sernesi: E. CECCHI, *Ritratto di Raffaello Sernesi*, Vita Artistica II 1927, p. 21 etc.; *Ottocento pittorico: Sernesi, Abbati, D'Ancona*, Frontespizio XII 1940, p. 202 etc. F. WITTGENS, *Dodici opere di Raffaello Sernesi nella raccolta Stramezzi*, Milan 1951.

Giuseppe Abbati: E. CECCHI, *Per un catalogo di Giuseppe Abbati*, Vita Artistica II, August-September 1927; *Ottocento pittorico: Sernesi, Abbati, D'Ancona*, Frontespizio XII 1940, p. 202 etc. R. BALDACCINI, *Contributi alla pittura italiana dell'Ottocento*, Florence 1947.

Vito d'Ancona: E. SOMARÉ, *Vito d'Ancona*, L'Esame IV 1925, p. 595 etc. E. CECCHI, *Vito d'Ancona*, Bollettino d'arte VI, series II 1926/27, p. 291 etc.; *Ottocento pittorico: Sernesi, Abbati, D'Ancona*, Frontespizio XII 1940, p. 202 etc.

Gioacchino Toma: G. TOMA, *Ricordi di un orfano*, Naples 1886. D. ANGELI, *Un pittore napoletano dimenticato, Gioacchino Toma*, Emporium XXII 1905, p. 153 etc. F. SAPORI, *Gioacchino Toma*, Turin 1919. E. QUARDASCIONE, *Gioacchino Toma*, Il colore in pittura, Bari 1924. M. TINTI, *Gioacchino Toma*, Vita Artistica II 1927, p. 117 etc. M. BIANCALE, *Gioacchino Toma*, Rome 1933. S. ORTOLANI, *Gioacchino Toma*, Rome 1934. A. DE RINALDIS, *Gioacchino Toma*, Verona 1934.

Michele Cammarano: M. BIANCALE, *Michele Cammarano*, Vita Artistica II 1927, p. 139 etc. F. GIROSI, *Michele Cammarano*, Rome 1934. M. BIANCALE, *Michele Cammarano*, Milan 1934; *Courbet e Cammarano*, Nuova Antologia 1935, N° 1519.

XXth CENTURY

GENERAL

F. FLORA, *Dal romanticismo al futurismo*, Milan 1925. G. SCHEIWILLER, *Art Italien moderne*, Paris 1930. G. CASTELFRANCO, *La pittura moderna*, Florence 1934. V. COSTANTINI, *Pittura italiana contemporanea*, Milan 1934. G. PAGANO, *Arte decorativa italiana*, Milan 1938. R. CARRIERI, *Fantasia degli italiani*, Domus 1939. V. E. BARBAROUX, *G. Giani. Arte italiana contemporanea*, Milan 1940. C. CARRÀ, *Il rinnovamento delle arti in Italia*, Milan 1945.

S. Cairola, *Arte italiana del nostro tempo*, Bergamo 1946. U. Nebbia, *La pittura del novecento*, Milan 1946. L. Venturi, *La peinture contemporaine*, Milan 1947. J. Thrall Soby, A. H. Barr Jr., *Twentieth Century Italian Art*, New York 1949. *Un demi-siècle d'art italien*, Cahiers d'art No 25, I, 1950. U. Apollonio, *Pittura moderna italiana*, Venice 1950. L. Venturi, *Prémisses théoriques de l'art moderne*, Preuves, May 1952, Special Number.

FUTURISM

Documents: F. U. Boccioni, *Pittura, scultura futuriste (dinamismo plastico)*, Milan 1914 ; *Opera completa*, Foligno 1927. F. Marinetti, *Le futurisme*, Paris 1911 ; *Manifesti del futurismo*, Milan n. d. ; *Futurismo e Fascismo*, Foligno n. d. G. Papini, *Lacerba* (Official Review of the Futurists), January 1913, May 1915 ; *Esperienza futurista*, Florence 1919. C. Carrà, *Guerra pittura*, Milan 1915 and 1916 ; *Pittura metafisica*, Florence 1919 and 1945 ; *La mia vita*, Rome 1932 ; *Artisti moderni*, Florence 1943 ; *Il rinnovamento delle arti in Italia*, Milan 1945 ; *Quarante ans d'art italien*, Lausanne 1947. (Carrà has also published numerous historical and critical studies in book form, in reviews like Lacerba and Valori Plastici and in newspapers.) G. de Chirico, *Sull'arte metafisica*, Valori Plastici I 1919 ; *Piccolo trattato di tecnica pittorica*, Milan 1928 ; *Hebdomeros*, Paris 1929, Milan 1942 ; *Le Silence*, Minotaure Nº 5, Paris 1934 ; *Memorie della mia vita*, Rome 1945. G. de Chirico and Isabella Far, *Commedia dell'arte moderna*, Rome 1945. (As well as other critical and polemical articles.) G. Severini, *Du cubisme au classicisme*, Paris 1921 ; *Ragionamenti sulle arti figurative*, Milan 1936 ; *Arte indipendente, arte borghese, arte sociale*, Rome 1944 ; *Tutta la vita di un pittore*, Cernusco sul Naviglio 1946 ; *Cinquante peintres italiens d'aujourd'hui*, Paris 1951. A. Soffici, *Rete mediterranea*, Florence n. d. ; *Primi principi di una estetica futurista*, Florence 1920 ; *Scoperte e massacri, scritti sull'arte*, Florence 1929 ; *Ricordi di vita artistica e letteraria*, Florence 1930 ; *Selva-Arte*, Florence 1943 ; *Trenta artisti moderni italiani e stranieri*, Florence 1950.

GENERAL

G. Coquiot, *Cubistes, futuristes, passéistes*, Paris 1914. A. J. Eddy, *Cubists and Post-impressionism*, Chicago 1919. G. Apollinaire, *Anecdotiques*, Paris 1926. C. Pavolini, *Futurismo, cubismo, impressionismo*, Florence 1926. A. G. Bragaglia, *Futurismo*, Rome. Fillia, *Il futurismo*, Milan 1932. C. Zervos, *Histoire de l'art contemporain*, Cahiers d'art 1938. Tato, *Raccontato da Tato 20 anni di futurismo*, Milan 1941. R. Benet, *Futurismo y Dada*, Barcelona 1950. G. C. Argan, *Il Futurismo*, Ulisse II, XII, 1950, p. 667 etc. *Catalogo della Mostra nazionale delle pittura e scultura futurista*, Bologna 1951.

Gino Severini: A. Behne, *G. Severini*, Der Sturm Nos 172-173, Berlin 1913. U. Boccioni, *I futuristi plagiati in Francia*, Lacerba, Florence 1913. P. A. Birot, *G. Severini*, Sic, Paris 1916. A. Salmon, *G. Severini*, L'art vivant, Paris 1920. Ch. Fegdal, *Ateliers d'artistes*, vol. I, Paris 1925. R. Landau, *Der unbestechliche Minos*, Hamburg 1925. M. Raynal, *Anthologie de la peinture en France de 1906 à nos jours*, Paris 1927. P. Courthion, *Gino Severini*, Milan 1930. J. Maritain, *G. Severini*, Paris 1930. C. Carrà, *Artisti d'oggi*, L'Ambrosiano November 6, Milan 1930. O. Freundlich, *G. Severini A bis Z*, Cologne 1931. J. Cassou, *G. Severini*, Paris 1933. M. Besson, *Opere di G. Severini nella decorazione di chiese svizzere*, L'Illustrazione Vaticana, March, Rome 1935. P. Fierens, *Gino Severini*, Paris-Milan 1936. A. H. Barr, *Cubism and Abstract Art*, Museum of Modern Art, New York 1936. L. Servolini, *G. Severini*, Thieme-Becker, vol. 30, Leipzig 1936. P. M. Bardi, *G. Severini*, Stile, Milan 1942. B. Wall, *Gino Severini*, London 1946.

Umberto Boccioni: R. Longhi, *U. Boccioni*, La Voce, Florence 1913-1914. G. Coquiot, *Cubistes, Futuristes, Passéistes*, Paris 1914. A. de Witt, *Su Boccioni, acquafortista*, Dedalo, 1914. C. Carrà, *U. Boccioni*, Milan 1916. F. T. Marinetti, *U. Boccioni*, 1924. H. Walden, *Einblick in Kunst*, Berlin 1924. A. de Witt, *Umberto Boccioni incisore*, Dedalo XIII, 1933, p. 116 etc. *Amour de l'art*, Paris 1934 (bio-bibliographical notice). A. H. Barr, *Cubism and Abstract Art*, New York 1936. F. Pastonchi, *Boccioni*, Cahiers d'art, Paris 1950. J. Th. Soby and A. H. Barr, *Twentieth-Century Italian Art*, New York 1950.

Carlo Carrà: G. Raimondi, *Carlo Carrà*, Bologna 1916. A. Soffici, *Carlo Carrà*, Milan 1928. P. M. Bardi, *Carrà e Soffici*, Milan 1930. R. Longhi, *Carlo Carrà*, Milan 1937. G. Raimondi, *Disegni di Carlo Carrà*, Milan 1942. P. Torriano, *Carlo Carrà*, Milan 1942. C. L. Ragghianti, *C. Carrà*, La Critica d'arte, 1936, p. 251 etc. S. Catalano, *Carlo Carrà*, Milan 1945. G. Pacchioni, *Carlo Carrà*, Milan 1945 (with bibliography). R. Longhi, *Carlo Carrà*, Milan 1945. L. Vitali, *Variazioni metafisiche di Carrà*, Le Tre Arti I, 3, 1945. F. Arcangeli, *Carlo Carrà*, Rassegna d'Italia III 1948, p. 593 etc. J. Lassaigne, in *History of Modern Painting*, Vol. III, Geneva 1950. G. Raimondi, *La congiuntura metafisica Morandi-Carrà*, Paragone XIX, 1951, p. 18 etc.

Giorgio de Chirico: J. Cocteau, *Dodici opere di G. de Chirico*, Rome 1919. R. Vitrac, *Georges de Chirico*, Paris 1927. P. Courthion, *L'art de Georges de Chirico*, Antwerp 1928. W. George, *G. de Chirico*, Paris 1928. B. Ternovetz, *Giorgio De Chirico*, Milan 1928. J. Cocteau, *Le mystère Laïc*, Paris 1928. C. L. Ragghianti, *De Chirico*, La critica d'arte I, 1935. G. Lo Duca, *Giorgio de Chirico*, Milan 1936 (with bibliography). J. Thrall Soby, *The Early Chirico*, New York 1941. R. Carrieri, *De Chirico*, Milan 1942 (with bibliography). A. D. Pica, *Giorgio de Chirico*, Milan 1944. R. Gaffé, *Georges de Chirico, le voyant*, Brussels 1946. I. Faldi, *Il primo De Chirico*, Venice 1949. J. Lassaigne, in *History of Modern Painting*, Vol. III, Geneva 1950.

Giorgio Morandi: G. de Chirico, *Giorgio Morandi*, Florence 1922. A. Soffici, *Giorgio Morandi*. G. Scheiwiller, *Giorgio Morandi*, Turin. A. Beccaria, *Morandi*, Milan 1939 (with bibliography). L. Bartolini, *Morandi incisore*, Emporium XCL, 1940, p. 173. C. Brandi, *Giorgio Morandi*, Florence 1942. G. Marchiori, *G. Morandi*, Genoa 1945. C. Gnudi, *Giorgio Morandi*, Florence 1946. M. Ramous, *I disegni di Giorgio Morandi*, Bologna 1949. S. Solmi, *Giorgio Morandi*, Milan 1949. G. Raimondi, *Le stampe di Giorgio Morandi*, Proporzioni II, 1948, Florence, p. 147 etc. J. Lassaigne, in *History of Modern Painting*, Vol. III, Geneva 1950.

Amedeo Modigliani: A. Salmon, *Modigliani, sa vie, son œuvre*, Paris 1926. M. Schwarz, *Modigliani*, Paris 1927. G. Scheiwiller, *A. Modigliani*, Milan 1927, 1950 (with bibliography). M. Dale, *Modigliani*, New York 1929. A. Pfannstiel, *Modigliani*, Paris 1929. L. Vitali, *Disegni di Modigliani*, Arte Moderna Italiana XV, Milan 1929. G. Scheiwiller, *Omaggio a Modigliani*, Milan 1930. A. Basler, *Modigliani*, Paris 1931. S. Taguchi, *Modigliani*, Tokyo 1936. L. Bartolini, *Modi*, Venice 1938. R. Franchi, *Modigliani*, Florence 1944, 1946. N. Apra, *Tormento di Modigliani*, Milan 1945. R. Carrieri, *Dodici opere di Amedeo Modigliani*, Milan 1947, 1949. G. di san Lazzaro, *Modigliani : Peintures*, Paris 1947. J. Lassaigne, in *History of Modern Painting*, Vol. III, Geneva 1950. M. Raynal, *Modigliani*, Geneva 1951. P. Descargues, *A. Modigliani*, Paris 1951. E. Carli, *Modigliani*, Rome 1952. N. Ponente, *Modigliani*, Commentari III, 1952, p. 146 etc.

INDEX OF NAMES

This Index of Names covers all three volumes of our history of ITALIAN PAINTING: The Creators of the Renaissance (I),
The Renaissance (II), From Caravaggio to Modigliani (III).

THIS

THE SEVENTH VOLUME OF THE COLLECTION

PAINTING ○ COLOUR ○ HISTORY

WAS PRINTED

BOTH TEXT AND COLORPLATES

BY THE

SKIRA

COLOR STUDIO

AT IMPRIMERIES RÉUNIES S. A.

LAUSANNE

FINISHED THE THIRTIETH DAY OF SEPTEMBER
NINETEEN HUNDRED AND FIFTY-TWO

*All the work produced by the Skira Color Studio
is carried out by the technical staff of
Editions d'Art Albert Skira.*

PRINTED IN SWITZERLAND